An Expositor's Handbook to the Greek Text of Matthew

An Expositor's Handbook to the Greek Text of Matthew

Daniel M. Gurtner

CASCADE Books • Eugene, Oregon

AN EXPOSITOR'S HANDBOOK TO THE GREEK TEXT OF MATTHEW

Copyright © 2025 Daniel M. Gurtner. All rights reserved. Except for brief quotations in critical publications or reviews, no part of this book may be reproduced in any manner without prior written permission from the publisher. Write: Permissions, Wipf and Stock Publishers, 199 W. 8th Ave., Suite 3, Eugene, OR 97401.

Cascade Books
An Imprint of Wipf and Stock Publishers
199 W. 8th Ave., Suite 3
Eugene, OR 97401

www.wipfandstock.com

PAPERBACK ISBN: 979-8-3852-3015-0
HARDCOVER ISBN: 979-8-3852-3016-7
EBOOK ISBN: 979-8-3852-3017-4

Cataloguing-in-Publication data:

Names: Gurtner, Daniel M., author.

Title: An expositor's handbook to the Greek text of Matthew / Daniel M. Gurtner.

Description: Eugene, OR: Cascade Books, 2025. | Includes index.

Identifiers: ISBN 979-8-3852-3015-0 (paperback). | ISBN 979-8-3852-3016-7 (hardcover). | ISBN 979-8-3852-3017-4 (ebook).

Subjects: LCSH: Bible.—Matthew—Commentaries.

Classification: BS2575.53 G87 2025 (print). | BS2575.553 (ebook).

VERSION NUMBER 04/17/25

Greek text is from the Nestle-Aland, *Novum Testamentum Graece*, 28th Revised Edition, edited by Barbara and Kurt Aland, Johannes Karavidopoulos, Carlo M. Martini, and Bruce M. Metzger in cooperation with the Institute for New Testament Textual Research, Münster/Westphalia, © 2012 Deutsche Bibelgesellschaft, Stuttgart. Used by permission.

From the time I came to faith in Christ (Spring, 1993), I was discipled in the classroom. I never knew a day in my early faith in which I did not have the patient, careful, and expert guidance of a Godly man to direct me in page after page of the Bible, which at that time I had hardly ever opened. That gift of faithful instruction came from Dr. James Bibza, who for decades has done nothing short of instruct young men and women in the study of the Bible—patiently, insightfully, and carefully, at Grove City College, Pennsylvania. Words fail me to express how much I owe to this man. Most importantly, it was Dr. Bibza who first taught me to know and love the Lord through the study of His Word, and to ζητεῖτε . . . πρῶτον τὴν βασιλείαν τοῦ θεοῦ . . . (Matt 6:33).

To Dr. James Bibza
With profound gratitude

Contents

Preface | ix
Introduction | xi
List of Abbreviations | xiii

§1 The Birth of Jesus: Matthew 1:18–25 | 1
§2 The Temptation of the Son of God: Matthew 4:1–11 | 24
§3 On Being Blessed: Matthew 5:1–12 | 54
§4 Where Are Your Treasures? Matthew 6:19–25 | 77
§5 What Sort of a Person Is Jesus? Matthew 8:23–27 | 101
§6 Good Soil or Bad? Matthew 13:3–9, 18–23 | 116
§7 What *Kind* of Savior? Matthew 16:13–23 | 150
§8 What Do I Still Lack? Matthew 19:16–22 | 185
§9 Behold, Your King! Matthew 21:1–11 | 207
§10 Jesus' Authority: Matthew 21:23–27 | 238
§11 Lord's Supper: Matthew 26:26–29 | 258
§12 (Mostly) True Accusations and Their Effects: The Death of Jesus: Matthew 27:32–50 | 272
§13 The Empty Tomb: Matthew 28:1–10 | 311
§14 From Jesus' Mission to Our Great Commission: Matthew 28:16–20 | 340

Biblical and Ancient Text Index | 355

Preface

On April 21, 2020, I was informed that I was among nine faculty members and some thirty staff laid off from my institution due to the Covid-19 pandemic. After fifteen years of seminary teaching, and with a family of five to sustain, this came as a complete shock. Shortly thereafter I was invited by a publisher to write this volume, and the opportunity to pore over selections of the Greek Text of Matthew for equipping preachers was the boon to my faith I hoped it would be. My work was finished by the summer of 2021, my soul was refreshed, but the publisher was overworked, understaffed, and too far behind with other demands to take up the task of turning my manuscript into a book for some weeks, which became months, which became two years. By then that overworked publisher was bought out by another publisher, whose business model seemed to have no place for an obscure little book written to equip pastors to make better use of the Greek text of Matthew for biblical exposition. In the end, it seemed to me, I would not get my little book published or a tool in the hands of pastors. But through the worshipful study of God's word, the self-reflection that comes from the Spirit of God when we come to Him eagerly and expectantly, and through the generous helping of humility that comes to a man on the cusp of puffing out his chest in self-righteous pride when he receives a document from the publisher titled "Termination Agreement," through all this, I got more of Christ. For that I am grateful. The exegetical content of this book is borne from years of study and teaching. The pastoral application arises from the crucible of hardship and loss. And, finding still *more* of Christ. Through it, I learned that previously I had only *wanted* Christ. But I didn't need Him. Now I needed Him. And He is *glorious*.

Introduction

An Expositor's Handbook to the Greek Text of Matthew is designed to help any expositor—primarily a Sunday morning preacher—who may have learned some Greek but is not presently in command of its fine points—make use of the Greek text of a selection of common passages from the Gospel of Matthew. It is for preachers whose Greek has gotten a little rusty. They still want to use it, but they need a little help. But this is not a technical, full-blown *exegetical guide* to all the finer points of grammar and syntax. This book is much more modest in that it covers only a *selection* of passages, not the whole gospel, and only *basic grammar*, unless more complicated constructions require explanation. Nor is this a *commentary* to explain the entirety of the passage. My focus here is only on the Greek itself and what that language contributes particularly to understand a passage. I want to help readers use *Greek*, while other tools can aid in addressing other matters. What I aim to do, then, is supply readers with *An Expositor's Handbook to the Greek Text of Matthew*. As such, this book addresses fourteen Preaching Units, each numbered as a Chapter, corresponding to a passage from the Gospel of Matthew, and given a title drawn from the main idea of that particular passage. Each passage ranges from five to nineteen verses long, with an average of about eleven verses. The passages are selected based on their general popularity or around their importance in the breadth of Christian church traditions—Christmas, Easter, Palm Sunday, etc. At the beginning of each Chapter the reference to Matthew is listed, along with the title of the passage, followed by an Introductory paragraph explaining the primary exegetical subject matter of the passage in clear, accessible, but precise language. The heart of the *Expositor's Handbook* are the exegetical notations, intended to aid the expositor in grasping the sense of the language and its features at a glance

INTRODUCTION

for preaching without reading lengthy comments or explanations. Where necessary, more complicated Greek constructions are explained. After the exegetical notations and at the end of each preaching unit, I furnish readers with some suggestions on preaching the unit of text in a segment called "Preaching the Text." Here I give (1) a brief phrase summarizing the main idea of the passage; (2) a few key points about specific aspects of the text itself that can be highlighted or explained in the sermon; and (3) a "Tip for Preaching" statement—usually a few sentences or a paragraph—with some suggestions to the expositor on aspects of sermon delivery particular to this passage.

Abbreviations

Grammatical Terms in Greek Parsings:

1st	first person
2nd	second person
3rd	third person
acc	accusative case
act	active voice
adj	adjective
adv	adverb
aor	aorist tense
conj	conjunction
dat	dative case
dem pron	demonstrative pronoun
fem	feminine (grammatical gender)
fut	future tense
gen	genitive case
impf	imperfect tense
imv	imperative tense
ind	indicative mood
indecl	indeclinable
indef pron	indefinite pronoun
inf	infinitive
interr pron	interrogative pronoun
masc	masculine (grammatical gender)

ABBREVIATIONS

mid	middle voice
neg particle	negative particle
neut	neuter (grammatical gender)
nom	nominative case
pass	passive voice
perf	perfect tense
pers	person
pers pron	personal pronoun
pl	plural
prep	preposition
pron	pronoun
ptcp	participle
reflexive pron	reflexive pronoun
rel pron	relative pronoun
sg	singular
subj	subjunctive mood
voc	vocative case

Texts and Translations of the Bible

ESV	English Standard Version
KJV	King James Version
LXX	Septuagint (Greek OT)
MT	Masoretic Text
NETS	New English Translation of the Septuagint
NIV	New International Version
NRS	New Revised Standard Version
RSV	Revised Standard Version

ABBREVIATIONS

Biblical Texts

Old Testament

Gen	Genesis
Exod	Exodus
Lev	Leviticus
Num	Numbers
Deut	Deuteronomy
Josh	Joshua
Judg	Judges
1 Sam	1 Samuel
2 Sam	2 Samuel
2 Kgs	2 Kings
1 Chron	1 Chronicles
2 Chron	2 Chronicles
Neh	Nehemiah
Ps/Pss	Psalms
Prov	Proverbs
Isa	Isaiah
Jer	Jeremiah
Lam	Lamentations
Ezek	Ezekiel
Dan	Daniel
Hos	Hosea
Joel	Joel
Amos	Amos
Mic	Micah
Hab	Habakkuk
Zeph	Zephaniah

New Testament

Matt	Matthew
Mark	Mark
Luke	Luke
John	John
Acts	Acts
1 Cor	1 Corinthians
2 Cor	2 Corinthians
Gal	Galatians
Eph	Ephesians
Heb	Hebrews
James	James
1 Pet	1 Peter
Rev	Revelation

Ancient Jewish Texts

Sir	Sirach
1 Macc	1 Maccabees
Pss Sol	Psalms of Solomon
Josephus, *War*	Josephus, *Jewish War*
m. Menaḥ	Mishnah Menaḥot

1
Matthew 1:18–25
The Birth of Jesus

Introduction: At the beginning of his gospel, Matthew outlines the genealogical origins of Jesus (1:1–17). There he listed the names of some reputable figures, some disreputable, but all showing that Jesus is in the line of Judah and heir to the kingship of David. In this passage (1:18–25) the evangelist turns to more specific and personal origins of Jesus. In doing so Matthew shows the personal origin of Jesus with some very important features: The account is told largely from Joseph's perspective, though of course Mary is introduced and the circumstances of her pregnancy are explained. Surprisingly, an angel of the Lord appears to Joseph and explains the situation personally to him. It is important to note that in all instances Joseph is a "righteous" man, first wanting to treat Mary honorably and second in his unconditional and prompt obedience to the commands of the angel. If he had more questions for the angel, Matthew does not record them for us. But all these events are orchestrated by the Lord, both through the intervention of his angel and in fulfillment of his Scriptures.

18a Τοῦ δὲ Ἰησοῦ Χριστοῦ ἡ γένεσις οὕτως ἦν.
Lit: *But of Jesus Christ the genesis thus was.*
Now the origin of Jesus Christ was like this:

Τοῦ   of
article: gen sg masc ὁ "of the"

δέ	Now
conj:	(postpositive. It will always appear second in a sentence) δέ "but"/ "now"
Ἰησοῦ	Jesus
noun:	gen sg masc Ἰησοῦς "of Jesus"
Χριστοῦ	Christ
noun:	gen sg masc Χριστός "of Christ"
ἡ	the
article:	nom sg fem ὁ
γένεσις	origin
noun:	nom sg fem γένεσις "a generation/origin"
οὕτως	like this
adv:	οὕτως "thus/ in this manner"
ἦν	was
verb:	impf act ind 3rd sg εἰμί "he/she/it (continually) was"

Explanation: Previously (1:1) Matthew gave an account of the origins (γένεσις) of Jesus, listing his genealogy (1:1–17). Here the origins (γένεσις) pertains to his birth. οὕτως is an adverb describing what the origins of Jesus was like. Though it is a faithful account of what occurred, it is by no means exhaustive and Matthew is selective in what he records.

18b μνηστευθείσης τῆς μητρὸς αὐτοῦ Μαρίας τῷ Ἰωσήφ,
Lit: having been betrothed of mother his Mary to Joseph,
When his mother was betrothed to Joseph,

μνηστευθείσης	betrothed
ptcp:	aor pass ptcp gen sg fem μνηστεύω "of (her) having been betrothed/ engaged"

MATTHEW 1:18-25

τῆς	the
article:	gen sg fem ὁ "of the"

μητρὸς	mother
noun:	gen sg fem μήτηρ "of (a) mother"

αὐτοῦ	his
personal pron:	gen sg masc αὐτός "of him/it" (a pronoun) he, she, it, him, they, self, etc.

Μαρίας	Mary
noun:	gen sg fem Μαρία "of Mary"

τῷ	to
article:	dat sg masc ὁ "to the"

Ἰωσήφ	Joseph
noun:	indecl Ἰωσήφ "Joseph"

Explanation: μνηστευθείσης τῆς μητρός is a "genitive absolute," which means τῆς μητρός acts like the subject and μνηστευθείσης acts like a finite verb.

18c πρὶν ἢ συνελθεῖν αὐτοὺς
Lit: before or to come together they.
before they came together

πρὶν	before
adv:	πρίν "before"

ἤ	not translated
particle:	ἤ "(or/than)"

συνελθεῖν	to come together
verb:	aor act inf συνέρχομαι "to come together"

αὐτοὺς   they
pers pron: acc pl masc αὐτός "they/them"

Explanation: The phrase πρὶν ἢ συνελθεῖν literally means "before or to come together," and is an idiom. αὐτούς, even though it is in the accusative case is the subject of the verb infinitive συνελθεῖν, and translated "they came together." πρίν ἢ simply means "before," and so the whole verse means "before they came together." The verb for coming together (συνελθεῖν) means sexual union. Matthew is clarifying that Mary was found to be pregnant before Joseph and Mary engaged in sexual intercourse.

18d εὑρέθη ἐν γαστρὶ ἔχουσα ἐκ πνεύματος ἁγίου.
Lit: she was found in the womb having from the Holy Spirit.
She was found to be pregnant by the Holy Spirit.

εὑρέθη   she was found
verb: aor pass ind 3rd sg εὑρίσκω "(he/she/it) was found"

ἐν   in
prep: ἐν "in/by/with"

γαστρὶ   the womb
noun: dat sg fem γαστήρ "to a womb/belly"

ἔχουσα   having
verb: pres act ptcp nom sg fem ἔχω "(one) having"

ἐκ   from
prep: ἐκ "from/out of"

πνεύματος the spirit
noun: gen sg neut πνεῦμα "of a spirit"

ἁγίου   holy
adj: gen sg neut ἅγιος "of a holy"

Explanation. The phrase ἐν γαστρὶ ἔχουσα is a common expression for pregnancy, literally meaning "having in the womb." Matthew does not say who discovered Mary's pregnancy, simply that it was εὑρέθη, "found" or "discovered." But he is also careful to point out at the outset that her pregnancy is by the Holy Spirit. Naturally it could not be kept secret for very long.

19a Ἰωσὴφ δὲ ὁ ἀνὴρ αὐτῆς,
Lit. Joseph but the husband of her,
But Joseph, her husband,

Ἰωσὴφ	Joseph
noun:	indecl Ἰωσήφ "Joseph"

δὲ	but
conj:	δέ "but/now"

ὁ	the
article:	nom sg masc ὁ "the"

ἀνὴρ	husband
noun:	nom sg masc ἀνήρ "a man/ husband"

αὐτῆς	her
pers pron:	gen sg fem αὐτός "of her"

Explanation. Joseph is described as "her husband" (ὁ ἀνὴρ αὐτῆς) even though they are merely betrothed (Μνηστευθείσης). Betrothals were legally binding and required a divorce to break.

19b δίκαιος ὢν καὶ μὴ θέλων αὐτὴν δειγματίσαι,
Lit: righteous being and not desiring her to disgrace publicly,
being righteous and not willing to publicly disgrace her,

δίκαιος	righteous
adj:	nom sg masc δίκαιος "righteous/just"

ὤν	being
ptcp:	pres act ptcp nom sg masc εἰμί "(one) being"

καί	and
conj:	καί "and"

μή	not
neg particle:	μή "no/not"

θέλων	willing
ptcp:	pres act ptcp nom sg masc θέλω "(one) willing"

αὐτήν	her
pers pron:	acc sg fem αὐτός "her"

δειγματίσαι	to disgrace publicly
verb:	aor act inf δειγματίζω "to begin to exhibit/expose"

Explanation. Joseph is described as "righteous" (δίκαιος) perhaps because he had in mind refraining from marriage to what he regarded as a defiled woman. Or it may be because of his nobility in refusing to disgrace Mary publicly.

19c ἐβουλήθη λάθρᾳ ἀπολῦσαι αὐτήν.
Lit. he determined secretly to divorce her.
he determined to divorce her secretly.

ἐβουλήθη	he determined / resolved
verb:	aor pass ind 3rd sg βούλομαι "(he/she/it) willed/determined"

λάθρᾳ	privately / secretly
adv:	λάθρᾳ "privately/ secretly"

ἀπολῦσαι	to divorce
verb:	aor act inf ἀπολύω "to begin to loose from/divorce"

αὐτήν   her
pers pron: acc sg fem αὐτός "her"

Explanation. Readers are here told of the inner contemplations of Joseph, that his resolved (ἐβουλήθη) to make the matter a private affair. Here readers are told about his inner-thinking in response to the situation.

20a Ταῦτα δὲ αὐτοῦ ἐνθυμηθέντος
Lit. These but of him having considered
But as he considered these things

Ταῦτα   these (things)
dem pron: acc pl neut οὗτος "these/these (things)"

δὲ   but
conj: δέ "but/now"

αὐτοῦ   he
pers pron: gen sg masc αὐτός "of him/it"

ἐνθυμηθέντος   while considering
ptcp: aor pass ptcp gen sg masc ἐνθυμέομαι "of (him) having been considered/pondered"

Explanation. αὐτοῦ ἐνθυμηθέντος is a genitive absolute, which means αὐτοῦ acts like a subject and the genitive participle ἐνθυμηθέντος like a finite verb. As an "absolute" it can stand on its own in a sentence. The action is concurrent—while thinking these things (v. 20a), the angel intercedes (v. 20b).

20b ἰδοὺ ἄγγελος κυρίου κατ' ὄναρ ἐφάνη αὐτῷ λέγων·
Lit: Behold, angel of the Lord according to a dream appeared to him saying;
Behold! An angel of the Lord appeared to him in a dream, saying,

ἰδοὺ	Behold!
verb:	aor mid imv 2nd sg ὁράω "begin (you for yourself) to see"

ἄγγελος	angel
noun:	nom sg masc ἄγγελος "an angel/angel"

κυρίου	of the Lord
noun:	gen sg masc κύριος "of the Lord/a lord"

κατ'	according to
prep:	κατά "according to/down/against"

ὄναρ	a dream
noun:	indecl ὄναρ "dream"

ἐφάνη	he appeared
verb:	aor pass ind 3rd sg φαίνω "(he/she/it) was shining/appearing"

αὐτῷ	to him
pers pron:	dat sg masc αὐτός "to him"

λέγων	saying
ptcp:	pres act ptcp nom sg masc λέγω "(one) saying"

Explanation. ἰδού is commonly used in Matthew to draw the reader's attention to something that is unexpected in the narrative. Matthew's κατ' ὄναρ, "according to a dream" simply means "by means of" or "in" a dream.

20c Ἰωσὴφ υἱὸς Δαυίδ,
Lit. Joseph son of David
Joseph, son of David

Ἰωσὴφ	Joseph
noun:	indecl Ἰωσήφ "Joseph"

υἱός	son
noun:	nom sg masc υἱός "a son/son"

Δαυίδ	of David
pron:	indecl Δαυίδ "David"

Explanation. "Son of David" refers to a promise given to King David (2 Sam 7) that a descendant from his kingly line ("house") will sit on the throne forever. Joseph is in that line, and Jesus will be, too. A few decades before this time, Jewish authors wrote a series of psalms that speak, among other things, about what they anticipate in a "son of David." This writing, called the Psalms of Solomon, depicts a militant, even violent "son of David" who will come into Jerusalem and destroy unrighteous rulers (Pss Sol 17). The son of David here did not come to destroy, but to save.

20d μὴ φοβηθῇς παραλαβεῖν Μαρίαν τὴν γυναῖκά σου·
Lit. Do not fear to take Mary the wife of you;
do not fear to take Mary as your wife,

μή	not
neg particle: μή "no/not"	

φοβηθῇς	you should be afraid
verb:	aor pass subj 2nd sg φοβέω "(you) should begin to be feared/afraid"

παραλαβεῖν	to take
verb:	aor act inf παραλαμβάνω "to begin to receive/take alongside"

Μαρίαν	Mary
noun:	acc sg fem Μαρία "Mary"

τὴν   the
article: acc sg fem ὁ "the"

γυναῖκά   wife
noun: acc sg fem γυνή "a woman/wife"

σου   your
pers pron: 2nd gen sg σύ "of you/your"

Explanations. It is not clear why Joseph would fear (φοβέω) to take Mary as his wife, except the likely social stigma that it would entail. παραλαβεῖν is a complementary infinitive, completing the action of and describing the main verb φοβηθῇς.

20e τὸ γὰρ ἐν αὐτῇ γεννηθὲν ἐκ πνεύματός ἐστιν ἁγίου·
Lit. The for in her conceived from spirit is holy;
for that which is conceived in her is from the Holy Spirit.

τὸ   the
article: nom sg neut ὁ "the"

γὰρ   for
conj: γάρ "for/because"

ἐν   in
prep: ἐν "in/by/with"

αὐτῇ   her
pers pron: dat sg fem αὐτός "to her"

γεννηθὲν   being conceived
ptcp: aor pass ptcp nom sg neut γεννάω "(it) having been given birth/fathered/born"

ἐκ   from
prep: ἐκ "from/out of"

πνεύματός	spirit
noun:	gen sg neut πνεῦμα "of a spirit"

ἐστιν	is
verb:	pres act ind 3rd sg εἰμί "(he/she/it) is"

ἁγίου	holy
adj:	gen sg neut ἅγιος "of a holy"

Explanation. In this verse the angel explains to Joseph the reason (γάρ) his otherwise understandable reservations about marriage to Mary should not be a hindrance. Her pregnancy is not the result of immoral relations; quite the contrary. It comes from the Holy Spirit.

21a τέξεται δὲ υἱὸν, καὶ καλέσεις τὸ ὄνομα αὐτοῦ Ἰησοῦν·
Lit. *She but son, and you will call the name of him Jesus;*
And she will bear a son, and you will call his name Jesus;

τέξεται	she will bear / give birth to
verb:	fut mid ind 3rd sg τίκτω "(he/she/it) will (for oneself) bear/give birth to"

δὲ	and
conj:	δέ "but/now"

υἱὸν	son
noun:	acc sg masc υἱός "a son/ son"

καὶ	and
conj:	καί "and"

καλέσεις	you (sg) will call
verb:	fut act ind 2nd sg καλέω "(you) will call/invite"

τὸ	the
article:	acc sg neut ὁ "the"

ὄνομα name
noun: acc sg neut ὄνομα "a name/name"

αὐτοῦ of him / his
pers pron: gen sg masc αὐτός "of him/it"

Ἰησοῦν Jesus / Joshua
noun: acc sg masc Ἰησοῦς "Jesus"

Explanation. Joseph is instructed to name the child Ἰησοῦν, which in Greek as well as Hebrew is identical to the biblical "Joshua." The significance of this name is explained next.

21b αὐτὸς γὰρ σώσει τὸν λαὸν αὐτοῦ ἀπὸ τῶν ἁμαρτιῶν αὐτῶν.
Lit. *He for will save the people of him from sins of them.*
for he will save his people from their sins.

αὐτὸς he
pers pron: nom sg masc αὐτός "he"

γὰρ for
conj: γάρ "for/because"

σώσει he will save
verb: fut act ind 3rd sg σῴζω "(he/she/it) will save/deliver"

τὸν the
article: acc sg masc ὁ "the"

λαὸν people
noun: acc sg masc λαός "a people/ people"

αὐτοῦ of him / his
pers pron: gen sg masc αὐτός "of him/it"

ἀπό	from
prep:	ἀπό "(away) from"

τῶν	the
article:	gen pl fem ὁ "of the (ones)"

ἁμαρτιῶν	sins
noun:	gen pl fem ἁμαρτία "of sins"

αὐτῶν	of them / their
pers pron:	gen pl masc αὐτός "of them/ their"

Explanation. The angel explains to Joseph the reason (γάρ) Joseph should give him the name Ἰησοῦς, and it has everything to do with the name Ἰησοῦς in Hebrew, which is *yehōšua* (יְהוֹשֻׁעַ), and in Hebrew means "YHWH is salvation" or "YHWH saves." So, Jesus is named "Jesus" because his name has significance, meaning that YHWH saves and Jesus himself will save his people (τὸν λαὸν αὐτοῦ). In Matthew "his people" is largely defined by allegiance to and faith in Jesus, not merely ethnicity. The salvation that Jesus comes to bring is from their sins (ἀπὸ τῶν ἁμαρτιῶν αὐτῶν).

22 τοῦτο δὲ ὅλον γέγονεν ἵνα πληρωθῇ τὸ ῥηθὲν ὑπὸ κυρίου διὰ τοῦ προφήτου λέγοντος

Lit. These but whole occurred in order that it might be fulfilled the word by the Lord through of the prophet saying

Now all this occurred in order that the saying by the Lord through the prophet may be fulfilled, saying

τοῦτο	this
dem pron: nom sg neut οὗτος "this/ this (thing)"	

δέ	now
conj:	δέ "but/now"

ὅλον	all / whole
adj:	nom sg neut ὅλος "all/whole"

γέγονεν	occurred
verb:	perf act ind 3rd sg γίνομαι "(he/she/it) has become/occurred"

ἵνα	in order that
conj:	ἵνα "in order that"

πληρωθῇ	it might be fulfilled
verb:	aor pass subj 3rd sg πληρόω "(he/she/it) should begin to be filled/fulfilled"

τὸ	the
article:	nom sg neut ὁ "the"

ῥηθὲν	saying
ptcp:	aor pass ptcp nom sg neut ἐρέω "(it) having been said"

ὑπὸ	by
prep:	ὑπό "by/under"

κυρίου	the Lord
noun:	gen sg masc κύριος "of the Lord/a lord"

διὰ	through
prep:	διά "through/because of"

τοῦ	the
article:	gen sg masc ὁ "of the/ the"

προφήτου	prophet
noun:	gen sg masc προφήτης "of a prophet/ prophet"

λέγοντος	saying
ptcp:	pres act ptcp gen sg masc λέγω "of (one) saying/ say"

Explanation. Matthew's ἵνα plus a subjunctive verb (πληρωθῇ) is common in his gospel and denotes purpose.

23a ἰδοὺ ἡ παρθένος ἐν γαστρὶ ἕξει καὶ τέξεται υἱόν,
Lit. Behold! The virgin in womb will be and will give birth to a son,
Behold! The virgin will be pregnant and will give birth to a son,

ἰδοὺ	Behold!
verb:	aor mid imv 2nd sg ὁράω "begin (you for yourself) to see/ see"
ἡ	the
article:	nom sg fem ὁ "the"
παρθένος	virgin
noun:	nom sg fem παρθένος "a virgin/ virgin"
ἐν	in
prep:	ἐν "in/by/with"
γαστρὶ	womb
noun:	dat sg fem γαστήρ "to a womb/belly"
ἕξει	will have
verb:	fut act ind 3rd sg ἔχω "(he/she/it) will have"
καὶ	and
conj:	καί "and"
τέξεται	will give birth to
verb:	fut mid ind 3rd sg τίκτω "(he/she/it) will (for oneself) bear/give birth to"
υἱόν	son
noun:	acc sg masc υἱός "a son/son"

23b καὶ καλέσουσιν τὸ ὄνομα αὐτοῦ Ἐμμανουήλ,
Lit. and they will call the name of him Emmanouēl,
And they will call his name Emmanuel,

καί   and
conj: καί "and"

καλέσουσιν   they will call
verb: fut act ind 3rd pl καλέω "(they) will call/invite"

τό   the
article: acc sg neut ὁ "the"

ὄνομα   name
noun: acc sg neut ὄνομα "a name"

αὐτοῦ   of him / his
pers pron: gen sg masc αὐτός "of him/it"

Ἐμμανουήλ   Emmanuel
noun: indecl Ἐμμανουήλ "Emmanuel"

Explanation. Ἐμμανουήλ is written in Greek letters but it is not a Greek word. Instead, it is a Hebrew word *Immānû ēl* (עִמָּנוּ אֵל) put into Greek letters from the Old Testament passage which Matthew cites (Isa 7:14). The context of Isaiah 7 pertains to the house of David and the birth of a child of promise to give some indication of God's intervention among his people, so the appeal to that context with respect to Jesus is fitting for Matthew's interests. The setting is the siege of Jerusalem and Ahaz king of Judah by Rezin king of Syria and Pekah king of Israel (Isa 7:1–2). The Lord instructs Isaiah to meet Ahaz and exhort him to courage because the plans of his enemies will not come to pass (Isa 7:3–9). The Lord himself assures Ahaz with a sign: "Behold, the virgin shall conceive and bear a son, and shall call his name Immanuel" (Isa 7:14 ESV). It is this child, the message continues, who shall not yet be old enough to know good from evil before "the land whose two kings you dread will be deserted" (Isa 7:16 ESV). Here Ahaz has in view trusting his nation's fate to the Assyrians rather than Israel's God—a foolish rejection by the unbelieving house of David. While a child was indeed born in Ahaz's time, it foreshadowed something later. For Matthew,

MATTHEW 1:18–25

Jesus is that expected child who will establish David's kingdom with security, righteousness, and justice.

23c ὅ ἐστιν μεθερμηνευόμενον μεθ' ἡμῶν ὁ θεός.
Lit. which is being translated with us God.
which is, when translated, God with us.

    ὅ   which
    rel pron: nom sg neut ὅς "which"

    ἐστιν   is
    verb: pres act ind 3rd sg εἰμί "(he/she/it) is"

    μεθερμηνευόμενον when translated
    ptcp: pres pass ptcp nom sg neut μεθερμηνεύω "(one) being fully interpreted"

    μεθ'   with
    prep: μετά "with/after"

    ἡμῶν   us
    pers pron: 1st gen pl ἐγώ "of us/our"

    ὁ   the
    article: nom sg masc ὁ "the"

    θεός   God
    noun: nom sg masc θεός "God/a god"

Explanation. Here Matthew explains for his readers, lest they miss the point, that the promise of a child to establish the Davidic kingdom is found in the child, but that is not all. This assurance is also borne out by the presence of God *himself* with his people. Jesus is *both* the promised child *and* God himself.

24a ἐγερθεὶς δὲ ὁ Ἰωσὴφ ἀπὸ τοῦ ὕπνου ἐποίησεν ὡς προσέταξεν αὐτῷ ὁ ἄγγελος κυρίου

Lit. After rising but Joseph from sleep he did as he commanded to him the angel of the Lord.

And after rising up from sleep Joseph did as the angel of the Lord commanded him

ἐγερθεὶς	after rising up
ptcp:	verb aor pass ptcp nom sg masc ἐγείρω "(he) having been raised up"
δὲ	and
conj:	δέ "but/now"
ὁ	the
article:	nom sg masc ὁ "the"
Ἰωσὴφ	Joseph
noun:	indecl Ἰωσήφ "Joseph"
ἀπὸ	from
prep:	ἀπό "(away) from"
τοῦ	the
article:	gen sg masc ὁ "of the"
ὕπνου	sleep
noun:	gen sg masc ὕπνος "of a deep sleep/rest"
ἐποίησεν	he did
verb:	aor act ind 3rd sg ποιέω "he/she/it did/made"
ὡς	as
adv:	ὡς "as"

MATTHEW 1:18-25

προσέταξεν   commanded
verb: aor act ind 3rd sg προστάσσω "he/she/it commanded/ ordered towards"

αὐτῷ   him
pers pron: dat sg masc αὐτός "to him"

ὁ   the
article: nom sg masc ὁ "the"

ἄγγελος   angel
noun: nom sg masc ἄγγελος "an angel"

κυρίου   of the Lord
noun: gen sg masc κύριος "of the Lord/a lord"

24b καὶ παρέλαβεν τὴν γυναῖκα αὐτοῦ,
Lit. and he took the wife of him,
And he took his wife,

καὶ   and
conj: καί "and"

παρέλαβεν   he took
verb: aor act ind 3rd sg παραλαμβάνω "he/she/it received/ took alongside"

τὴν   the
article: acc sg fem ὁ "the"

γυναῖκα   wife
noun: acc sg fem γυνή "a woman/wife"

αὐτοῦ   his
pers pron: gen sg masc αὐτός "of him/it"

Explanation. By saying Joseph "took his wife" (παρέλαβεν τὴν γυναῖκα αὐτοῦ) Matthew is simply saying he obeyed the angel's commands and married Mary.

25a καὶ οὐκ ἐγίνωσκεν αὐτὴν ἕως οὗ ἔτεκεν υἱόν·
Lit. and not he did know her until she gave birth to a son;
And he did not know her until she gave birth to a son;

καὶ   and
conj: καί "and"

οὐκ   not
neg particle: οὐ "no/not"

ἐγίνωσκεν   know
verb: impf act ind 3rd sg γινώσκω "(he/she/it) continually knew"

αὐτὴν   her
pers pron: acc sg fem αὐτός "her"

ἕως   until
adv: ἕως "until/while" "until/while"

οὗ   which
rel pron: gen sg masc ὅς "of which"

ἔτεκεν   she gave birth to
verb: aor act ind 3rd sg τίκτω "he/she/it bore/gave birth to"

υἱόν   son
noun: acc sg masc υἱός "a son"

Explanation. The verb ἐγίνωσκεν is an imperfect, meaning a continuous past action. So, Joseph "not knowing" Mary in sexual union was a continuous state until the birth of the son.

25b καὶ ἐκάλεσεν τὸ ὄνομα αὐτοῦ Ἰησοῦν.
Lit. and he called the name of him Jesus.
and he called his name Jesus.

καὶ	and
conj:	καί "and"

ἐκάλεσεν	called
verb:	aor act ind 3rd sg καλέω "he/she/it called/invited"

τὸ	the
article:	acc sg neut ὁ "the"

ὄνομα	name
noun:	acc sg neut ὄνομα "a name"

αὐτοῦ	of him/ his
pers pron:	gen sg masc αὐτός "of him/it"

Ἰησοῦν	Jesus
noun:	acc sg masc Ἰησοῦς "Jesus"

Preaching the Text

1. **Main idea:** God Saves through Jesus
2. **Text to Sermon:**
   a. The name "Jesus" only appears three times in this passage; elsewhere he is simply called "the child" or "a son." But like all of Matthew the passage is singularly about Jesus. So, it is important to notice what Matthew is telling readers about Jesus. There are certainly circumstances regarding the nature of his conception and birth (vv. 18), but this really serves to point to Jesus' "origin" from the Holy Spirit (v. 20). Not only is Jesus *from* God he also *is* God; God *with us*. This is the incarnation. Tied to his identity as God is Jesus' function and purpose: his very name is a banner announcing his significance—Jesus is YHWH's means of salvation for his people. And, whatever else Jesus may do for his people—and he does a great deal—the main function here is to save them from their sins.
   b. The story from Mary's perspective is found in the gospel of Luke. Here Matthew chooses to focus on the account from Joseph's perspective. Here there are two things that are remarkable: First, how little Joseph really knows about the situation. If there was more dialogue between Joseph and the angel giving some further explanation or clarification of instructions, Matthew did not record it. That means that it was not necessary for Matthew's purpose. Second, how promptly and unquestioningly Joseph obeys. No doubt he had responsibilities with work, caring for extended family, etc. But Matthew focuses on a simple instruction-obey formula. That is Joseph's faith in action.
   c. Readers are given the impression that it would be natural and expected that Joseph would divorce Mary. Presumably she was guilty of adultery, which called for punishment (Deut 22:20–24). When Mary's pregnancy became known, it was likely a public experience for her with considerable shame and disgrace for herself and her family. In obedience to the angel of the Lord, Joseph willingly aligns himself with Mary by taking her as his wife.
   d. The information given to Joseph about Mary's child is of course a private affair that occurs in a dream, but its implications are by

MATTHEW 1:18–25

no means limited to him and his new, small family. It is for all "his people." But for now, only Joseph knows that.

3. **Tip for Preaching:** Matthew condenses events that probably took months to occur into a passage that takes less than a minute to read. There is a great deal that is *unsaid* in this or any passage in Matthew. Our task is to focus on what *is said* by Matthew, and avoid speculating about other things. There is plenty here to discuss.

2

Matthew 4:1–11

The Temptation of the Son of God

What is the "temptation" about? Not surprisingly, it is about Jesus! Recall that Mark's gospel has almost nothing about this event (Mark 1:14) and Luke's account has a slightly different ordering of events (Luke 4:1–13). In Matthew's narrative Jesus was just baptized by John, who was in the wilderness of Judea (Matt 3:1), and a voice from heaven—clearly God's— declares Jesus to be his "beloved son" with whom he is "well pleased" (Matt 3:17). Being declared the son of God evokes Ps 2:7, a psalm utilized for the enthronement of a king. This is essential for the temptation account, because it is precisely as the "son of God" that Jesus is tempted. Notice that everything Satan asks of Jesus has to do with Jesus being "Son of God." But does Satan really *doubt* that Jesus is the Son of God? No, he is doing something much more subtle and poignant. He is enticing Jesus to use his status as God's son to provide for his own particular needs in response to a particular request. Furthermore, Matthew is crafting his narrative of the events to portray Jesus like a "new Moses," whose teachings are authoritative for the people of God. And in other ways, Jesus is like a "New Israel," being tested in the wilderness and succeeding where the first Israel failed. Ultimately, though, the temptation account will show us that Jesus is the Son of God in a class of His own, that only He can fill.

1a   Τότε ὁ Ἰησοῦς ἀνήχθη εἰς τὴν ἔρημον ὑπὸ τοῦ πνεύματος
Lit. Then Jesus was led into the wilderness by the Spirit
Then Jesus was led into the wilderness by the Spirit

MATTHEW 4:1–11

Τότε	then
adv:	τότε "then"

ὁ	the
article:	nom sg masc ὁ "the"

Ἰησοῦς	Jesus
noun:	nom sg masc Ἰησοῦς "Jesus"

ἀνήχθη	was lead
verb:	aor pass ind 3rd sg ἀνάγω "(he/she/it) was lead/brought up"

εἰς	into
prep:	εἰς "into/for"

τὴν	the
article:	acc sg fem ὁ "the"

ἔρημον	wilderness/ deserted region
adj:	acc sg fem ἔρημος "deserted/wild"

ὑπὸ	by
prep:	ὑπό "by/under"

τοῦ	the
article:	gen sg neut ὁ "of the"

πνεύματος	spirit
noun:	gen sg neut πνεῦμα "of a spirit"

Explanation. Both Matthew (4:1–11) and Luke (4:1–13) have the account of three temptations. Mark merely records that the temptation happened (Mark 1:12–13). But the order of the temptations differs between Matthew and Luke, with the latter recording (1) stones to bread, (2) kingdoms of the world, and (3) high point of the temple. Matthew's account also has (1) stones to bread, but then reverses the order from Luke to read (2) high point of the temple, and then (3) kingdoms of the world. Matthew alone uses the word τότε in these accounts, and so indicates that his is the sequential order, suggesting that Luke's is arranged topically.

ἀνάγω means "I lead," and in the aorist passive third singular form here, ἀνήχθη, it means Jesus "was lead." Matthew leaves no question about how Jesus got into the wilderness. He did not meander there one day by chance; He was led by the Spirit (ὑπὸ τοῦ πνεύματος).

The word ἔρημον, "wilderness," also means "deserted place." One should not think of a wooded forest, but rather a barren, dry desert-like area where very few things live. This wilderness is adjacent the Dead Sea, which is the lowest place on earth and near the site of Kirbet Qumran, the ruins of Qumran, where the Dead Sea Scrolls were discovered. There a group of about 200 men lived in seclusion, with their own distinctive interpretation of the Torah, in hopes that their piety would "prepare the way of the Lord" (Isa 40:3).

1b πειρασθῆναι ὑπὸ τοῦ διαβόλου.
Lit. to be tempted by the devil
to be tempted by the devil.

πειρασθῆναι to be tempted
verb: aor pass inf πειράζω "to begin to be tested"

ὑπὸ by
prep: ὑπό "by/under"

τοῦ the
article: gen sg masc ὁ "of the"

διαβόλου devil
adj: gen sg masc διάβολος "of a slanderous (devil)"

Explanation. πειρασθῆναι is an infinitive, indicating purpose. Jesus was brought to the wilderness for no other purpose than the temptation by the devil.

MATTHEW 4:1-11

Just as the Spirit was the means of the leading (ὑπὸ τοῦ πνεύματος, 1a), the devil is the means of the tempting (ὑπὸ τοῦ διαβόλου).

2a καὶ νηστεύσας ἡμέρας τεσσεράκοντα καὶ νύκτας τεσσεράκοντα
Lit. and after fasting days forty and nights forty
and after fasting forty days and forty nights

καὶ   and
conj: καί "and"

νηστεύσας   after fasting
ptcp: aor act ptcp nom sg masc νηστεύω "(he) having fasted"

ἡμέρας   days
noun: acc pl fem ἡμέρα "days"

τεσσεράκοντα   forty
adj: num τεσσαράκοντα "forty"

καὶ   and
conj: καί "and"

νύκτας   nights
noun: acc pl fem νύξ "nights"

τεσσεράκοντα   forty
adj: num τεσσαράκοντα "forty"

Explanation. Luke's account simply says Jesus did not eat anything (Luke 4:2). Matthew alone says that Jesus was actively fasting (νηστεύω), which in Matthew is a deliberate act of righteousness suitable for Jesus (Matt 6:16-18).

ἡμέρας τεσσεράκοντα καὶ νύκτας τεσσεράκοντα seems redundant; but it does not simply mean that Jesus also fasted at night. Instead, it is intended to remind readers of Moses, who was also on a mountain forty days and forty nights (Exod 34:28). In some ways, Jesus is very much like Moses in this narrative.

2b ὕστερον ἐπείνασεν.
Lit. afterward he hungered.
afterward, he hungered.

<blockquote>

ὕστερον   afterward
adv: ὕστερον "afterward/later"

ἐπείνασεν   he hungered
verb: aor act ind 3rd sg πεινάω "he/she/it hungered"

</blockquote>

Explanation. ὕστερον indicates season of fasting was at its end, and Jesus as a result ἐπείνασεν, hungered. But it is not yet time for him to eat, as the ensuing narrative clarifies. Being fully human, Jesus experienced the limitations of human needs like hunger.

3a καὶ προσελθὼν ὁ πειράζων εἶπεν αὐτῷ·
Lit. And approaching the tempter said to him;
And, approaching, the tempter said to him;

<blockquote>

καὶ   and
conj: καί "and"

προσελθὼν   approaching
ptcp: aor act ptcp nom sg masc προσέρχομαι "(he) having come toward"

ὁ   the
article: nom sg masc ὁ "the"

πειράζων   one tempting/ tempter
ptcp: pres act ptcp nom sg masc πειράζω "(one) testing"

</blockquote>

εἶπεν said
verb: aor act ind 3rd sg λέγω "he/she/it said"

αὐτῷ to him
pers pron: dat sg masc αὐτός "to him"

Explanation. The devil is called ὁ πειράζων, which is a participle from the verb πειράζω, "I test" or "I tempt." As a participle, then, it means "the one tempting" or simply "the tempter." This designates the devil's function in the temptation account; his principal role is that of tempting Jesus.

3b εἰ υἱὸς εἶ τοῦ θεοῦ,
Lit. Since you are the son of God
Since you are the son of God

εἰ if / since
conditional: εἰ "if/since"

υἱὸς son
noun: nom sg masc υἱός "a son/son"

εἶ you are
verb: pres act ind 2nd sg εἰμί "(you) are"

τοῦ of the
article: gen sg masc ὁ "of the"

θεοῦ god
noun: gen sg masc θεός "of God/a god"

Explanation. εἰ and εἶ are different words in Greek. The former, εἰ, is a conditional term meaning "if," and often followed by a verb in the subjunctive mood. The word εἶ is that verb in the subjunctive mood, and it comes from the verb εἰμί, "to be." So, the phrase εἰ . . . εἶ means "if you are" or "if you should be." Here the question pertains to Jesus being υἱὸς θεοῦ, "son of God."

εἰ as a conditional term which can translate "if" or "since." The context suggests that the devil is by no means uncertain about Jesus' identity. That is, he is not questioning *whether* Jesus is the son of God. Rather, he is *presuming* that he is the son of God, and enticing him to do utilize that unique and powerful status to care for his own affairs. So, it is best translated here not "if" you are the son of God, but "since" you are the son of God.

3c εἰπὲ ἵνα οἱ λίθοι οὗτοι ἄρτοι γένωνται.
Lit. Say that the stones these breads may become.
Speak, that these stones may become bread.

εἰπὲ	speak
verb:	aor act imv 2nd sg λέγω "begin (you) to say"

ἵνα	that/ in order that
conj:	ἵνα "that/in order that"

οἱ	the
article:	nom pl masc ὁ "the (ones)/the"

λίθοι	stones
noun:	nom pl masc λίθος "stones"

οὗτοι	these
dem pron:	nom pl masc οὗτος "these"

ἄρτοι	bread
noun:	nom pl masc ἄρτος "breads/loaves"

γένωνται	may become
verb:	aor mid subj 3rd pl γίνομαι "(they) should begin to be (for themselves) become/occurred"

Explanation. The temptation here is for Jesus to use his status as son of God to feed himself by supernatural means. Satan knows that merely by speaking (εἰπόν), Jesus could turn the stones to bread (ἵνα οἱ λίθοι οὗτοι ἄρτοι γένωνται) and solve the problem of his hunger (Matt 4:2). Jesus' supernatural power is not only recognized but presumed, and yet nowhere in this passage does Jesus use those powers. He is instead entirely dependent on "every word that comes from the mouth of God," meaning the Scripture that he cites in response to Satan each time.

4a ὁ δὲ ἀποκριθεὶς εἶπεν·
Lit. The but answering he said,
But, answering, he said,

ὁ	the
article:	nom sg masc ὁ "the"

δὲ	but
conj:	δέ "but/now"

ἀποκριθεὶς	answering
ptcp:	aor pass ptcp nom sg masc ἀποκρίνομαι "(he) having been answered"

εἶπεν	he said
verb:	aor act ind 3rd sg λέγω "he/she/it said"

4b γέγραπται· οὐκ ἐπ' ἄρτῳ μόνῳ ζήσεται ὁ ἄνθρωπος,
Lit. "It has been written; not upon bread only he shall live a person,
"It has been written, 'A person does not live on bread only,

γέγραπται	it has been written
verb:	perf pass ind 3rd sg γράφω "(he/she/it) has been written"

οὐκ	not
neg particle:	οὐ "no/not"

ἐπ'   on/ upon
prep: ἐπί "upon"

ἄρτῳ   bread
noun: dat sg masc ἄρτος "to a bread/loaf"

μόνῳ   only
adj: dat sg masc μόνος "to an alone/only"

ζήσεται shall live/ will live
verb: fut mid ind 3rd sg ζάω "(he/she/it) will (for oneself) live"

ὁ   the
article: nom sg masc ὁ "the"

ἄνθρωπος man/ person/ human being
noun: nom sg masc ἄνθρωπος "a man/person"

Explanation. γέγραπται is a passive voice verb, indicating it was written by someone not named. Perhaps it is inferred that it is written by God, or at least Moses.

The command is quoted from Deut 8:3. This is part of a larger passage in Deuteronomy where Moses recounts to Israel the instructions which God gave to him, and which he in turn was to give to Israel (see Deut 5:1).

The commands taken from the Old Testament, such as ζήσεται, "you will live," are in the future tense most likely because the Hebrew text from which it comes is in the qal imperfect (יִהְיֶה) which alone can connote a future sense, but when it is negated, like here (לֹא . . . יִהְיֶה), takes a strong imperatival sense. Like the Ten Commandments (Exod 20:1–17), it means, *you shall never!*

English translations traditionally render ἄνθρωπος as "man," but the term is a general one for human being and is not here gender-specific.

MATTHEW 4:1-11

4c ἀλλ' ἐπὶ παντὶ ῥήματι ἐκπορευομένῳ διὰ στόματος θεοῦ.
Lit. *but upon every word proceeding through the mouth of God."*
but upon every word proceeding through the mouth of God."

ἀλλ'	but
conj:	ἀλλά "but"

ἐπὶ	upon
prep:	ἐπί "upon"

παντὶ	all / every
adj:	dat sg neut πᾶς "to an all"

ῥήματι	saying/ word
noun:	dat sg neut ῥῆμα "to a saying"

ἐκπορευομένῳ	proceeding out of
ptcp:	pres mid/pass ptcp dat sg neut ἐκπορεύομαι "to (one) proceeding/going out"

διὰ	through
prep:	διά "through/because of"

στόματος	mouth
noun:	gen sg neut στόμα "of the mouth"

θεοῦ	of God
noun:	gen sg masc θεός "of God/a god"

5a Τότε παραλαμβάνει αὐτὸν ὁ διάβολος εἰς τὴν ἁγίαν πόλιν
Lit. *Then he took him the devil into the holy city*
Then the devil took him along into the holy city

Τότε	then
adv:	τότε "then"

παραλαμβάνει   took along
verb: pres act ind 3rd sg παραλαμβάνω "(he/she/it) receives/ takes alongside"

αὐτὸν   him
pers pron: acc sg masc αὐτός "him"

ὁ   the
article: nom sg masc ὁ "the"

διάβολος   devil
adj: nom sg masc διάβολος "slanderous (devil)"

εἰς   into
prep: εἰς "into/for"

τὴν   the
article: acc sg fem ὁ "the"

ἁγίαν   holy
adj: acc sg fem ἅγιος "holy"

πόλιν   city
noun: acc sg fem πόλις "a city/ city"

Explanation. The "holy city" is Jerusalem (see Neh 11:1; Isa 52:1; Matt 27:53; Rev 11:2; 21:2, 10; 22:19).

5b   καὶ ἔστησεν αὐτὸν ἐπὶ τὸ πτερύγιον τοῦ ἱεροῦ
Lit. and he stood him upon the highest point of the temple
and he stood him upon the highest point of the temple

καὶ   and
conj: καί "and"

MATTHEW 4:1-11

ἔστησεν	he stood
verb:	aor act ind 3rd sg ἵστημι "he/she/it stood"

αὐτὸν	him
pers pron:	acc sg masc αὐτός "him"

ἐπὶ	upon
prep:	ἐπί "upon"

τὸ	the
article:	acc sg neut ὁ "the"

πτερύγιον	pinnacle/ highest point
noun:	acc sg neut πτερύγιον "a pinnacle/ highest point"

τοῦ	of the
article:	gen sg neut ὁ "of the"

ἱεροῦ	temple
noun:	gen sg neut ἱερόν "of a temple"

Explanation. The action of standing Jesus (ἔστησεν) is done by the devil. Notice how "passive" Jesus is here and throughout the passage; presumably allowing the devil to lead in this and the other encounters.

The τὸ πτερύγιον τοῦ ἱεροῦ is not an architectural feature of the temple, rather it is a way of indicating a high and precarious position.

6a καὶ λέγει αὐτῷ· Εἰ υἱὸς εἶ τοῦ θεοῦ,
Lit. and he said to him, "If son you are of God,
and he said to him, "Since you are the son of God,

καὶ	and
conj:	καί "and"

λέγει he says/ said
verb: pres act ind 3rd sg λέγω "(he/she/it) says"

αὐτῷ to him
pers pron: dat sg masc αὐτός "to him"

Εἰ if/ since
conditional: εἰ "if"

υἱὸς son
noun: nom sg masc υἱός "a son"

εἶ you are
verb: pres act ind 2nd sg εἰμί "(you) are"

τοῦ of the
article: gen sg masc ὁ "of the"

θεοῦ God
noun: gen sg masc θεός "of God/a god"

Explanation. λέγει is a "historical present," meaning its form is in the present tense but the context, by use of the aorists beforehand, indicate the action of the whole scene takes place in the past.

6b βάλε σεαυτὸν κάτω·

Lit. throw yourself down;

throw yourself down;

βάλε throw/ cast
verb: aor act imv 2nd sg βάλλω "begin (you) to throw/cast"

σεαυτὸν yourself
reflexive pron: 2nd acc sg masc σεαυτοῦ "yourself"

κάτω   down/ downward/ below
adv: κάτω "below"

Explanation. κάτω is an adverb of place, indicating a downward direction.

6c γέγραπται γὰρ ὅτι τοῖς ἀγγέλοις αὐτοῦ ἐντελεῖται περὶ σοῦ

Lit. it has been written for that to the angels of him he will command concerning of you

for it has been written, 'He will command his angels concerning you

γέγραπται   it has been written
verb: perf pass ind 3rd sg γράφω "(he/she/it) has been written"

γὰρ   for
conj: γάρ "for/because"

ὅτι   introduces a quotation, acts like an English quotation mark, or it may be part of the quotation from Ps 91:11 (90:11 LXX).
conj: ὅτι "because/that"

τοῖς   to the ones/ the
article: dat pl masc ὁ "to the (ones)"

ἀγγέλοις   angels
noun: dat pl masc ἄγγελος "to angels"

αὐτοῦ   of him/ his
pers pron: gen sg masc αὐτός "of him/it/ his"

ἐντελεῖται   he will command
verb: fut mid/pass ind 3rd sg ἐντέλλω "(he/she/it) will command"

περὶ   concerning
prep: περί "concerning/around"

σοῦ   you
pers pron: 2nd gen sg σύ "of you"

Explanation. The quotation comes from Ps 90:11 in the LXX, which corresponds to Ps 91:11 in the Hebrew (and modern translations).

Τοῖς ἀγγέλοις is in the front of the sentence quoted for emphasis. They are the agents of the ensuing activity.

The subject of ἐντελεῖται is implied, God. It is *God* who commands *his* angels concerning *you* (Jesus).

6d καὶ ἐπὶ χειρῶν ἀροῦσίν σε,
Lit. *and upon the hands they will bear you,*
and upon hands they will bear you,

καὶ   and
conj: καί "and"

ἐπὶ   upon
prep: ἐπί "upon"

χειρῶν   hands
noun: gen pl fem χείρ "of hands"

ἀροῦσίν   they will bear up/ take away/ lift up
verb: fut act ind 3rd pl αἴρω "(they) will take away/lift up"

σε   you
pers pron: 2nd acc sg σύ "you"

Explanation. The subject of the plural verb ἀροῦσίν is the angels (v. 6a).

6e μή ποτε προσκόψῃς πρὸς λίθον τὸν πόδα σου.
Lit. not at some time you should stroke to stone the foot of you."
lest you strike your foot against a stone.'"

μή	not

neg particle: μή "no/not (stop)"

ποτε	at some time

particle: ποτέ "former/when"

προσκόψῃς	you stumble/ strike upon

verb: aor act subj 2nd sg προσκόπτω "you should begin to stumble/strike upon"

πρὸς	toward

prep: πρός "toward"

λίθον	stone

noun: acc sg masc λίθος "a stone"

τὸν	the

article: acc sg masc ὁ "the"

πόδα	foot

noun: acc sg masc πούς "a foot"

σου	of you/ your

pers pron: 2nd gen sg σύ "of you/ your"

Explanation. μή ποτε, sometimes written as a single word μήποτε is a common expression meaning "lest" or "so that not," meaning what occurs afterwards is something that is undesirable and to be avoided.

The angels from Ps 91:11 (90:11 LXX) are instructed by God concerning Jesus in such a manner as to prevent him from striking his foot against a stone. This is likely a metaphor for protecting him in his comings and goings.

7a ἔφη αὐτῷ ὁ Ἰησοῦς·
Lit. he said to him Jesus;
Jesus said to him,

> ἔφη he said
> verb: impf act ind 3rd sg φημί "(he/she/it) continually stated/claimed"
>
> αὐτῷ to him
> pers pron: dat sg masc αὐτός "to him"
>
> ὁ the
> article: nom sg masc ὁ "the"
>
> Ἰησοῦς Jesus
> noun: nom sg masc Ἰησοῦς "Jesus"

Explanation. The form ἔφη could be aorist or imperfect. The context here suggests the aorist is in view.

7b πάλιν γέγραπται·
Lit. "Again it has been written
"Again, it has been written,

> πάλιν again
> adv: πάλιν "again"
>
> γέγραπται it has been written
> verb: perf pass ind 3rd sg γράφω "(he/she/it) has been written"

Explanation. πάλιν is an adverb indicating a repetition in the same manner, meaning that what he is about to quote is written in the same manner as what he quoted previously.

MATTHEW 4:1–11

7c οὐκ ἐκπειράσεις κύριον τὸν θεόν σου.
Lit. Not you shall test the Lord the God of you."
'You shall not test the Lord your God.'"

οὐκ   not
neg particle: οὐ "no/not"

ἐκπειράσεις   you (sg) will test/ tempt
verb: fut act ind 2nd sg ἐκπειράζω "(you) will tempt/test"

κύριον   Lord
noun: acc sg masc κύριος "Lord/lord"

τὸν   the
article: acc sg masc ὁ "the"

θεόν   God
noun: acc sg masc θεός "God/god"

σου   of you/ your
pers pron: 2nd gen sg σύ "of you"

Explanation. The future indicative ἐκπειράσεις is sometimes called an "imperatival future."

Κύριον and θεόν are both nouns in the accusative case. The first, Κύριον, is the direct object of the verb ἐκπειράσεις. The second noun, θεόν, is in apposition to Κύριον, meaning it is restating it. So, it translates "the Lord God."

The response by Jesus comes from Deut 6:16, which comes from the same context as the passage above, where Moses is passing on to Israel the instructions given to him by God (Deut 5:1).

8a Πάλιν παραλαμβάνει αὐτὸν ὁ διάβολος εἰς ὄρος ὑψηλὸν λίαν
Lit. Again he took him the devil into mountain high exceedingly,
Again, the devil took him to an exceedingly high mountain,

Πάλιν again
adv: πάλιν "again"

παραλαμβάνει he took/ took along
verb: pres act ind 3rd sg παραλαμβάνω "(he/she/it) receives/takes alongside"

αὐτὸν him
pers pron: acc sg masc αὐτός "him"

ὁ the
article: nom sg masc ὁ "the"

διάβολος devil
adj: nom sg masc διάβολος "slanderous (devil)"

εἰς into/ to
prep: εἰς "into/for"

ὄρος mountain
noun: acc sg neut ὄρος "a mountain"

ὑψηλὸν high
adj: acc sg neut ὑψηλός "high"

λίαν greatly/ exceedingly
adv: λίαν "exceedingly"

Explanation. παραλαμβάνω is a compound verb, built from the preposition παρα "beside, in the presence of, alongside of" and the verb λαμβάνω, "to take." Here the compound is used because the devil takes Jesus *with* him. That is, they go together.

The description of the height of the mountain (ὄρος) is emphatic. First, it is "high" (ὑψηλὸν) and, second, its height is "exceedingly" or "extreme" (λίαν).

8b καὶ δείκνυσιν αὐτῷ πάσας τὰς βασιλείας τοῦ κόσμου καὶ τὴν δόξαν αὐτῶν

Lit. and he showed to him all the kingdoms of the world and the glory of them

and he showed him all the kingdoms of the world and their glory

καὶ and
conj: καί "and"

δείκνυσιν   he showed
verb: pres act ind 3rd sg δεικνύω "(he/she/it) shows"

αὐτῷ   to him/ him
pers pron: dat sg masc αὐτός "to him"

πάσας   all
adj: acc pl fem πᾶς "all (ones)"

τὰς   the
article: acc pl fem ὁ "the (ones)"

βασιλείας   kingdoms
noun: acc pl fem βασιλεία "kingdoms"

τοῦ   of the
article: gen sg masc ὁ "of the"

κόσμου world
noun: gen sg masc κόσμος "of the world"

καὶ   and
conj: καί "and"

τὴν   the
article: acc sg fem ὁ "the"

δόξαν   glory
noun: acc sg fem δόξα "glory"

αὐτῶν   of them/ their
pers pron: gen pl fem αὐτός "of them"

Explanation. The manner in which the devil showed (δείκνυσιν) Jesus the kingdoms and their glory is not specified.

The word βασιλεία in Matthew occurs fifty-six times, and forms a central part of Jesus' teaching. With the coming of Jesus, God's kingdom has come near (Matt 4:17). This kingdom is where Jesus reigns as king, and the advancement of the kingdom is an advancement of his kingship.

9a καὶ εἶπεν αὐτῷ·
Lit. and he said to him;
and he said to him,

καί   and
conj: καί "and"

εἶπεν   he said
verb: aor act ind 3rd sg λέγω "he/she/it said"

αὐτῷ   to him
pers pron: dat sg masc αὐτός "to him"

Explanation. αὐτῷ is in the dative because the words spoken are *to* "him" (Jesus). If Matthew used the accusative αὐτόν it would mean he "spoke him," which gives no sense.

9b ταῦτά σοι πάντα δώσω, ἐὰν πεσὼν προσκυνήσῃς μοι.
Lit. "These to you all I will give if falling down you should worship me."
"All these things to you I will give, if, falling down, you should worship me."

ταῦτά   these (things)
dem pron: acc pl neut οὗτος "these"

σοι   you/ to you
pers pron: 2nd dat sg σύ "to you"

πάντα   and
adj: acc pl neut πᾶς "all (ones)"

δώσω   I will give
verb: fut act ind 1st sg δίδωμι "(I) will give"

ἐάν   if
conditional: ἐάν "if"

πεσών   falling down
ptcp: aor act ptcp nom sg masc πίπτω "(he) having fallen"

προσκυνήσῃς   you should worship
verb: aor act subj 2nd sg προσκυνέω "you should begin to worship/prostrate"

μοι   me
pers pron: 1st dat sg ἐγώ "to me"

Explanation. Putting the demonstrative pronoun ταῦτα at the beginning of the sentence is for emphasis: it is "*these things*"–meaning the kingdoms of the world and their glory—the devil will give to Jesus.

ἐάν indicates the condition for the first part of the sentence, giving Jesus the kingdoms and their glory, to come true. ἐάν is typically followed by a subjunctive verb, as here (προσκυνήσῃς), meaning "if you should worship me." The participle πεσών describes the verb; the devil is asking Jesus to worship him, falling down or prostrating himself. It is not two actions—falling down and worshipping—it is a worship characterized by prostration.

10a τότε λέγει αὐτῷ ὁ Ἰησοῦς·
Lit. then he said to him Jesus;
then Jesus said to him,

τότε	then
adv:	τότε "then"

λέγει	he said
verb:	pres act ind 3rd sg λέγω "(he/she/it) says"

αὐτῷ	to him
pers pron:	dat sg masc αὐτός "to him"

ὁ	the
article:	nom sg masc ὁ "the"

Ἰησοῦς	Jesus
noun:	nom sg masc Ἰησοῦς "Jesus"

Explanation. Regardless of word order, Matthew puts ὁ Ἰησοῦς in the nominative case, which means only it can be the subject of the verb λέγει.

10b ὕπαγε, σατανᾶ· γέγραπται γάρ· κύριον τὸν θεόν σου προσκυνήσεις
Lit. "Go, Satan! It has been written for Lord the God of you shall worship
"Go, Satan! For it has been written, 'The Lord your God you shall worship

ὕπαγε	Go!
verb:	pres act imv 2nd sg ὑπάγω "depart/go forth (you)"

σατανᾶ	Satan
noun:	voc sg masc σατανᾶς "O Satan!"

γέγραπται it has been written
verb: perf pass ind 3rd sg γράφω "(he/she/it) has been written"

γάρ for
conj: γάρ "for/because"

κύριον Lord
noun: acc sg masc κύριος "Lord/lord"

τὸν the
article: acc sg masc ὁ "the"

θεόν God
noun: acc sg masc θεός "God/god"

σου of you/ your
pers pron: 2nd gen sg σύ "of you/ your"

προσκυνήσεις you shall worship
verb: fut act ind 2nd sg προσκυνέω "(you) will worship/prostrate"

Explanation. Jesus' emphatic command to depart (ὕπαγε) is grounded (γάρ) in the command of scripture. That is, the reason Jesus commands his departure, and implicitly and emphatically refuses the devil's offer, is the clear command of scripture. What the devil is asking for—προσκυνέω–is owed exclusively to God.

The quotation here comes from either Deut 6:13a or 10:20a, which say exactly the same thing: κύριον τὸν θεόν σου φοβηθήση. But Matthew replaces "fear" (φοβηθήση) with "worship" (προσκυνήσεις), understanding the devil's request to worship him as appropriately addressed by this verse.

10c καὶ αὐτῷ μόνῳ λατρεύσεις.
Lit. and to him only you shall serve.
and him only you shall serve.'"

καί	and
conj:	καί "and"

αὐτῷ	him/ to him
pers pron:	dat sg masc αὐτός "to him"

μόνῳ	alone/ alone
adj:	dat sg masc μόνος "to an alone/only"

λατρεύσεις	you (sg) will serve
verb:	fut act ind 2nd sg λατρεύω "(you) will render service"

Explanation. The quotation here comes from either Deut 6:13b or 10:20b, which say exactly the same thing: καὶ αὐτῷ λατρεύσεις. Notice that Matthew adds the emphatic and exclusive "alone" (μόνῳ), surely implied by not stated in Deuteronomy.

11a Τότε ἀφίησιν αὐτὸν ὁ διάβολος,
Lit. Then he left him the devil,
Then the devil left him,

Τότε	then
adv:	τότε "then"

ἀφίησιν	left
verb:	pres act ind 3rd sg ἀφίημι "(he/she/it) dismisses/forsakes"

αὐτόν	him
pers pron:	acc sg masc αὐτός "him"

ὁ   the
article: nom sg masc ὁ "the"

διάβολος devil
adj: nom sg masc διάβολος "slanderous (devil)"

Explanation. The devil leaves Jesus at this point, but his influence is still felt sometimes by the misunderstanding of Jesus' own disciples ("Get behind me, Satan!" Matt 16:23 NRSV) or even by those who observe him on the cross, enticing him with the same phrase used by Satan: "save yourself! *If you are the Son of God*, come down from the cross" (Matt 27:40 NRSV).

11b καὶ ἰδοὺ ἄγγελοι προσῆλθον
Lit. and behold angels came
and behold angels came

    καὶ   and
    conj: καί "and"

    ἰδοὺ   behold
    verb: aor mid imv 2nd sg ὁράω "begin (you for yourself) to see"

    ἄγγελοι   angels
    noun: nom pl masc ἄγγελος "angels"

    προσῆλθον came
    verb: aor act ind 3rd pl προσέρχομαι "they came toward"

Explanation. Now the angels which the devil evoked in the temptation in v. 6 come to Jesus not by coercion but to minister to him (11c).

11c καὶ διηκόνουν αὐτῷ.
Lit. and they waited upon him.
and they were ministering to him.

καὶ   and
conj: καί "and"

διηκόνουν   they were ministering
verb: impf act ind 3rd pl διακονέω "(they) continually ministered/served"

αὐτῷ   to him
pers pron: dat sg masc αὐτός "to him"

Explanation. διηκόνουν is an imperfect verb, indicating that the action of "ministering" was a continuous past action. It was ongoing, not simply a single time. Notice that Satan quotes scripture regarding the angels bearing him up, and Jesus refuses to test God. Here those very angels attend to Jesus' needs upon the successful completion of his test.

Preaching the Text

1. **Main idea:** Jesus is the Tested Son of God

2. The devil's statements are about Jesus—"if you are the son of God." But the devil knows who Jesus is; that is not in question. The question is, and what the devil prods Jesus to do, is to *act upon* His identity, precisely because He *is* the son of God. So, this passage is about Jesus—who He is and what He came to do. In a sense, we can all relate because we all face temptations (see 1 Cor 10:13; Heb 4:15). Yet in another sense these are entirely unique, because none of us are tempted as Son of God. Here are a few salient points:

3. **Text to Sermon:**

    a. First Temptation: The quote in v. 4 comes from Deut 8:3. This is a reminder by Moses to Israel about the Lord's provision: ² "Remember the long way that the LORD your God has led you these forty years in the wilderness, in order to humble you, testing you to know what was in your heart, whether or not you would keep his commandments. ³ He humbled you by letting you hunger, then by feeding you with manna, with which neither you nor your ancestors were acquainted, in order to make you understand that one does not live by bread alone, but by every word that comes from the mouth of the LORD" (Deut 8:2–3 NRSV). In Luke's account the quotation simply reads "one does not live by bread alone" (Luke 4:4). Matthew alone continues the quotation to underscore living "upon every word proceeding through the mouth of God" (Matt 4:4). Matthew's emphasis is on the abiding authority of the Scriptures of the Old Testament, and how they are continually brought to their fullness in Jesus.

    b. Second Temptation: Satan tempts Jesus to throw himself down from a high point of the temple (vv. 5–6) and so claim a promise from Ps 91:11–12. The problem with Satan's use of this passage is explained by Jesus himself, when he retorts that what Satan is really asking Jesus to do is put the Lord to the test (v. 7). This response is itself a quotation from Deut 6:16 and clearly indicates that Jesus regarded obedience to Satan's instruction as sinning against God. How? The appeal to Psalm 91 is taken by the devil completely out of context. It addresses those who "live in the shelter of the Most

High" (91:1) regard the Lord as their "refuge" and "fortress" (91:2), and so is followed by a litany of promises to that person (91:3–16), including the promises quoted by Satan (91:11–12). It is *not* a promise to those who go *looking* to put themselves at risk in order to *force God's hand* to respond. This kind of manipulation, Jesus says, is sin. It would be sin for Jesus, and sin for us. Obligating God is making a claim upon a promise by deliberately putting out something so as to attempt to force God to respond. It reminds me somewhat of playing checkers: I barely know the rules, but I once played a friend who was a competitive checkers champion! He knew how to move his pieces in such a way that would leave me with no choice but to move my pieces where he wanted me. It was very frustrating in a board game; in a life of faith to use against God it's evil.

c. Third Temptation: In the third temptation the devil shows Jesus the kingdoms of the world and their splendor (v. 8). He offers to give them to Jesus on the condition that Jesus would worship the devil (v. 9). Notice that Jesus does not argue the point; the devil does (temporarily) have the kingdoms and their splendor. Moreover, Jesus will himself one day have them for himself. The temptation, then, is for Jesus to have them *now* and not *through the suffering of the cross*. It is only *after* the crucifixion and resurrection that "all authority in heaven and on earth" will be given to Jesus (Matt 28:18). But the condition is too steep; it is to give to the devil what belongs to God alone, and here Jesus quotes from Deut 6:13; 10:20.

d. In the end, Satan is trying to get Jesus to avoid the way of the cross. But he is not alone. Peter's notion of Jesus' mission that balks at suffering and death is attributed to Satan (Matt 16:23), and even at the cross Jesus is chided by onlookers and opponents alike with the *very words of the devil* to come down off the cross "if you are the son of God" (Matt 27:40; cf. 27:43).

4. **Tip for Preaching:** We have noted that Jesus is rather "passive," allowing the devil to take him here and there, show him this and that. But notice that though Jesus has at his disposal more twelve legions of angels (Matt 26:53), at no point during this narrative does Jesus use any of *his supernatural powers*. The only power he uses is Scripture.

MATTHEW 4:1-11

We too can memorize scripture, and if it's good enough for the Son of God to combat the devil, it is surely good enough for us to fight our sins. But notice too that the devil can quote Scripture, so some degree of understanding and not simply exploiting is necessary to follow the example of the faithful Son of God.

3

Matthew 5:1–12

On Being Blessed

Want to be blessed? Of course, we all do. But how does *Jesus* define being "blessed"? And what does it mean to be "blessed"? In Matthew's Gospel Jesus moves from the temptation account (4:1–11) to the beginning of his public ministry (4:12–17). The theme of the latter is simply this: "Repent, for the kingdom of heaven has come near" (4:17, NRSV). Jesus first ministers around Galilee, gathering disciples and proclaiming the kingdom of God (4:18–25). With a crowd around him, Jesus ascends a mountain, sits down, and teaches his disciples about the nature of that kingdom (Matt 5:1). Throughout the Sermon on the Mount (Matt 5–7) there are many paradoxes and ways in which the kingdom of God operates with respect to the kingdoms of the earth. This begins in the Beatitudes (Matt 5:2–12). Here Jesus pronounces as "blessed" many things which we spend a lot of energy trying to avoid. But the hardships of Jesus' kind of blessedness is the path of Jesus. Throughout the Beatitudes there is a kind of unexplained correspondence between the believers' behavior and his/ her standing before God. One who mourns will be comforted by God; one who shows mercy will be shown mercy by God, etc.

1a Ἰδὼν δὲ τοὺς ὄχλους ἀνέβη εἰς τὸ ὄρος
    Lit. Seeing but the crowds (he) ascended into the mountain;
    Now seeing the crowds, he ascended the mountain;

Ἰδών	seeing/ beholding
ptcp:	aor act ptcp nom sg masc ὁράω "(he) having seen"

δὲ	but/ now
conj:	δέ "but/now"

τοὺς	the
article:	acc pl masc ὁ "the (ones)"

ὄχλους	crowds
noun:	acc pl masc ὄχλος "crowds"

ἀνέβη	he ascended/ went up
verb:	aor act ind 3rd sg ἀναβαίνω "he/she/it went up/ascended"

εἰς	into
prep:	εἰς "into/for"

τὸ	the
article:	acc sg neut ὁ "the"

ὄρος	mountain
noun:	acc sg neut ὄρος "a mountain"

Explanation. ὄχλους is a plural noun; it also appears in the singular, ὄχλος. The former is "crowds," the latter is "crowd" and both connote a group by the very meaning of the word. In Matthew the crowds are often depicted as curious onlookers who have not yet made up their minds about Jesus to the point of becoming disciples.

Jesus here is presented like Moses, who ascends Mount Sinai. Matthew's use of a form of ἀναβαίνω and the phrase εἰς τὸ ὄρος is used of Moses in similar contexts (Exod 19:3; 24:18, 34:4). Like in the Temptation account (Matt 4:1–11), Jesus is a "new Moses." But Jesus is not a new giver of a new law, but one who explains the true meaning and intent of the Law given to Moses. This is born out most in the so-called "antitheses," where Jesus says "You have heard that it was said . . . ," often quotes the Old Testament, and then says, "But I say to you . . ." Here he is not contrasting or contradicting the Old Testament, but rather explaining what it has always meant–getting to the heart of the believer.

1b καὶ καθίσαντος αὐτοῦ προσῆλθαν αὐτῷ οἱ μαθηταὶ αὐτοῦ·
Lit. and sitting down of him they came to him the disciples of him;
And when he sat down his disciples came to him,

καὶ   and
conj: καί "and"

καθίσαντος   after sitting down/ when he sat down
ptcp: aor act ptcp gen sg masc καθίζω "of (him) having sat down"

αὐτοῦ   of him/ he
pers pron: gen sg masc αὐτός "of him/it"

προσῆλθαν   they came
verb: aor act ind 3rd pl προσέρχομαι "they came toward"

αὐτῷ   to him
pers pron: dat sg masc αὐτός "to him"

οἱ   the
article: nom pl masc ὁ "the (ones)"

μαθηταὶ   disciples
noun: nom pl masc μαθητής "disciples"

αὐτοῦ   of him/ his
pers pron: gen sg masc αὐτός "of him/it"

Explanation. καθίσαντος αὐτοῦ is a "genitive absolute," with the genitive case αὐτοῦ acting as a subject and the participle καθίσαντος as a finite verb.

MATTHEW 5:1-12

Previously (4:12-25) Jesus walked around Galilee and gathered a following. Here the grammar insists that it is the disciples who come to him (προσῆλθαν αὐτῷ οἱ μαθηταί).

2   καὶ ἀνοίξας τὸ στόμα αὐτοῦ ἐδίδασκεν αὐτοὺς λέγων·
    Lit. and opening the mouth of him he was teaching them saying
    And opening his mouth he was teaching them, saying,

καὶ   and
conj: καί "and"

ἀνοίξας   opening
ptcp: aor act ptcp nom sg masc ἀνοίγω "(he) having opened"

τὸ   the
article: acc sg neut ὁ "the"

στόμα   mouth
noun: acc sg neut στόμα "the mouth"

αὐτοῦ   of him/ his
pers pron: gen sg masc αὐτός "of him/it"

ἐδίδασκεν   he was teaching
verb: impf act ind 3rd sg διδάσκω "(he/she/it) continually taught"

αὐτοὺς   them
pers pron: acc pl masc αὐτός "them"

λέγων   saying
ptcp: pres act ptcp nom sg masc λέγω "(one) saying"

Explanation. ἐδίδασκεν is an imperfect tense verb, indicating that the teaching was a continuous past action. Perhaps it is a reference to an extended period of time in which the Sermon on the Mount is given. It may suggest elaboration on points beyond what is recorded in the Sermon on the Mount, or it may indicate the giving of the content of the Sermon was given on more than one occasion. The verb tense allows for all these options.

Matthew commonly uses an adverbial participle, like ἀνοίξας, and places it before the verb it modifies, here ἐδίδασκεν.

3a Μακάριοι οἱ πτωχοὶ τῷ πνεύματι,
Lit. Blessed the poor to spirit,
"Blessed are the poor in spirit,

Μακάριοι Blessed
adj: nom pl masc μακάριος "blessed/happy (ones)"

οἱ   the
article: nom pl masc ὁ "the (ones)"

πτωχοὶ   poor/ poor ones
adj: nom pl masc πτωχός "poor (ones)"

τῷ   to
article: dat sg neut ὁ "to the"

πνεύματι spirit
noun: dat sg neut πνεῦμα "to a spirit"

Explanation. Μακάριοι is the predicate adjective, placed at the front for emphasis. The subject is designated by the definitive article, "the poor" (οἱ πτωχοί).

The meanings and translations of μακάριοι are many. It is most often translated "blessed," but also "fortunate," "happy" or even "privileged." The term suggests that the one upon whom it is pronounced is in a very favorable situation.

There is no verb stated in this sentence. In Greek the sense of the passage supplies it for the English translation, and so here one presumes a form of εἰμί, namely εἰσίν, "they are."

οἱ πτωχοὶ τῷ πνεύματι indicates a poverty with reference to, or with respect to the spirit (see Isa 61:1). It may be that the poor in general have no recourse but to trust in God's provision, and those poor in a spiritual sense are likewise dependent upon God.

3b ὅτι αὐτῶν ἐστὶν ἡ βασιλεία τῶν οὐρανῶν.
Lit. because of them is the kingdom of the heavens.
because the kingdom of the heavens is theirs.

ὅτι	because
conj:	ὅτι "because/that"

αὐτῶν	of them/ their
pers pron:	gen pl masc αὐτός "of them"

ἐστὶν	is
verb:	pres act ind 3rd sg εἰμί "(he/she/it) is"

ἡ	the
article:	nom sg fem ὁ "the"

βασιλεία	kingdom
noun:	nom sg fem βασιλεία "a kingdom"

τῶν	of the/ the
article:	gen pl masc ὁ "of the (ones)"

οὐρανῶν	heavens
noun:	gen pl masc οὐρανός "of heavens"

Explanation. Matthew uses ὅτι to give the reason why one who is poor in spirit is to be regarded favorably. The use of the present tense verb ἐστίν indicates present reality.

αὐτῶν is placed after ὅτι and before the rest of the sentence for emphasis. In their spiritual poverty they are now in possession of—it is theirs—the kingdom of the heavens. For the disciples, to whom this is addressed, that is how the kingdom works, and so they are pronounced "blessed."

4a μακάριοι οἱ πενθοῦντες,
Lit. Blessed the ones mourning,
Blessed are those who are mourning,

μακάριοι	blessed
adj:	nom pl masc μακάριος "blessed/happy (ones)"

οἱ	the
article:	nom pl masc ὁ "the (ones)"

πενθοῦντες	ones who are mourning
ptcp:	pres act ptcp nom pl masc πενθέω "(those) mourning"

Explanation. πενθοῦντες is a present participle, which with the definite article οἱ is acting like a substantival adjective. This means that the action of the verbal root πενθέω ("I mourn") turns into a noun: "the ones mourning" (οἱ πενθοῦντες). Nothing is said about what causes the person to mourn; the application then is quite broad.

4b ὅτι αὐτοὶ παρακληθήσονται.
Lit. because they will be comforted.
because they will be comforted.

ὅτι	because
conj:	ὅτι "because/that"

αὐτοὶ they
pers pron: nom pl masc αὐτός "they"

παρακληθήσονται	will be comforted
verb:	fut pass ind 3rd pl παρακαλέω "they will be comforting/consoling/encouraging"

MATTHEW 5:1-12

Explanation. παρακληθήσονται is a passive voice verb, indicating the action will be done *to* the subject. They *will be* comforted. This is sometimes called a "divine passive," meaning it is implied that God is the one doing the comforting.

5a   μακάριοι οἱ πραεῖς,
     Lit. *Blessed the meek,*
     Blessed are the meek

   μακάριοι   Blessed
   adj: nom pl masc μακάριος "blessed/happy (ones)"

   οἱ   the
   article: nom pl masc ὁ "the (ones)"

   πραεῖς   meek/ gentle (ones)
   adj: nom pl masc πραΰς "meek/gentle (ones)"

Explanation. πραεῖς is only used of Jesus elsewhere in Matthew (11:29; 21:5) and, in the Old Testament, Moses (Num 12:3). It can also connote a gentleness that accompanies those who do not regard themselves too highly, and has a gentleness that is pleasing in God's sight (cf. 1 Pet 3:4; Ps 34:3 [33:3 LXX]; 37:11 [36:11 LXX]; 76:10 [75:10 LXX]; 147:6 [146:6 LXX]; 149:4).

5b   ὅτι αὐτοὶ κληρονομήσουσιν τὴν γῆν.
     Lit. *because they will inherit the earth.*
     because they will inherit the earth.

   ὅτι   because
   conj: ὅτι "because/that"

   αὐτοὶ   they
   pers pron: nom pl masc αὐτός "they"

κληρονομήσουσιν will inherit
verb: fut act ind 3rd pl κληρονομέω "(they) will inherit"

τὴν the
article: acc sg fem ὁ "the"

γῆν earth
noun: acc sg fem γῆ "earth/land"

Explanation. κληρονομήσουσιν future tense verb and so connotes a future rather than present expectation. So, the pronouncement of blessedness upon the meek is grounded in a future promise.

v. 5 is almost identical to the Greek (LXX) of Ps 36:11, which reads οἱ δὲ πραεῖς κληρονομήσουσιν τὴν γῆν ("The meek shall inherit the land."). This psalm exhorts the righteous to delight in the Lord and his ways rather than being envious of the wicked and lawless.

6a   μακάριοι οἱ πεινῶντες καὶ διψῶντες τὴν δικαιοσύνην,
Lit. blessed the ones hungering and thirsting righteousness,
Blessed are those hungering and thirsting for righteousness,

μακάριοι Blessed
adj: nom pl masc μακάριος "blessed/happy (ones)"

οἱ the
article: nom pl masc ὁ "the (ones)"

πεινῶντες those hungering/ the ones hungering
ptcp: pres act ptcp nom pl masc πεινάω "(those) hungering"

καὶ and
conj: καί "and"

διψῶντες those thirsting/ the ones thirsting
ptcp: pres act ptcp nom pl masc διψάω "(those) thirsting"

MATTHEW 5:1–12

τὴν   the
article: acc sg fem ὁ "the"

δικαιοσύνην   righteousness
noun: acc sg fem δικαιοσύνη "righteousness"

Explanation. The single definite article (οἱ) accompanies both participles (πεινῶντες and διψῶντες), suggesting *both* hungering and thirsting are in view together, not either one or the other. It is a statement of extreme longing. There are very few things for which one *both* hungers *and* thirsts.

In Matthew δικαιοσύνη is always a desirable attribute for the disciple (Matt 5:6, 10, 20; 6:1, 33), exhibited by John the Baptist (21:32) and Jesus (3:15). It is among the things Jesus commands the disciple to seek (Matt 6:33). For the disciple, it must be possessed in a measure that surpasses that of the scribes and Pharisees to even see the kingdom of the heavens (5:20). Yet here Jesus declares blessed the ones desperately longing for righteousness (v. 6a) and the reason for that declaration (v. 6b) is that their longing will be satisfied *by* God.

6b   ὅτι αὐτοὶ χορτασθήσονται.
Lit. because they will be satisfied.
because they will be satisfied.

ὅτι   because
conj: ὅτι "because/that"

αὐτοὶ   they
pers pron: nom pl masc αὐτός "they"

χορτασθήσονται   will be satisfied
verb: fut pass ind 3rd pl χορτάζω "they will be satisfied/satiated"

Explanation. Jesus pronounces those who hunger and thirst for δικαιοσύνη as blessed. And the reason is the promise that comes with it: χορτασθήσονται. The verb is a future "divine passive" indicating their eating to the full will be supplied by God.

In Psalm 107 (LXX 106) the Psalmist reflects on those redeemed by the Lord, who were hungry and thirsty (πεινῶντες καὶ διψῶντες 106:5). They cried out to the Lord in their distress (106:6a), and they should acknowledge him for his mercies because he "fed an empty soul" (ἐχόρτασεν ψυχὴν κενὴν) and "a hungry soul he filled with good things" (ψυχὴν πεινῶσαν ἐνέπλησεν ἀγαθῶν, Ps 106:9). Here it is the same Lord and God who satisfies the hungers and thirsts of the Psalmist who satisfies what is lacking in the believer's longed-for righteousness.

7a μακάριοι οἱ ἐλεήμονες,
Lit. Blessed the merciful,
Blessed are the merciful,

μακάριοι Blessed
adj: nom pl masc μακάριος "blessed/happy (ones)"

οἱ the
article: nom pl masc ὁ "the (ones)"

ἐλεήμονες merciful/ those who are merciful/ merciful ones
adj: nom pl masc ἐλεήμων "merciful (ones)"

Explanation. ἐλεήμονες is an adjective, and οἱ is its definite article. This means that the adjective is functioning substantivally, or as a noun: the merciful (ones).

A verb third personal plural verb from εἰμί, "are" (εἰσίν) is implied and needs to be supplied for English translation.

7b ὅτι αὐτοὶ ἐλεηθήσονται.
Lit. because they will receive mercy.
because they will receive mercy.

ὅτι　　　because
conj:　　ὅτι "because/that/ "

αὐτοὶ　　they
pers pron: nom pl masc αὐτός "they"

ἐλεηθήσονται　will receive mercy
verb:　　fut pass ind 3rd pl ἐλεέω "they will be having mercy"

Explanation. Though ἐλεήμονες is an adjective (v. 7a) and ἐλεηθήσονται is a verb (v. 7b), they both come from the same root.

ἐλεηθήσονται is a future passive verb, a "divine passive" indicating the reception of mercy comes from God.

8a　μακάριοι οἱ καθαροὶ τῇ καρδίᾳ,
Lit. Blessed the pure to heart,
Blessed are the pure in heart,

μακάριοι　Blessed
adj:　　nom pl masc μακάριος "blessed/happy (ones)"

οἱ　　　the
article:　nom pl masc ὁ "the (ones)"

καθαροὶ　clean (ones)/ pure (ones)
adj:　　nom pl masc καθαρός "clean/pure (ones)"

τῇ　　　the
article:　dat sg fem ὁ "to the"

καρδίᾳ　heart
noun:　　dat sg fem καρδία "to a heart"

Explanation. A verb third personal plural verb from εἰμί, "are" (εἰσίν) is implied and needs to be supplied for English translation.

τῇ καρδίᾳ is a dative of reference, indicating purity with reference to the heart.

According to Ps 24:4 (23:4 LXX), the pure in heart (καθαρὸς τῇ καρδίᾳ) are among those who will ascend the mountain of the Lord (Ps 24:3), receive his blessing and mercy (Ps 24:5).

8b ὅτι αὐτοὶ τὸν θεὸν ὄψονται.
Lit. because they God they will see.
because they will see God.

ὅτι	because
conj:	ὅτι "because/that"

αὐτοὶ	they
pers pron:	nom pl masc αὐτός "they"

τὸν	the
article:	acc sg masc ὁ "the"

θεὸν	God
noun:	acc sg masc θεός "God/god"

ὄψονται	will see
verb:	fut mid ind 3rd pl ὁράω "(they) will (for themselves) see"

Explanation. ὄψονται is a middle voice verb but can be translated like a simple active.

No one could see God's face and live (Exod 33:20), and yet the righteous in heavenly bliss will see his face (Rev 22:4).

9a μακάριοι οἱ εἰρηνοποιοί,
Lit. Blessed the peacemakers,
Blessed are the peacemakers,

μακάριοι blessed
adj: nom pl masc μακάριος "blessed/happy (ones)"

οἱ   the
article: nom pl masc ὁ "the (ones)"

εἰρηνοποιοί   peacemakers/ ones making peace
adj: nom pl masc εἰρηνοποιός "peacemaking (ones)"

Explanation. A verb third personal plural verb from εἰμί, "are" (εἰσίν) is implied and needs to be supplied for English translation.

εἰρηνοποιοί is a compound word, joining "peace" (εἰρήνη) and the noun "doer" (ποιητής) or probably more likely the verb "I do" (ποιέω).

9b ὅτι αὐτοὶ υἱοὶ θεοῦ κληθήσονται.
Lit. because they sons of God will be called.
because they will be called sons of God.

ὅτι   because
conj: ὅτι "because/that"

αὐτοὶ   they
pers pron: nom pl masc αὐτός "they"

υἱοὶ   sons
noun: nom pl masc υἱός "sons"

θεοῦ   of God
noun: gen sg masc θεός "of God/a god"

κληθήσονται   will be called
verb: fut pass ind 3rd pl καλέω "they will be calling/inviting"

Explanation. 9b gives the reason (ὅτι) why peacemakers are blessed.

κληθήσονται is a future passive verb, indicating the designation is not present but in the future. Presumably too, like in other future passives in this passage, the passive voice is a divine passive, indicating God will be the ones designating the people as sons. The verb καλέω is a designation or appointment as sons; with God giving the designation of people who are his sons.

10a μακάριοι οἱ δεδιωγμένοι ἕνεκεν δικαιοσύνης,

Lit. Blessed are the ones having been persecuted on account of righteousness,

Blessed are the ones having been persecuted on account of righteousness,

μακάριοι Blessed
adj: nom pl masc μακάριος "blessed/happy (ones)"

οἱ   the
article: nom pl masc ὁ "the (ones)"

δεδιωγμένοι   ones having been persecuted
ptcp: perf pass ptcp nom pl masc διώκω "(those) having been persecuted/pursued"

ἕνεκεν   on account of/ for the sake of
prep: ἕνεκα "because/sake of"

δικαιοσύνης   righteousness
noun: gen sg fem δικαιοσύνη "of righteousness"

Explanation. A verb third personal plural verb from εἰμί, "are" (εἰσίν) is implied and needs to be supplied for English translation.

οἱ δεδιωγμένοι is a substantival participle, meaning it is acting like a noun. It is built upon the verb διώκω, meaning "I persecute." When made into a passive-voice participle it becomes "being persecuted." The presence of the definite article clarifies that it is substantival, "the ones being persecuted." Nothing is said about who is doing the persecuting, rather the focus is on the character of the one persecuted.

δεδιωγμένοι is not unqualified, but is on account of or for the sake of (ἕνεκεν) δικαιοσύνη. In other words, mere persecution is not in view here. The same idea is advocated in 1 Peter 2:20.

10b ὅτι αὐτῶν ἐστὶν ἡ βασιλεία τῶν οὐρανῶν.
Lit. because of them is the kingdom of the heavens.
because theirs is the kingdom of the heavens.

ὅτι	because
conj:	ὅτι "because/that/ "

αὐτῶν	of them/ theirs
pers pron:	gen pl masc αὐτός "of them"

ἐστὶν	is
verb:	pres act ind 3rd sg εἰμί "(he/she/it) is"

ἡ	the
article:	nom sg fem ὁ "the"

βασιλεία	kingdom
noun:	nom sg fem βασιλεία "a kingdom"

τῶν	of the
article:	gen pl masc ὁ "of the (ones)"

οὐρανῶν	heavens
noun:	gen pl masc οὐρανός "of heavens"

Explanation. Here Jesus gives the reason (ὅτι) one being persecuted for the sake of righteousness is blessed. The αὐτῶν is at the front of the sentence for emphasis; *theirs* is the kingdom of the heavens. Note that this is a present reality; it is *presently* theirs, not merely a future promise.

τῶν οὐρανῶν is a plural noun, "of the heavens," perhaps reflecting the Hebrew, where "heaven" is always plural (שָׁמַיִם).

11 μακάριοί ἐστε ὅταν ὀνειδίσωσιν ὑμᾶς καὶ διώξωσιν καὶ εἴπωσιν πᾶν πονηρὸν καθ' ὑμῶν ψευδόμενοι ἕνεκεν ἐμοῦ.

Lit. Blessed are you when they disparage you and they persecute you and they say all evil against you falsely on account of me.

Blessed are you (pl) when they disparage you (pl) and they persecute and they say all (kinds of) evil against you falsely on account of me.

μακάριοί blessed
adj: nom pl masc μακάριος "blessed/happy (ones)"

ἐστε you are
verb: pres act ind 2nd pl εἰμί "(you [pl]) are"

ὅταν when/ whenever
conj: ὅταν "when/whenever"

ὀνειδίσωσιν they insult/ disparage
verb: aor act subj 3rd pl ὀνειδίζω "they should begin to insult/disparage"

ὑμᾶς you (pl)
pers pron: 2nd acc pl σύ "you (pl)"

καὶ and
conj: καί "and"

διώξωσιν they persecute
verb: aor act subj 3rd pl διώκω "they should begin to persecute/pursue"

καὶ and
conj: καί "and"

εἴπωσιν   they say
verb: aor act subj 3rd pl λέγω "they should begin to say"

πᾶν   all (kinds)
adj: acc sg neut πᾶς "all"

πονηρὸν   evil (things)
adj: acc sg neut πονηρός "evil"

καθ'   against
prep: κατά "according to/down/against"

ὑμῶν   you (pl)
pers pron: 2nd gen pl σύ "of you (pl)"

ψευδόμενοι   falsely
ptcp: pres mid/pass ptcp nom pl masc ψεύδομαι "(those) lying/speaking falsely"

ἕνεκεν   on account of/ for the sake of
prep: ἕνεκα "because/sake of"

ἐμοῦ   of me
pers pron: 1st gen sg ἐγώ "of me/my"

Explanation. καθ' is from the preposition κατά. It is an abbreviated through elision, which is when a contracted form is used and an apostrophe inserted to aid in pronunciation of the next word, in this case ὑμῶν. It is more natural for a native Greek-speaker to say καθ' ὑμῶν than κατά ὑμῶν.

All of the previous beatitudes are pronounced in the third person—to those poor in spirit, etc. Here Jesus changes to directly address his disciples in the second person (plural), "you." This is addressed to a community of people.

Previously (v. 10) the persecution was on account of (ἕνεκεν) righteousness; here all the hardship is on account of (ἕνεκεν) Jesus.

ἐμοῦ is an emphatic form of μοῦ.

Here all the slanderous things are hurled at the disciple are explicitly said to be false (ψευδόμενοι). There is no provision or blessing pronounced upon those for whom the accusations are true.

12a χαίρετε καὶ ἀγαλλιᾶσθε,
Lit. Rejoice and exult,
Rejoice and exult!

χαίρετε	rejoice
verb:	pres act imv 2nd pl χαίρω "rejoice (you [pl])"
καὶ	and
conj:	καί "and"
ἀγαλλιᾶσθε	exult/ rejoice
verb:	pres mid/pass imv 2nd pl ἀγαλλιάω "rejoice/exult (you [pl])"

Explanation. The verbs, χαίρετε and ἀγαλλιᾶσθε, are generally synonymous. They are also both in the imperative, indicating commands. The commands are in the circumstances of the hardships of v. 11, and the reason is given in v. 12b.

12b ὅτι ὁ μισθὸς ὑμῶν πολὺς ἐν τοῖς οὐρανοῖς·
Lit. because the reward of you great in the heavens;
Because your reward in the heavens is much.

ὅτι	because
conj:	ὅτι "because/that/ "
ὁ	the
article:	nom sg masc ὁ "the"

μισθὸς	reward/ wage	
noun:	nom sg masc μισθός "a reward/wage"	

ὑμῶν	of you (pl)/ your	
pers pron:	2nd gen pl σύ "of you (pl)"	

πολὺς	much/ many	
adj:	nom sg masc πολύς "much"	

ἐν	in	
prep:	ἐν "in/by/with"	

τοῖς	the	
article:	dat pl masc ὁ "to the (ones)"	

οὐρανοῖς	heavens	
noun:	dat pl masc οὐρανός "to heavens"	

Explanation. μισθός occurs several times in Matthew and is often translated "reward" (Matt 5:46; 6:1, 2, 5, 16; 10:41, 42), but also refers to an earned wage (Matt 20:8).

The location of the μισθός is in the heavens, but it is a present rather than future reality. A present tense verb seems to be implied, though not stated.

12c οὕτως γὰρ ἐδίωξαν τοὺς προφήτας τοὺς πρὸ ὑμῶν.

Lit. Thusly for they persecuted the prophets which before you."

For in this manner they persecuted the prophets who (were) before you (pl)."

οὕτως	thus/ in this manner	
adv:	οὕτως "thus/in this manner"	

γὰρ	for	
conj:	γάρ "for/because"	

ἐδίωξαν	they persecuted
verb:	aor act ind 3rd pl διώκω "they persecuted/pursued"

τοὺς	the
article:	acc pl masc ὁ "the (ones)"

προφήτας	prophets
noun:	acc pl masc προφήτης "prophets"

τοὺς	the (ones)
article:	acc pl masc ὁ "the (ones)"

πρὸ	before
prep:	πρό "(time) before"

ὑμῶν	you (pl)
pers pron:	2nd gen pl σύ "of you (pl)"

Explanation. οὕτως indicates manner, meaning the manner in which they (who are undefined here) persecute the disciples is the same manner in which they persecuted the prophets. Their suffering is in good company!

τούς here acts like a relative pronoun, "the (ones)"

πρό ὑμῶν is sequential, indicating they preceded the disciples in time.

Preaching the Text

1. **Main idea:** Am I blessed?

    a. How do you define "blessed"? Most of us would say something about health, perhaps a good job, a family, friends, even a good church home. In the Beatitudes, Jesus inverts all our notions of blessedness. The good things we have are blessings, no doubt, and we should be grateful for them. But we also need to recognize that Jesus regards blessings not simply as spiritualized worldly blessings, but as something other-worldly, even ironic or paradoxical to the ways we may think. Jesus includes among the blessed those who are poor in spirit, who mourn, the meek, and those who hunger and thirst *for righteousness*. And here we have to remember that all of this is addressed to disciples (5:2). Yes, others do overhear Jesus' teachings here and are touched by them (7:28–29), but these declarations of blessings are for those within the kingdom. It will look completely upside down in the eyes of the world because in God's Kingdom things are right-side up. He also acclaims the blessedness of the merciful, the pure in heart, and the peacemakers. But what about those who are persecuted for the sake of righteousness? Yes, those too are blessed. And so are those who are reviled, persecuted, and falsely slandered. For these people Jesus has a command: rejoice. That's the path of Jesus.

    b. Recall that to say someone is "Blessed" in this sense is a statement of special favor; it is almost *congratulatory*. One interpreter has understood them as "Good for you!"

    c. The blessedness given throughout is always given by God; they are not earned, but characteristics of Kingdom-minded disciples.

    d. The crux of the Beatitudes is its turn from the third to the second person, where Jesus makes general statements about people to specific addresses to his gathered disciples. Importantly, these outline hardships experienced at the hands of false accusations specifically on account of Jesus (Matt 5:11). And, the result in a heavenly reward and indicate the path of the prophets before them (Matt 5:12).

2. **Tip for Preaching:** Most of the Beatitudes have reasons. That is, a statement that one is blessed, and then an explanation as to why. The

explanation is always something Kingdom-oriented. And always remember, Jesus is expressly addressing *disciples* (Matt 5:1-2), people who already gave up their lives to follow Him (Matt 4:20, 22). So, the promises here are made for Christians.

4
Matthew 6:19–25

Where Are Your Treasures?

Matthew 6 has few commands, but those few are explained very clearly. First, Jesus warns his disciples to "beware" of the traps of hypocritical acts of piety—giving (vv. 2–4), praying (vv. 5–15), and fasting (vv. 16–18). All these should be done with a secrecy that only God can see (vv. 4, 6, 18) and rewards accordingly. In this way the disciples' true intent and heart is exposed. The second command is to store up treasures (vv. 19–20), but where they are stored makes all the difference (v. 21). Then, Jesus gives illustrations about the role of one's eye (vv. 22–23) and serving masters (vv. 24–25), all of which illustrate the orientation of one's heart. Why such heavenward attention? It is all bound up in the character of God, who cares for the wellbeing of the tiniest bird which we may never notice (vv. 26–27) and a flower of the field (vv. 28–30). This leads to two off-setting conclusions: do not worry about provisions, but strive for the kingdom of God (vv. 31–34). This passage urges an unrestricted investment of all our affections towards God and His purposes.

Part I

19a Μὴ θησαυρίζετε ὑμῖν θησαυροὺς ἐπὶ τῆς γῆς,
Lit. "Not you treasure up to you treasures upon earth,
"Do not treasure up for yourselves treasures upon earth,

Μὴ   not
neg particle: μή "no/not (stop)"

θησαυρίζετε   store up/ save up
verb: pres act imv 2nd pl θησαυρίζω "save/store (you [pl])"

ὑμῖν   your (pl)/ of you (pl)
pers pron: 2nd dat pl σύ "to you (pl)"

θησαυροὺς   treasures
noun: acc pl masc θησαυρός "treasuries"

ἐπὶ   upon
prep: ἐπί "upon"

τῆς   the
article: gen sg fem ὁ "of the"

γῆς   earth
noun: gen sg fem γῆ "of earth/land"

Explanation. ὑμῖν is a dative plural, meaning "for yourselves."

The command here is indeed to store up treasures for one's self, but not ἐπὶ τῆς γῆς.

θησαυρίζω . . . θησαυρός are verb and noun forms of the same word, and refer to treasuring up treasures. The presumption seems to be that one will surely store up treasures somewhere, the choice remains to the individual as to where.

19b ὅπου σὴς καὶ βρῶσις ἀφανίζει
Lit. where moth and vermin destroy
where moth and vermin destroy

ὅπου   where
adv: ὅπου "where"

4
Matthew 6:19–25
Where Are Your Treasures?

Matthew 6 has few commands, but those few are explained very clearly. First, Jesus warns his disciples to "beware" of the traps of hypocritical acts of piety—giving (vv. 2–4), praying (vv. 5–15), and fasting (vv. 16–18). All these should be done with a secrecy that only God can see (vv. 4, 6, 18) and rewards accordingly. In this way the disciples' true intent and heart is exposed. The second command is to store up treasures (vv. 19–20), but where they are stored makes all the difference (v. 21). Then, Jesus gives illustrations about the role of one's eye (vv. 22–23) and serving masters (vv. 24–25), all of which illustrate the orientation of one's heart. Why such heavenward attention? It is all bound up in the character of God, who cares for the wellbeing of the tiniest bird which we may never notice (vv. 26–27) and a flower of the field (vv. 28–30). This leads to two off-setting conclusions: do not worry about provisions, but strive for the kingdom of God (vv. 31–34). This passage urges an unrestricted investment of all our affections towards God and His purposes.

Part I

19a Μὴ θησαυρίζετε ὑμῖν θησαυροὺς ἐπὶ τῆς γῆς,
Lit. "Not you treasure up to you treasures upon earth,
"Do not treasure up for yourselves treasures upon earth,

Μὴ   not
neg particle: μή "no/not (stop)"

θησαυρίζετε   store up/ save up
verb: pres act imv 2nd pl θησαυρίζω "save/store (you [pl])"

ὑμῖν   your (pl)/ of you (pl)
pers pron: 2nd dat pl σύ "to you (pl)"

θησαυροὺς   treasures
noun: acc pl masc θησαυρός "treasuries"

ἐπὶ   upon
prep: ἐπί "upon"

τῆς   the
article: gen sg fem ὁ "of the"

γῆς   earth
noun: gen sg fem γῆ "of earth/land"

Explanation. ὑμῖν is a dative plural, meaning "for yourselves."

The command here is indeed to store up treasures for one's self, but not ἐπὶ τῆς γῆς.

θησαυρίζω ... θησαυρός are verb and noun forms of the same word, and refer to treasuring up treasures. The presumption seems to be that one will surely store up treasures somewhere, the choice remains to the individual as to where.

19b ὅπου σὴς καὶ βρῶσις ἀφανίζει
Lit. where moth and vermin destroy
where moth and vermin destroy

ὅπου   where
adv: ὅπου "where"

MATTHEW 6:19–25

σής	moth
noun:	nom sg masc σής "a moth"

καὶ	and
conj:	καί "and"

βρῶσις	vermin
noun:	nom sg fem βρῶσις "eating/food"

ἀφανίζει	ruin/ destroy
verb:	pres act ind 3rd sg ἀφανίζω "(he/she/it) ruins/vanishes"

Explanation. βρῶσις is often translated "rust" (KJV, NRSV, ESV) but can also refer to "eating" and whatever destroys by eating. Hence "vermin."

The notion of "moth and rust" destroying is an illustration, indicating that earthly treasures are inevitably vulnerable. Here the illustration indicates their subjection to decay or vermin.

19c καὶ ὅπου κλέπται διορύσσουσιν καὶ κλέπτουσιν·
Lit. and where thieves break in and steal;
and where thieves break in and steal;

καὶ	and
conj:	καί "and"

ὅπου	where
adv:	ὅπου "where"

κλέπται	thieves
noun:	nom pl masc κλέπτης "thieves"

διορύσσουσιν	break in
verb:	pres act ind 3rd pl διορύσσω "(they) break in/ dig through"

καὶ   and
conj: καί "and"

κλέπτουσιν   steal
verb: pres act ind 3rd pl κλέπτω "(they) steal"

Explanation. κλέπται is a noun and κλέπτουσιν is a verb, but they come from the same root, and could be translated "thieves."

The illustration here is that earthly treasures are subject to theft. In both illustrations (v. 19b and 19c), the point is that earthly treasures are insecure, and that storing up treasures in an insecure location is contrasted with storing them in a secure location in heaven.

20a θησαυρίζετε δὲ ὑμῖν θησαυροὺς ἐν οὐρανῷ
Lit. treasure up but to you treasures in to heaven
but treasure up for yourselves treasures in heaven

θησαυρίζετε   treasure up
verb: pres act imv 2nd pl θησαυρίζω "save/store (you [pl])"

δὲ   But
conj: δέ "but/now"

ὑμῖν   for yourselves
pers pron: 2nd dat pl σύ "to you (pl)"

θησαυροὺς   treasures
noun: acc pl masc θησαυρός "treasuries"

ἐν   in
prep: ἐν "in/by/with"

οὐρανῷ   heaven
noun: dat sg masc οὐρανός "to the heaven"

Explanation. θησαυρίζω . . . θησαυρός are verb and noun forms of the same word, and refer to treasuring up treasures.

δέ, when used in contrasts, is usually rather weak. Here the context suggests a stronger contrast.

ὑμῖν is a dative plural, meaning "for yourselves."

The command here will indeed be to store up treasures for one's self, but here it is ἐν οὐρανῷ. In heaven the treasures are under the immutable supervision of God. It is this kind of heavenly treasure that is offered to the rich young man, if he would be sell all his goods, give the money to the poor, and follow Jesus (Matt 19:21). But he went away sorrowful because he was unwilling, it seems, to part with his great possessions (Matt 19:22). This is an excellent illustration of Jesus' point here in Matthew 6.

20b ὅπου οὔτε σὴς οὔτε βρῶσις ἀφανίζει

Lit. where neither moth nor vermin destroy

where neither moth nor vermin destroy

ὅπου	Where
adv:	ὅπου "where"
οὔτε	neither
neg conj:	οὔτε "nor/not even"
σὴς	moth
noun:	nom sg masc σής "a moth"
οὔτε	nor
neg conj:	οὔτε "nor/not even"
βρῶσις	vermin
noun:	nom sg fem βρῶσις "eating/food"
ἀφανίζει	destroy
verb:	pres act ind 3rd sg ἀφανίζω "(he/she/it) ruins/vanishes"

Explanation οὔτε . . . οὔτε means neither . . . nor. Treasures stored up in heaven are threatened by nothing because they are in the direct care of God.

Notice that ἀφανίζει is a singular verb, with two subjects.

20c καὶ ὅπου κλέπται οὐ διορύσσουσιν οὐδὲ κλέπτουσιν·
Lit. and where thieves no break in nor steal;
and where thieves neither break in nor steal;

καὶ	and
conj:	καί "and"

ὅπου	where
adv:	ὅπου "where"

κλέπται	thieves
noun:	nom pl masc κλέπτης "thieves"

οὐ not
neg particle: οὐ "no/not"

διορύσσουσιν	break in
verb:	pres act ind 3rd pl διορύσσω "(they) break in/ dig through"

οὐδὲ nor
neg conj: οὐδέ "nor/not even"

κλέπτουσιν	steal
verb:	pres act ind 3rd pl κλέπτω "(they) steal"

Explanation. οὐ . . . οὐδέ means "not . . . nor." Here neither the treat of break-ins nor theft are felt by those keeping treasures in heaven.

21 ὅπου γάρ ἐστιν ὁ θησαυρός σου, ἐκεῖ ἔσται καὶ ἡ καρδία σου.
Lit. where for is the treasure of you, there is also the heart of you."
for where your treasure is, there will your heart be also."

ὅπου	where
adv:	ὅπου "where"
γάρ	for
conj:	γάρ "for/because"
ἐστιν	is
verb:	pres act ind 3rd sg εἰμί "(he/she/it) is"
ὁ	the
article:	nom sg masc ὁ "the"
θησαυρός	treasure
noun:	nom sg masc θησαυρός "a treasury"
σου	of you/ your
pers pron:	2nd gen sg σύ "of you"
ἐκεῖ	there
adv:	ἐκεῖ "there"
ἔσται	will be
verb:	fut mid ind 3rd sg εἰμί "(he/she/it) will (for oneself) be"
καὶ	also
conj:	καί "and"
ἡ	the
article:	nom sg fem ὁ "the"
καρδία	heart
noun:	nom sg fem καρδία "a heart"

σου   of you/ your
pers pron: 2nd gen sg σύ "of you"

Explanation. καί means "and, also, namely." The context here makes no sense with "and," and clearly indicates an additional idea. So "also" is the preferred translation.

This is the main point of the segment (vv. 19–21). In ancient thought the "heart" (καρδία) was not the seat of emotion, but a metaphor for the center of a person's being. Notice also the tense change in the verbs—where your treasure *is presently* (ἐστιν) there your heart *will be* (ἔσται) in the future. The present esteem of one's treasure is inextricably linked to one's eternal destination.

Part II

22a Ὁ λύχνος τοῦ σώματός ἐστιν ὁ ὀφθαλμός.
Lit. "The lamp of the body is the eye."
"The lamp of the body is the eye."

Ὁ   the
article: nom sg masc ὁ "the"

λύχνος   lamp
noun: nom sg masc λύχνος "a lamp"

τοῦ   of the
article: gen sg neut ὁ "of the"

σώματός   body
noun: gen sg neut σῶμα "of a body"

ἐστιν   is
verb: pres act ind 3rd sg εἰμί "(he/she/it) is"

ὁ   The
article: nom sg masc ὁ "the"

ὀφθαλμός   eye
noun: nom sg masc ὀφθαλμός "an eye"

Explanation. The word order of the Greek in this sentence suggests "the lamp of the body" is the subject, and so comes first. The "eye" here, like the treasures above (vv. 19–21), is metaphorical.

22b ἐὰν οὖν ᾖ ὁ ὀφθαλμός σου ἁπλοῦς,
Lit. If then should be the eye of you sound,
If then your eye should be sound,

ἐὰν   if
conditional: ἐάν "if"

οὖν   then
conj: οὖν "therefore"

ᾖ   should be
verb: pres act subj 3rd sg εἰμί "(he/she/it) should be"

ὁ   the
article: nom sg masc ὁ "the"

ὀφθαλμός   eye
noun: nom sg masc ὀφθαλμός "an eye"

σου   of you/ your
pers pron: 2nd gen sg σύ "of you"

ἁπλοῦς   whole
adj: nom sg masc ἁπλοῦς "single"

Explanation. ᾖ is a subjunctive verb from εἰμί. With the conditional particle ἐὰν is understood "if . . . it should be."

οὖν is an inferential particle, indicating the natural implications of the previous sentence (v. 22a).

ἁπλοῦς means "single," could possible suggest a singleness of purpose (cf. Eph 6:5). But the contrast with πονηρός in v. 23 suggests the notion of wholeness. The "whole" eye is not to be confused with a healthy eye, but is a metaphor for a good or generous outlook, and likely indicates "seeing" in a spiritual sense.

22c ὅλον τὸ σῶμά σου φωτεινὸν ἔσται·
Lit. whole the body of you full of light will be;
your whole body will be full of light;

ὅλον	whole
adj:	nom sg neut ὅλος "whole"

τὸ	the
article:	nom sg neut ὁ "the"

σῶμά	body
noun:	nom sg neut σῶμα "a body"

σου	of you/ your
pers pron:	2nd gen sg σύ "of you"

φωτεινὸν	full of light/ bright
adj:	nom sg neut φωτεινός "full of light/bright"

ἔσται	will be
verb:	fut mid ind 3rd sg εἰμί "(he/she/it) will (for oneself) be"

Explanation. ὅλον is at the front of the sentence for emphasis. The "light" here is also non-literal, but rather one of "seeing" in a sense connoted from discipleship. In other words, only an outlook ("eye") that adopts a kingdom mindset would be able to appropriate ("see") that investment in heavenly treasure is better than earthly treasure (vv. 19–21). This is a decidedly kingdom perspective that orients the entirety of one's being.

23a ἐὰν δὲ ὁ ὀφθαλμός σου πονηρὸς ᾖ,
Lit. if but the eye of you evil should be,
but if your eye should be evil,

ἐὰν	if
conditional:	ἐάν "if"

δὲ	but
conj:	δέ "but/now"

ὁ	the
article:	nom sg masc ὁ "the"

ὀφθαλμός	eye
noun:	nom sg masc ὀφθαλμός "an eye"

σου	of you/ your
pers pron:	2nd gen sg σύ "of you"

πονηρὸς	evil
adj:	nom sg masc πονηρός "evil"

ᾖ	should be/ may be
verb:	pres act subj 3rd sg εἰμί "(he/she/it) should be"

Explanation. ᾖ is a subjunctive verb from εἰμί. With the conditional particle ἐάν is understood "if . . . it should be."

Again, the eye is metaphorical. The "eye" is one's outlook, and if that is evil and does not adopt the kingdom perspective espoused in the Sermon on the Mount, then the entire body is in darkness (v. 23b).

23b ὅλον τὸ σῶμά σου σκοτεινὸν ἔσται.
Lit. whole the body of you darkness will be.
your whole body will be in darkness.

ὅλον	whole
adj:	nom sg neut ὅλος "whole"

τὸ	the
article:	nom sg neut ὁ "the"

σῶμά	body
noun:	nom sg neut σῶμα "a body"

σου	of you/ your
pers pron:	2nd gen sg σύ "of you"

σκοτεινὸν	dark/ in darkness
adj:	nom sg neut σκοτεινός "dark/in darkness"

ἔσται	will be
verb:	fut mid ind 3rd sg εἰμί "(he/she/it) will (for oneself) be"

Explanation. "Darkness" is always a sign of unbelief and judgment in Matthew (Matt 4:16; 8:12; 10:27; 22:13; 24:29; 25:30; 27:45). It likely draws from the judgment upon the land of Egypt at the Exodus (Exod 10:21, 22; 14:20), and elsewhere in the Old Testament too it can be used for unbelief and judgment (cf. Deut 28:29; Prov 20:20; Isa 8:22; 50:10; Lam 3:2). Moving from darkness to light is a common metaphor for belief and faith (cf. 2 Sam 22:29; Isa 29:18; 42:16; Mic 7:8; Acts 26:18; 1 Pet 2:9).

23c εἰ οὖν τὸ φῶς τὸ ἐν σοὶ σκότος ἐστίν,
Lit. if then the light the in to you darkness is,
If, then, the light which is in you is darkness,

εἰ	if
conditional:	εἰ "if"

οὖν	then, therefore
conj:	οὖν "therefore"

τὸ	the
article:	nom sg neut ὁ "the"

φῶς	light
noun:	nom sg neut φῶς "light"

τὸ	the
article:	nom sg neut ὁ "the"

ἐν	in
prep:	ἐν "in/by/with"

σοὶ	you
pers pron: 2nd dat sg σύ "to you"	

σκότος	darkness
noun:	nom sg neut σκότος "darkness"

ἐστίν	is
verb:	pres act ind 3rd sg εἰμί "(he/she/it) is"

Explanation. The second τό is a definite article but has no noun. Here it functions like a relative pronoun, "which."

23d τὸ σκότος πόσον.

Lit. the darkness how great?
how great the darkness?"

τὸ	the
article:	nom sg neut ὁ "the"

σκότος	darkness
noun:	nom sg neut σκότος "darkness"

πόσον	how much/ many/ great?
interr pron: nom sg neut πόσος "how much?"	

Explanation. There is no verb in Greek, and none is required in English. But it could just as well be translated "how great is the darkness?"

Part III

24a Οὐδεὶς δύναται δυσὶ κυρίοις δουλεύειν·
Lit. No one is able two lords to serve;
"No one is able to serve two masters;

Οὐδεὶς no one
adj: nom sg masc οὐδείς "no (one/thing)"

δύναται able
verb: pres mid/pass ind 3rd sg δύναμαι "(he/she/it) is able"

δυσὶ two
adj: dat pl masc δύο "to two"

κυρίοις lords/ masters
noun: dat pl masc κύριος "to lords"

δουλεύειν to serve
verb: pres act inf δουλεύω "to serve/slave"

Explanation. δυσί is a dative plural masculine adjective, meaning "two." All numbers are adjectives, and so if they are attributive match the nouns they modify in case, number, and gender, as is the case here with κυρίοις.

κύριος can mean "lord" as in a revered person, "Lord" as in God, or "master" as in an authoritative figure. It need not be a reference to God, but is at very least a reference to someone highly esteemed and revered to such a degree as to have one's loyalty and allegiance. Here the reference is likely to a slave and master relationship. The very nature of this phenomenon is unattested in antiquity, pointing to its impossibility. One master or the other would be neglected in such an arrangement, and so it simply was not done.

MATTHEW 6:19–25

24b ἢ γὰρ τὸν ἕνα μισήσει καὶ τὸν ἕτερον ἀγαπήσει,
Lit. either for the one s/he will hate and the other s/he will love,
for either the one s/he will hate and the other s/he will love,

ἢ	either
particle:	ἤ "or/than"

γὰρ	for
conj:	γάρ "for/because"

τὸν	the
article:	acc sg masc ὁ "the"

ἕνα	one
adj:	acc sg masc εἷς "one"

μισήσει	s/he will hate
verb:	fut act ind 3rd sg μισέω "(he/she/it) will hate"

καὶ	and
conj:	καί "and"

τὸν	the
article:	acc sg masc ὁ "the"

ἕτερον	other
adj:	acc sg masc ἕτερος "another/different"

ἀγαπήσει	s/he will love
verb:	fut act ind 3rd sg ἀγαπάω "(he/she/it) will love"

Explanation. ἢ . . . ἢ (vv. 24b, 24c) expresses two opposite alternatives, "either . . . or."

μισήσει is a third singular verb and requires a nominative singular subject. τὸν ἕνα is in the accusative, and so cannot be the subject but rather the object. The subject is an implied "he" or "she."

The language of "hate" is analogues to that used in Luke 14:26, "If any one comes to me and does not hate his own father and mother and wife and children and brothers and sisters, yes, and even his own life, he cannot be my disciple" (RSV). Matthew understands the "hate" language here as "love less than." This is clear in his own version of the same saying in Matt 10:37: "He who loves father or mother more than me is not worthy of me; and he who loves son or daughter more than me is not worthy of me" (RSV). Jesus is not advocating a strong emotional aversion and disregard to the master, as is implied by the English word "hate," but rather that there will be some natural bias in affection toward one master over the other.

24c ἢ ἑνὸς ἀνθέξεται καὶ τοῦ ἑτέρου καταφρονήσει.
Lit. or one s/he will hold firmly and the other s/he will despise.
or one s/he will hold firmly and of the other s/he will despise.

ἢ	either
particle:	ἢ "or/than"
ἑνὸς	one
adj:	gen sg masc εἷς "of a one"
ἀνθέξεται	hold firmly
verb:	fut mid ind 3rd sg ἀντέχω "(he/she/it) will (for oneself) hold firmly"
καὶ	and
conj:	καί "and"
τοῦ	the
article:	gen sg masc ὁ "of the"
ἑτέρου	other
adj:	gen sg masc ἕτερος "of another/a different"

καταφρονήσει despise
verb: fut act ind 3rd sg καταφρονέω "(he/she/it) will despise/scorn"

Explanation. ἤ ... ἤ (vv. 24b, 24c) expresses two opposite alternatives, "either ... or."

ἤ is a conjunction, different from the nominative feminine singular, which is ἡ.

ἑνός is an adjective and, like other adjectives, can be attributive or predicative. Here it is the latter, and acting like a noun. Its lexical form is εἷς, which is very different from the nearly identical preposition εἰς.

24d οὐ δύνασθε θεῷ δουλεύειν καὶ μαμωνᾷ.
Lit. not you (pl) are able to God to serve and to wealth.
You (pl) are not able to serve God and wealth."

οὐ not
neg particle: οὐ "no/not"

δύνασθε you (pl) are able
verb: pres mid/pass ind 2nd pl δύναμαι "(you [pl]) are able"

θεῷ God
noun: dat sg masc θεός "to God/a god"

δουλεύειν to serve
verb: pres act inf δουλεύω "to serve/slave"

καὶ and
conj: καί "and"

μαμωνᾷ wealth
noun: dat sg masc μαμωνᾶς "to mammon/money/wealth"

Explanation. δουλεύειν is a complementary infinitive, meaning it completes the thought of the verb it modifies, in this case δύνασθε ("able . . . to serve").

This is the main point of this unit (vv. 22–24). The subject of slaves and masters was metaphorical for disciples as the "slaves" and either God or money as the "master." The term μαμωνᾶς is a transliteration from the Aramaic word ממון, meaning "wealth" or "property."

Part IV

25a Διὰ τοῦτο λέγω ὑμῖν;
Lit. *Through this I say to you;*
"For this reason, I say to you;

Διὰ	Through
prep:	διά "through/because of"

τοῦτο	this
dem pron: acc sg neut οὗτος "this"	

λέγω	I say
verb:	pres act ind 1st sg λέγω "(I) say"

ὑμῖν	to you (pl)
pers pron: 2nd dat pl σύ "to you (pl)"	

Explanation. Διὰ τοῦτο literally means "through this," but is a common idiom meaning "for this reason." In other words, because one cannot serve both God and money. Or perhaps it infers the entirety of vv. 19–24. Regardless, the following (v. 25) gives the implications of the preceding truths to direct instructions for the disciples. It is primarily given here in terms of what not to be anxious about, with illustrations given (vv. 26–32), and a climactic statement what the disciple should be concerned about: seeking first the kingdom of God and its righteousness (Matt 6:33).

λέγω means "I say." The subject is implied in the verb, which does not need to be written out in Greek but does in English.

ὑμῖν is a plural indirect object, meaning the saying is directed toward more than just one person.

25b μὴ μεριμνᾶτε τῇ ψυχῇ ὑμῶν τί φάγητε ἢ τί πίητε,
Lit. do not have concern to the life of you, what you may eat or what you may drink,

do not have concern in your life, what you may eat or what you may drink,

μή	not

neg particle: μή "no/not (stop)"

μεριμνᾶτε	you (pl) have concern
verb:	pres act imv 2nd pl μεριμνάω "have concern (you [pl])"

τῇ	the
article:	dat sg fem ὁ "to the"

ψυχῇ	soul/ life
noun:	dat sg fem ψυχή "to a soul"

ὑμῶν	of you (pl)/ your (pl)

pers pron: 2nd gen pl σύ "of you (pl)"

τί	what?

interr pron: acc sg neut τίς "whom?/what?"

φάγητε	you (pl) may eat
verb:	aor act subj 2nd pl ἐσθίω "you (pl) should begin to eat"

ἤ	or
particle:	ἤ "or/than"

τί   what
interr pron: acc sg neut τίς "whom?/what?"

πίητε   you (pl) may drink
verb: aor act subj 2nd pl πίνω "you (pl) should begin to drink"

Explanation. The command not to have concern in one's soul pertains specifically to eating and drinking, as these are fundamental necessities of life. But this surely applies to other things as well.

25c μηδὲ τῷ σώματι ὑμῶν τί ἐνδύσησθε·
Lit. nor to the body of you what you may wear;
nor your body, what you may wear.

μηδὲ   nor
neg conj: μηδέ "not even/neither"

τῷ   the
article: dat sg neut ὁ "to the"

σώματι   body
noun: dat sg neut σῶμα "to a body"

ὑμῶν   your (pl)/ of you
pers pron: 2nd gen pl σύ "of you (pl)"

τί   what
interr pron: acc sg neut τίς "whom?/what?"

ἐνδύσησθε   you (pl) may wear
verb: aor mid subj 2nd pl ἐνδύω "(you [pl]) should begin to be (for yourselves) clothed"

Explanation. The governing (main) verb comes from v. 25c (μεριμνᾶτε).

MATTHEW 6:19–25

25d οὐχὶ ἡ ψυχὴ πλεῖόν ἐστιν τῆς τροφῆς καὶ τὸ σῶμα τοῦ ἐνδύματος;
Lit. not the life more than is of food and the body of clothing?
Is not life more than food and the body more than clothing?"

οὐχὶ	not
interr particle: οὐχί "not?"	
ἡ	the
article:	nom sg fem ὁ "the"
ψυχὴ	soul/ life
noun:	nom sg fem ψυχή "a soul"
πλεῖόν	much/ more
adj:	nom sg neut πολύς "much"
ἐστιν	is
verb:	pres act ind 3rd sg εἰμί "(he/she/it) is"
τῆς	the
article:	gen sg fem ὁ "of the"
τροφῆς	food
noun:	gen sg fem τροφή "of food/a supply"
καὶ	and
conj:	καί "and"
τὸ	the
article:	nom sg neut ὁ "the"
σῶμα	body
noun:	nom sg neut σῶμα "a body"
τοῦ	the
article:	gen sg neut ὁ "of the"

ἐνδύματος   clothing

noun: gen sg neut ἔνδυμα "of clothing"

Explanation. The presence of οὐχί at the head of the sentence and insertion by modern edition text editors of the ";"—which functions like a question mark—at the end indicates this is a question. It is often easiest to translate a question as a statement first, then reformulate it in English as a question. For example, "Life is more than food" as a statement turns into the question "Is not life more than food?" In the earliest manuscripts there was little or no punctuation. Sometimes there were no spaces between words or letters. By knowing the Greek text well, editors of our modern published editions of the Greek NT are able to discern word divisions easily enough and furnish punctuation to aid readers. Seldom is there any substantial issue of meaning at stake in such instances.

πλεῖόν is a comparative word, "more than" or "greater than." So, the phrase ἡ ψυχὴ πλεῖόν ἐστι τῆς τροφῆς means "life is more than food," meaning in colloquial English: "there is more to life than food."

τὸ σῶμα τοῦ ἐνδύματος implies the πλεῖόν is duplicated for this comparison as well, so as to read τὸ σῶμα (πλεῖόν) τοῦ ἐνδύματος, "the body is more than clothing." Or, colloquially, "there is more to the body than clothing."

Preaching the Text

1. **Main idea:** An undivided heart

2. **Text to Sermon:**

    a. Part 1: Matthew 6:19–21: Surprisingly, Jesus commands his disciples to store up treasures for themselves. The question is *where* will they be stored; on earth or in heaven? Every treasure treasured up on earth is subject to corruption, decay, or theft. Every treasure treasured up in heaven is entirely immune to any kind of corruption, loss, or decay. Peter says it this way: " . . . By [God's] great mercy he has given us a new birth into a living hope through the resurrection of Jesus Christ from the dead, and into an inheritance that is *imperishable, undefiled, and unfading, kept* in heaven for you" (1 Peter 1:3–4, NRSV; emphasis added).

    b. Part 2: Matthew 6:22–23: These verses are not clear and heavily debated. But since the verses before and after relate to money, these probably relate to money as well. Later Jesus will tell his disciples that if the eye causes one to sin, it is best to cut it out (Matt 18:9). So here the metaphor seems to be one of covetousness with regard to wealth. The healthy eye is not coveting wealth, but the unhealthy one is. And the covetous heart toward wealth has pervasive effects on one's discipleship to Jesus Christ.

    c. Part 3: Matthew 6:24: We all have many pressures pulling us in different ways in life, but only God can be our master. He must have our undivided loyalty, and does not allow for competition. God does not allow for any other gods, and is jealous for the exclusive covenant fidelity of His people (cf. Exod 34:14).

    d. Part 4: Matthew 6:25: This verse functions as a thematic summary for the whole. If one's allegiances to God are absolute—storing treasures in heaven, avoiding covetousness, and having God as our only master—provision for our material well-being is a natural consequence. God takes care of his own. He instructs his disciples not to care for such things, but rather focus on the kingdom of God and its righteousness, and trust in his provision for the other concerns.

3. **Tip for Preaching:** As different as these passages may seem at a surface level, they are all leading us to the same, singular point: an undivided

and singular allegiance to Christ and His kingdom, with a heavenward mindset and priorities aligned with His. Matthew 6:25 makes this apparent. And all the more so this is seen a little later on when Jesus instructs His disciples: "But seek first the kingdom of God and his righteousness, and all these things will be added to you" (Matt 6:33, ESV). If Matt 6:25 is a summary of the others, Matt 6:33 is a compass, pointing the hearts of the followers of Christ in the direction to which all of the other teachings in these verses are oriented.

5
Matthew 8:23–27
What Sort of a Person Is Jesus?

In this passage Jesus is in Capernaum (Matt 8:5), where he made his home (Matt 4:13). This is a small village on the northern shore of the Sea of Galilee. It is here that Jesus is approached by a Roman centurion, asking Jesus to heal his servant (Matt 8:5–6). As a centurion, he was a leader of 100 men, and knew what it was to be obeyed by subordinates, so for him there was simply no need for Jesus to come to his home. In his estimation, Jesus could just issue the command it and it would be done (Matt 8:7–9), and so it was (Matt 8:10–13). In Peter's house the fever of his mother-in-law and the unclean spirits obeyed Jesus' voice just as readily (Matt 8:14–17). When Jesus gives instructions to his disciples to cross the Sea of Galilee with him (Matt 8:18), Jesus teaches would-be followers that doing so may involve giving up the comforts of a home (vv. 19–20) and perhaps even the most intimate of familial obligations (vv. 21–22). It is after these statements—when the disciples overhear just how demanding it can be to follow Jesus—that they get into the boat for a memorable trip across the often-placid Sea of Galilee.

23 Καὶ ἐμβάντι αὐτῷ εἰς πλοῖον ἠκολούθησαν αὐτῷ οἱ μαθηταὶ αὐτοῦ.
Lit. And getting into to it in the boat they followed to him the disciples of him.
And getting into the boat with him, his disciples followed him.

Καὶ   and
conj: καί "and"

ἐμβάντι   going in/ getting in
ptcp: aor act ptcp dat sg masc ἐμβαίνω "to (him) having gone in"

αὐτῷ   with him
pers pron: dat sg masc αὐτός "to him"

εἰς   into
prep: εἰς "into/for"

τὸ   the
article: acc sg neut ὁ "the"

πλοῖον   boat
noun: acc sg neut πλοῖον "a boat/ship"

ἠκολούθησαν followed
verb: aor act ind 3rd pl ἀκολουθέω "they followed"

αὐτῷ   him
pers pron: dat sg masc αὐτός "to him"

οἱ   the
article: nom pl masc ὁ "the (ones)"

μαθηταὶ   disciples
noun: nom pl masc μαθητής "disciples"

αὐτοῦ   of him/ his
pers pron: gen sg masc αὐτός "of him/it"

Explanation. The αὐτῷ in ἠκολούθησαν αὐτῷ is in the dative case because the verb takes its direct object not in the accusative but dative case.

ἀκολουθέω in Matthew is typically used for discipleship (Matt 4:20, 22, 25; 8:1, 10, 19, 22-23; 9:9, 19, 27; 10:38; 12:15; 14:13; 16:24; 19:2, 21, 27-28; 20:29, 34; 21:9; 26:58; 27:55)

24a καὶ ἰδοὺ σεισμὸς μέγας ἐγένετο ἐν τῇ θαλάσσῃ,
Lit. And behold storm great came in the lake,
And behold a great storm came about on the lake,

καὶ	and
conj:	καί "and"
ἰδοὺ	behold
verb:	aor mid imv 2nd sg ὁράω "begin (you for yourself) to see"
σεισμὸς	a storm
noun:	nom sg masc σεισμός "an earthquake"
μέγας	great
adj:	nom sg masc μέγας "great"
ἐγένετο	occurred/ came about
verb:	aor mid ind 3rd sg γίνομαι "(one oneself) became/occurred"
ἐν	in
prep:	ἐν "in/by/with"
τῇ	the
article:	dat sg fem ὁ "to the"
θαλάσσῃ	sea/ lake
noun:	dat sg fem θάλασσα "to the sea"

Explanation. σεισμὸς is the same word used for an earthquake (Matt 24:7; 27:54; 28:2).

θαλάσσῃ is the Sea of Galilee, which is a freshwater lake approximately 8 miles wide and 13 miles long. In 1986, during a very dry year when the waters were very low on the Sea of Galilee, a boat emerged from the mud. It turned out to be a fishing boat from between 50 BC and AD 50. It measures 27 feet in length and 7 ½ feet in width. It was carefully removed and its remains are housed in the Yigal Allon Museum in Kibbutz Ginosar. Though there is no way of knowing whether or not Jesus made use of this particular boat, it does give us an indication of the dimensions of boats from that time.

24b ὥστε τὸ πλοῖον καλύπτεσθαι ὑπὸ τῶν κυμάτων,
Lit. so that the boat was being hidden under the waves,
so that the boat was being hidden by the waves,

ὥστε	so that
conj:	ὥστε "so that"
τὸ	the
article:	nom sg neut ὁ "the"
πλοῖον	boat
noun:	nom sg neut πλοῖον "a boat/ship"
καλύπτεσθαι	was being concealed/ was being hidden
verb:	pres pass inf καλύπτω "to be concealed/hid"
ὑπὸ	by/ under
prep:	ὑπό "by/under"
τῶν	the
article:	gen pl neut ὁ "of the (ones)"
κυμάτων	waves
noun:	gen pl neut κῦμα "of waves"

Explanation. The perspective here is one in which the boat is so overcome in sizable waves that it is no longer visible. It is not under the water, yet.

24c αὐτὸς δὲ ἐκάθευδεν.
Lit. he but was sleeping.
but he was sleeping.

αὐτός	He
pers pron:	nom sg masc αὐτός "he"

δὲ	but
conj:	δέ "but/now"

ἐκάθευδεν	was sleeping
verb:	impf act ind 3rd sg καθεύδω "(he/she/it) continually slept"

Explanation. αὐτός is emphatic; *He* was sleeping. The sentence makes perfect sense without the αὐτός.

δέ is somewhat contrastive, introducing something unexpected—presumably readers are to regard the tumultuous setting in vv. 24a and 24b is insufficiently disturbing to prevent Jesus' restful sleep. He sees no cause for alarm.

ἐκάθευδεν is an imperfect verb, indicating a continuous past action. Sleep was sometimes regarded as the blessings associated with trust in God (cf. Job 11:18–19; Ps 3:5–6; Prov. 3:24–26).

25a καὶ προσελθόντες ἤγειραν αὐτὸν λέγοντες·
Lit. And coming they awakened him saying,
And coming towards (him) they awakened him, saying,

καὶ	and
conj:	καί "and"

προσελθόντες   coming toward
ptcp: aor act ptcp nom pl masc προσέρχομαι "(the men) having come toward"

ἤγειραν   they raised up/ awakened him
verb: aor act ind 3rd pl ἐγείρω "they raised up"

αὐτὸν   him
pers pron: acc sg masc αὐτός "him"

λέγοντες   saying
ptcp: pres act ptcp nom pl masc λέγω "(those) saying" "say"

Explanation. Matthew commonly puts adverbial particles, like προσελθόντες, before the main verb in a sentence, like ἤγειραν.

25b κύριε, σῶσον, ἀπολλύμεθα.
Lit. Lord, save, we are perishing.
Lord, save, we are perishing!

κύριε   Lord
noun: voc sg masc κύριος "O Lord!"

σῶσον   save
verb: aor act imv 2nd sg σῴζω "begin (you) to save/deliver"

ἀπολλύμεθα   we are perishing
verb: pres mid ind 1st pl ἀπόλλυμι "(we ourselves) destroy"

Explanation. κύριε is a vocative, meaning it is a direct address, here in urgency.

Notice the terse language brought about by the crisis: The verb has no direct object (save *us*) and Matthew omits his customary "for" (*for* we are perishing). The verb is pregnant with meaning, and typically refers to more than physical peril (cf. Matt 1:21; 18:11; 19:25).

ἀπόλλυμι is a present tense verb and not a historical present, indicating it is a present continuous action. It is not that they *will* perish, but they are then in the very process of perishing.

26a καὶ λέγει αὐτοῖς· τί δειλοί ἐστε, ὀλιγόπιστοι;
Lit. And he said to them, "Why cowardly you are, O little-faith-ones!
And he said to them, "Why are you cowardly? O little-faith-ones!

καί	and
conj:	καί "and"

λέγει	he said
verb:	pres act ind 3rd sg λέγω "(he/she/it) says"

αὐτοῖς	to them
pers pron:	dat pl masc αὐτός "to them"

τί	why
interr pron:	nom sg neut τίς "whom?/what?"

δειλοί	cowardly
adj:	nom pl masc δειλός "cowardly/timid (ones)"

ἐστε	you are
verb:	pres act ind 2nd pl εἰμί "(you [pl]) are"

ὀλιγόπιστοι	O little-faith-ones!
adj:	voc pl masc ὀλιγόπιστος "O-little-faith-(ones)!"

Explanation. Jesus is not concerned that they are "afraid" (φοβέω, Matt 1:20; 2:22; 9:8, etc.) but they are δειλός, "cowardly" or "faint of heart" (cf. Rev 21:8; LXX Deut 20:8; Judg 7:3; 2 Chron 13:7).

Jesus does not say "you have little faith," but he calls them a single adjective, here acting like a noun, ὀλιγόπιστοι, "little-faith-ones." The vocative case indicates direct address, "O little-faith-ones!"

Τί is an interrogative pronoun, the meaning of which is determined by the need of the context (e.g., why? what? etc.).

The question comes before Jesus rises to rebuke the storm (v. 26b). What Jesus expects of them is not explicitly stated, though it is clear that he regards their cowardice and lack of faith as inappropriate not because of the storm but because of him.

26b τότε ἐγερθεὶς ἐπετίμησεν τοῖς ἀνέμοις καὶ τῇ θαλάσσῃ,
Lit. Then rising he rebuked to the winds and to the sea,
Then, rising, he rebuked the winds and the sea,

τότε	then
adv:	τότε "then"
ἐγερθεὶς	raising
ptcp:	aor pass ptcp nom sg masc ἐγείρω "(he) having been raised up"
ἐπετίμησεν	he rebuked
verb:	aor act ind 3rd sg ἐπιτιμάω "he/she/it rebuked"
τοῖς	the
article:	dat pl masc ὁ "to the (ones)"
ἀνέμοις	winds
noun:	dat pl masc ἄνεμος "to winds"
καὶ	and
conj:	καί "and"
τῇ	the
article:	dat sg fem ὁ "to the"
θαλάσσῃ	sea
noun:	dat sg fem θάλασσα "to the sea"

Explanation. ἐπιτιμάω, "I rebuke," is the same language Jesus uses against those who would make him known before his time (Matt 12:16), Peter used against Jesus (Matt 16:23), Jesus used against a demon (Matt 17:18), the disciples against those who brought children to Jesus (Matt 19:13), and the crowds against the blind men hailing Jesus as Son of David (Matt 20:30–31).

26c καὶ ἐγένετο γαλήνη μεγάλη.
Lit. and there came calm great.
and there came a great calm.

καὶ	and
conj:	καί "and"

ἐγένετο	there came/ it came/
verb:	aor mid ind 3rd sg γίνομαι "(one oneself) became/occurred"

γαλήνη	calm
noun:	nom sg fem γαλήνη "a calm"

μεγάλη	great
adj:	nom sg fem μέγας "great"

Explanation. γαλήνη occurs only here and the parallels in Mark (4:39) and Luke (8:29) in the Bible. It does not occur in the LXX.

27a οἱ δὲ ἄνθρωποι ἐθαύμασαν λέγοντες,
Lit. The but people were amazed saying,
But the men were amazed, saying,

οἱ	The
article:	nom pl masc ὁ "the (ones)"

δὲ	But
conj:	δέ "but/now"

ἄνθρωποι   men
noun: nom pl masc ἄνθρωπος "men"

ἐθαύμασαν were amazed/ marveled
verb: aor act ind 3rd pl θαυμάζω "they were amazed/marveled"

λέγοντες   saying
ptcp: pres act ptcp nom pl masc λέγω "(those) saying"

Explanation. ἄνθρωπος typically refers to people in general, though it can, as here, refer to men in particular.

δέ is second in the sentence simply because it must be, even though it disrupts the definite article (οἱ) and its noun (ἄνθρωποι). δέ is called a "postpositive" because it occurs *after* the *first* word.

θαυμάζω, "I marvel, am amazed," is a common response to Jesus' miracles (Matt 15:31; 21:20; Mark 5:20; Luke 8:25; 9:43; 11:14; cf. Luke 24:12) or his teachings (Matt 22:22; Luke 20:26; 24:41; cf. Matt 27:14; Mark 15:5)

27b ποταπός ἐστιν οὗτος ὅτι καὶ οἱ ἄνεμοι καὶ ἡ θάλασσα αὐτῷ ὑπακούουσιν;

Lit. *What sort of this that and the winds and the sea to him they obey?*

"What sort of (person) is this, that even the winds and the sea obey him?"

ποταπός   what sort of?
adj: nom sg masc ποταπός "what sort of"

ἐστιν   is
verb: pres act ind 3rd sg εἰμί "(he/she/it) is"

οὗτος   this
dem pron: nom sg masc οὗτος "this"

ὅτι   that
conj: ὅτι "because/that"

καὶ   and/ even
conj: καί "and"

οἱ   the
article: nom pl masc ὁ "the (ones)"

ἄνεμοι   winds
noun: nom pl masc ἄνεμος "winds"

καὶ   and
conj: καί "and"

ἡ   the
article: nom sg fem ὁ "the"

θάλασσα sea
noun: nom sg fem θάλασσα "the sea"

αὐτῷ   him
pers pron: dat sg masc αὐτός "to him"

ὑπακούουσιν obey
verb: pres act ind 3rd pl ὑπακούω "(they) obey"

Explanation. ποταπός ἐστιν οὗτος, "what sort is this?" requires readers to supply an implied noun, "person" (ἄνθρωπος)

καὶ can be a conjunction ("and") or an adverb ("also"). Context for the first occurrence requires it to be an adverb; the conjunction makes no sense here. Context for the second requires it to be a conjunction, since an adverb makes no sense.

ὑπακούω only occurs here in Matthew, but it is used for the obedience of unclean spirits to Jesus (Mark 1:27). Notice the manner in which the winds and sea instantly respond to Jesus' voice.

This is the climax of the passage, and the disciples ask precisely what the reader is to ask (and answer) for him/herself. Behind this may lie various Psalms, such as:

- Psalm 89:8–9: "Who is like you, Lord God Almighty? You, Lord, are mighty, and your faithfulness surrounds you. You rule over the surging sea; when its waves mount up, you still them" (NIV).

- Psalm 65:5, 7: "You answer us with awesome and righteous deeds, God our Savior, the hope of all the ends of the earth and of the farthest seas, . . . who stilled the roaring of the seas, the roaring of their waves, and the turmoil of the nations" (NIV).

- Psalm 107:29: "He stilled the storm to a whisper; the waves of the sea were hushed" (NIV).

Preaching the Text

1. **Main idea:** What *sort of man* is Jesus?

2. **Text to Sermon:**

   a. This is not a story about a storm. Nor is it a story about the disciples, or even a miracle. Of course, it is a story about Jesus. And it is a miracle story about Jesus. The function of a miracle story is to call a person to faith in Jesus because of who he is as revealed in the miracle. This is key to the entire context of Matthew.

   b. The disciples know enough about Jesus to follow him into a boat (Matt 8:23), but apparently not enough to recognize that he can calm a storm, which comes as a complete shock to them (8:27). They questioned whether Jesus even cared that they were perishing in the storm (Matt 8:24–25), but Matthew says nothing about what they expected of him. Help to row to shore? Or perhaps to help bail out water from their sinking boat? Regardless, what happened was not what they expected.

   c. The main point of the passage is v. 27. Remember, Jesus' disciples have been with him for a while, and yet for some reason are not asking questions about who he is—that comes later (Matthew 16). They are asking instead *what* he is. Or at least what sort of person he is. He is certainly a person—they know that—but what kind of person does such a thing? Notice—and this is essential—Matthew *never answers the question*. The reader is supposed to *deduce from the evidence* what sort of person can do such a thing. Only God. Notice, however, that nowhere does Matthew say "Jesus is God!" And yet this passage makes it abundantly clear. That is how gospel narratives work; they depict the things they try to communicate to readers.

   d. Let's go back in history for a bit, and imagine you are a disciple on that boat. If you are among the twelve, there are eleven other men plus Jesus and the boat is a little crowded. A huge storm comes up, and everyone panics. Some of these guys are fisherman who grew up on the Sea of Galilee, so if *they* are scared, it must be a big deal. Yet there is Jesus. Asleep? Yes, asleep. Perplexed, the disciples try to get his help. What do they expect? Maybe grab a paddle or a bucket? We do not know. But what he does shocks them. He calms the storm *by words*. And there is a dead calm—the waves that were a moment ago so massive that they hid the boat from view are now smooth and calm as a sheet of glass. You may be panting from your labors, or fear, as you look around at the other disciples. What is going through their minds? It is *not* "Jesus can calm the storms in my life"! No, this is not a *metaphor*, it is a *miracle*, and we must encounter Christ as a miracle-working Christ if we are to grasp the implications of this story. So, the disciples ask one another the very question you and I are to ask: in light of what just occurred, *what sort of person is this, that even the wind and the sea obey him*? Be careful how you answer. If you say he is God, you are right, but you also cannot help following him. And following him comes with a cost, the cost of discipleship. Because the purpose of a miracle story is to call people to faith in Jesus because of who he is as revealed in the miracle.

e. The following context illustrates the point. When Jesus casts demons out of two men among the tombs at the Gadarenes, the people whose pigs the demons subsequently destroyed implored Jesus to leave (Matt 8:28–34). Upon returning to Capernaum Jesus healed a paralytic and the crowds responded with awe (Matt 9:1–8). Then, we get to Matt 9:9: "As Jesus was walking along, he saw a man called Matthew sitting at the tax booth; and he said to him, "Follow me." And he got up and followed him." Nothing is said about what Matthew knows about Jesus that causes this kind of immediate obedience. That is irrelevant. Matthew has given us as readers *all that we need to understand Matthew's response and the compulsion for us to do the same* by his succession of miracle stories. What sort of person is Jesus? A person to be followed; Jesus is God.

3. **Tip for Preaching:** This passage is not a metaphor, it is a miracle. And it is not about a storm, but about a man who calmed the storm. And it is about a man that even his closest disciples could not quite figure out. This passage is all about who Jesus is as revealed in the miracle. That is how Matthew ends this story, and that is how he wants his readers to experience it, and that is how we need to experience it as well. Until

we come to terms with who Jesus is as revealed in this miracle, we simply cannot understand who Jesus really is at all.

6
Matthew 13:3–9, 18–23
Good Soil or Bad?

Parables in the Gospels are stories taken from every-day life that Jesus uses to illustrate a moral or theological truth. But the stories are not from *our* everyday lives, but from those of Jesus' listeners and Matthew's readers. Nevertheless, they are usually pretty clear and illustrate important matters in simple terms—there are no plot twists, there are seldom more than a few characters, and readers never get lost in the story. Perhaps that is why we love them. Among the most prominent parables in Matthew is the parable of the sower. In it, Matthew gives us both an account of Jesus' telling of the parable itself (Matt 13:1–9) and his even longer explanation of it (Matt 13:18–23). Jesus teaches the parable to a crowd gathered around him from a boat on the Sea of Galilee (Matt 13:1–2). Matthew says that Jesus told them "many things in parables" (Matt 13:3), which includes what we have in Matthew but probably also much more. He tells of seed sown by a farmer that fell among different kinds of soil—rocky soil, soil choked by thorns, and good soil. Only the latter grows (Matt 13:3–9). In his explanation (Matt 13:18–23), Jesus clarifies that the seed is the "word of the kingdom" and that the differing soils correspond to the receptivity of the person to the kingdom message (Matt 13:8–22). The good soil represents one who not only hears the message, but understands it and bears corresponding fruit (Matt 13:12).

MATTHEW 13:3-9, 18-23

Part I

3a Καὶ ἐλάλησεν αὐτοῖς πολλὰ ἐν παραβολαῖς λέγων·
Lit. And he spoke to them many in to parables saying,
And he taught them many (things) in parables, saying,

καὶ   and
conj: καί "and"

ἐλάλησεν he spoke
verb: aor act ind 3rd sg λαλέω "he/she/it spoke"

αὐτοῖς   to them
pers pron: dat pl masc αὐτός "to them"

πολλὰ   much/ many (things)
adj: acc pl neut πολύς "many (ones)"

ἐν   in
prep: ἐν "in/by/with"

παραβολαῖς parables
noun: dat pl fem παραβολή "to parables"

λέγων   saying
ptcp: pres act ptcp nom sg masc λέγω "(one) saying"

Explanation. ἐλάλησεν is an aorist verb, whereas one would expect an imperfect verb to convey a continuous past action. But the fact that Jesus taught "many (things)" supplies the idea that there was much said here, and surely more than recorded in Matthew 13.

It is important to see how the grammar shows us how the various words and phrases relate to the verb, ἐλάλησεν ("he spoke"). The subject, "he," is implied in the verb and does not need to be stated in Greek like it does in English. αὐτοῖς is the indirect object, saying to whom Jesus spoke ("to them"). πολλά is the direct object, and so receives the action of the verb. It tells us what Jesus spoke. Here πολλά is an adjective ("many") acting substantivally, like a noun ("many [things]"). The ἐν παραβολαῖς is a prepositional phrase and explains the manner in which Jesus spoke—in parables.

3b ἰδοὺ ἐξῆλθεν ὁ σπείρων τοῦ σπείρειν.
Lit. "Behold he went out the sower of to sow.
"Behold a sower went out to sow.

ἰδοὺ	Behold
verb:	aor mid imv 2nd sg ὁράω "begin (you for yourself) to see"
ἐξῆλθεν	went out
verb:	aor act ind 3rd sg ἐξέρχομαι "he/she/it went/came out"
ὁ	the
article:	nom sg masc ὁ "the"
σπείρων	sower/ one sowing
ptcp:	pres act ptcp nom sg masc σπείρω "(one) sowing"
τοῦ	of the
article:	gen sg neut ὁ "of the"
σπείρειν	to sow
verb:	pres act inf σπείρω "to sow"

Explanation. σπείρειν is an infinitive verb, with the definite article τοῦ is an articular infinitive indicating purpose.

4a καὶ ἐν τῷ σπείρειν αὐτὸν ἃ μὲν ἔπεσεν παρὰ τὴν ὁδόν,
Lit. and in to the sowing him what he sowed alongside the path,
and as he was sowing, some (seeds) fell alongside the path,

καὶ	and
conj:	καί "and"

MATTHEW 13:3-9, 18-23

ἐν in
prep: ἐν "in/by/with"

τῷ the
article: dat sg neut ὁ "to the"

σπείρειν to sow
verb: pres act inf σπείρω "to sow"

αὐτὸν him
pers pron: acc sg masc αὐτός "him"

ἃ some
rel pron: nom pl neut ὅς "which (ones)"

μὲν indeed/ *untranslated*
particle: μέν "indeed"

ἔπεσεν fell
verb: aor act ind 3rd sg πίπτω "he/she/it fell"

παρὰ alongside/
prep: παρά "beside/alongside"

τὴν the
article: acc sg fem ὁ "the"

ὁδόν road/ way/ path
noun: acc sg fem ὁδός "a road/path/way"

Explanation. ἐν τῷ σπείρειν αὐτὸν is complicated. The verb σπείρειν is an infinitive, which here functions like a finite verb with the accusative-case pronoun αὐτόν as the subject. ἐν τῷ indicates timing, here contemporary action: "as he was sowing."

ἅ is a relative pronoun that is translated like a demonstrative, functioning like the subject of ἔπεσεν: "some fell." Notice that the subject is plural but the verb is singular. Perhaps this is because the subject implies a collective singular "seed," allowing for a singular verb.

μέν is simply a particle of anticipation, pointing forward to the progress of the narrative. It can be translated "indeed" or not translated at all.

4b καὶ ἐλθόντα τὰ πετεινὰ κατέφαγεν αὐτά.
Lit. and coming the birds devoured them.
and, coming, the birds devoured them.

καὶ	and
conj:	καί "and"

ἐλθόντα	coming
ptcp:	aor act ptcp nom pl neut ἔρχομαι "(those) having come"

τὰ	the
article:	nom pl neut ὁ "the (ones)"

πετεινὰ	birds
noun:	nom pl neut πετεινόν "birds"

κατέφαγεν	devoured
verb:	aor act ind 3rd sg κατεσθίω "he/she/it swallowed down/devoured"

αὐτά	them
pers pron:	acc pl neut αὐτός "them"

Explanation. Matthew commonly uses adverbial participles ahead of the verbs they modify, here ἐλθόντα before κατέφαγεν.

The verb κατέφαγεν, from κατεσθίω, is a compound verb combining ἐσθίω, "I eat" with the preposition, κατά to form κατεσθίω, "I eat up" or "I devour."

MATTHEW 13:3-9, 18-23

5a ἄλλα δὲ ἔπεσεν ἐπὶ τὰ πετρώδη ὅπου οὐκ εἶχεν γῆν πολλήν,

Lit. *others but fell upon the rocky ground were not they have ground much,*

and others fell on the rocky ground, where they did not have much soil,

ἄλλα	others
adj:	nom pl neut ἄλλος "other (ones)"
δὲ	and
conj:	δέ "but/now"
ἔπεσεν	fell
verb:	aor act ind 3rd sg πίπτω "he/she/it fell"
ἐπὶ	upon
prep:	ἐπί "upon"
τὰ	the
article:	acc pl neut ὁ "the (ones)"
πετρώδη	rocky soil
adj:	acc pl neut πετρώδης "rocky (soils)"
ὅπου	where
adv:	ὅπου "where"
οὐκ	not
neg particle:	οὐ "no/not"
εἶχεν	it was having
verb:	impf act ind 3rd sg ἔχω "(he/she/it) continually had"
γῆν	earth/ dirt/ soil
noun:	acc sg fem γῆ "earth/land"

πολλήν   much
adj: acc sg fem πολύς "much"

Explanation. ὅπου is an adverb, beginning an adverbial phrase which in full describes what occurs upon falling on the rocky soil.

Though εἶχεν is singular, the implied collective subject "seed" can infer in English a plural "they" for its subject.

5b καὶ εὐθέως ἐξανέτειλεν διὰ τὸ μὴ ἔχειν βάθος γῆς,
Lit. and immediately they sprung up through the not to have depth of earth,

and immediately they sprung up because they had no depth of soil,

καὶ   and
conj: καί "and"

εὐθέως   immediately
adv: εὐθέως "immediately/next"

ἐξανέτειλεν   it sprung up
verb: aor act ind 3rd sg ἐξανατέλλω "he/she/it sprung up"

διὰ   because of
prep: διά "through/because of"

τὸ   the
article: acc sg neut ὁ "the"

μὴ   not
neg particle: μή "no/not (stop)"

ἔχειν   to have
verb: pres act inf ἔχω "to have"

βάθος	depth
noun:	acc sg neut βάθος "a depth"

γῆς	of oil/ dirt/ land/ earth
noun:	gen sg fem γῆ "of earth/land"

Explanation. Though ἐξανέτειλεν is a singular verb, the collective singular nature of its implied subject, "seed," suggests a plural subject in English, "they."

διὰ indicates purpose, with τὸ ἔχειν, as an articular infinitive, acts like a finite verb.

6a ἡλίου δὲ ἀνατείλαντος ἐκαυματίσθη
Lit. of the sun but having risen it was scorched up
but when the sun rose, they were scorched

ἡλίου	of the sun
noun:	gen sg masc ἥλιος "of the sun"

δὲ	but
conj:	δέ "but/now"

ἀνατείλαντος	arising/ rising
ptcp:	aor act ptcp gen sg masc ἀνατέλλω "of (him) having arisen"

ἐκαυματίσθη	it was scorched/ burned up
verb:	aor pass ind 3rd sg καυματίζω "(he/she/it) was scorched/burnt up"

Explanation. ἡλίου ... ἀνατείλαντος is literally "rising of the sun." The participle connotes a temporal idea, so it is translated "when the sun rose."

ἐκαυματίσθη is a third singular, with a collective singular subject "seed" can be translated "they were scorched."

6b καὶ διὰ τὸ μὴ ἔχειν ῥίζαν ἐξηράνθη.
Lit. and through the not having root they were withered.
and, because they had no root, they were withered.

καὶ	and
conj:	καί "and"

διὰ	through/ because of
prep:	διά "through/because of"

τὸ	the
article:	acc sg neut ὁ "the"

μὴ	not
neg particle:	μή "no/not (stop)"

ἔχειν	to have
verb:	pres act inf ἔχω "to have"

ῥίζαν	root
noun:	acc sg fem ῥίζα "a root"

ἐξηράνθη	was withered/ dried up
verb:	aor pass ind 3rd sg ξηραίνω "(he/she/it) was dried up/withered"

Explanation. διὰ indicates purpose, with τὸ ἔχειν, as an articular infinitive, acts like a finite verb.

ἐξηράνθη is a third singular, with a collective singular subject "seed" can be translated "they were withered."

7a ἄλλα δὲ ἔπεσεν ἐπὶ τὰς ἀκάνθας,
Lit. others but fell upon the thorns,
and others fell among the thorns,

ἄλλα	others
adj:	nom pl neut ἄλλος "other (ones)"

δὲ	and
conj:	δέ "but/now"

ἔπεσεν	fell
verb:	aor act ind 3rd sg πίπτω "he/she/it fell"

ἐπὶ	upon/ among
prep:	ἐπί "upon"

τὰς	the
article:	acc pl fem ὁ "the (ones)"

ἀκάνθας	thorns
noun:	acc pl fem ἄκανθα "thorns"

Explanation. ἔπεσεν is a third singular verb, but the subject, ἄλλα, is plural presumably because it refers to the collective singular "seed."

7b καὶ ἀνέβησαν αἱ ἄκανθαι καὶ ἔπνιξαν αὐτά.
Lit. and they grew up the thorns and choked them.
and the thorns grew up and choked them.

καὶ	and
conj:	καί "and"

ἀνέβησαν	grew up
verb:	aor act ind 3rd pl ἀναβαίνω "they went up/ascended"

αἱ	the
article:	nom pl fem ὁ "the (ones)"

ἄκανθαι	thorns
noun:	nom pl fem ἄκανθα "thorns"

καί	and
conj:	καί "and"

ἔπνιξαν	strangled/ choked
verb:	aor act ind 3rd pl πνίγω "they strangled/choked"

αὐτά	them
pers pron:	acc pl neut αὐτός "them"

8a ἄλλα δὲ ἔπεσεν ἐπὶ τὴν γῆν τὴν καλὴν καὶ ἐδίδου καρπόν,

Lit. others but fell upon the ground the good and were producing fruit,

still others fell on the good soil and were producing fruit,

ἄλλα	others
adj:	nom pl neut ἄλλος "other (ones)"

δέ	and/ still
conj:	δέ "but/now"

ἔπεσεν	fell
verb:	aor act ind 3rd sg πίπτω "he/she/it fell"

ἐπί	on/ upon
prep:	ἐπί "upon"

τήν	the
article:	acc sg fem ὁ "the"

γῆν	soil/ earth
noun:	acc sg fem γῆ "earth/land"

τήν	the
article:	acc sg fem ὁ "the"

καλὴν	good
adj:	acc sg fem καλός "noble/good"

καὶ	and
conj:	καί "and"

ἐδίδου	was bearing/ was giving
verb:	impf act ind 3rd sg δίδωμι "(he/she/it) continually gave"

καρπόν	fruit
noun:	acc sg masc καρπός "a fruit"

Explanation. ἔπεσεν is a third singular verb, but the subject, ἄλλα, is plural presumably because it refers to the collective singular "seed."

ἐδίδου is an imperfect, indicating that the producing of fruit (ἐδίδου καρπόν) was a continuous past action.

ἐδίδου is a third singular verb, and its subject is a collective "seed." So, it translates "they were producing."

8b ὃ μὲν ἑκατὸν, ὃ δὲ ἑξήκοντα, ὃ δὲ τριάκοντα.
Lit. some one hundred, some but sixty, some but thirty.
some a hundred, some sixty, and some thirty (times what was sown).

ὃ	which/ some
rel pron:	nom sg neut ὅς "which"

μὲν	untranslated
particle:	μέν "indeed"

ἑκατὸν	one hundred
adj:	num ἑκατόν "one hundred"

ὃ	which/ some
rel pron:	nom sg neut ὅς "which"

δὲ	and
conj:	δέ "but/now"

ἑξήκοντα	sixty
adj:	num ἑξήκοντα "sixty"

ὃ	which/ some
rel pron:	nom sg neut ὅς "which"

δὲ	and
conj:	δέ "but/now"

τριάκοντα	thirty
adj:	num τριάκοντα "thirty"

Explanation. ὁ is a relative pronoun that is translated like a demonstrative, translated "some."

μέν is simply a particle of anticipation, pointing forward to the progress of the narrative. It can be translated "indeed" or not translated at all.

The remainder of the sentence is unstated in Greek, but implied, and can be rendered in English: "... times what was sown."

9 ὁ ἔχων ὦτα ἀκουέτω.
Lit. The one having hears let him hear.
Let the one having ears hear."

ὁ	the
article:	nom sg masc ὁ "the"

ἔχων	one having
ptcp:	pres act ptcp nom sg masc ἔχω "(one) having"

ὦτα	ears
noun:	acc pl neut οὖς "ears"

MATTHEW 13:3-9, 18-23

ἀκουέτω   let hear
verb: pres act imv 3rd sg ἀκούω "let (him/her/it) hear"

Explanation. ὁ ἔχων is a substantival participle with an object of ὦτα. So, the subject is "the one having ears."

Part II

18   Ὑμεῖς οὖν ἀκούσατε τὴν παραβολὴν τοῦ σπείραντος.
Lit. You then hear the parable of the sower.
"You, therefore, understand the parable of the sower."

Ὑμεῖς   you
pers pron: 2nd nom pl σύ "you (pl)"

οὖν   then/ therefore
conj: οὖν "therefore"

ἀκούσατε   hear/ understand
verb: aor act imv 2nd pl ἀκούω "begin (you [pl]) to hear"

τὴν   the
article: acc sg fem ὁ "the"

παραβολὴν   parable
noun: acc sg fem παραβολή "a parable"

τοῦ   the
article: gen sg masc ὁ "of the"

σπείραντος   one sowing
ptcp: aor act ptcp gen sg masc σπείρω "of (him) having sowed"

Explanation. Ὑμεῖς is emphatic, exhorting his hearers to attend to his explanation.

ἀκούω means "I hear." But given that his listeners have already heard it (vv. 1–9), it is best taken here as "understand," since he is about to give an explanation as to its meaning.

19a παντὸς ἀκούοντος τὸν λόγον τῆς βασιλείας καὶ μὴ συνιέντος
Lit. All the ones hearing the word of the kingdom and not understanding,

All the ones hearing the word of the kingdom and not understanding,

παντὸς   all
adj: gen sg masc πᾶς "of an all"

ἀκούοντος   ones hearing
ptcp: pres act ptcp gen sg masc ἀκούω "of (one) hearing"

τὸν   the
article: acc sg masc ὁ "the"

λόγον   word
noun: acc sg masc λόγος "a word"

τῆς   the
article: gen sg fem ὁ "of the"

βασιλείας   kingdom
noun: gen sg fem βασιλεία "of a kingdom" "kingdom"

καὶ   and
conj: καί "and"

μὴ   not
neg particle: μή "no/not (stop)"

συνιέντος understanding
ptcp: pres act ptcp gen sg masc συνίημι "of (one) understanding"

Explanation. παντὸς is the genitive subject of ἀκούοντος and συνιέντος.

19b ἔρχεται ὁ πονηρὸς καὶ ἁρπάζει τὸ ἐσπαρμένον ἐν τῇ καρδίᾳ αὐτοῦ,
Lit. comes the evil (one) and snatches that which is sown in the heart of him,
the evil (one) comes and snatches what had been sown in his heart,

ἔρχεται comes
verb: pres mid/pass ind 3rd sg ἔρχομαι "(he/she/it) comes"

ὁ the
article: nom sg masc ὁ "the"

πονηρὸς evil
adj: nom sg masc πονηρός "evil"

καὶ and
conj: καί "and"

ἁρπάζει seizes/ snatches
verb: pres act ind 3rd sg ἁρπάζω "(he/she/it) seizes/snatches"

τὸ the
article: acc sg neut ὁ "the"

ἐσπαρμένον being sown
ptcp: perf pass ptcp acc sg neut σπείρω "(one) having been sown"

ἐν   in
prep: ἐν "in/by/with"

τῇ   the
article: dat sg fem ὁ "to the"

καρδίᾳ   heart
noun: dat sg fem καρδία "to a heart"

αὐτοῦ   of him/ his
pers pron: gen sg masc αὐτός "of him/it"

Explanation. πονηρός is an adjective, but with the definite article and nothing for it to modify, it functions substantivally (like a noun). This means that instead of simply "evil" as an adjective, it becomes a noun, "the evil (one)."

ἐσπαρμένον is a participle from σπείρω. Its article τό shows that it is substantival, meaning it acts like a noun and translates "that which has been sown." The prepositional phrase ἐν τῇ καρδίᾳ αὐτοῦ indicates the location where the seed was sown. τῇ καρδίᾳ is in the dative case only because the preposition ἐν requires it, because the meaning of a preposition is determined by the case of its object. The dative object means that ἐν translates "in."

19c οὗτός ἐστιν ὁ παρὰ τὴν ὁδὸν σπαρείς.
Lit. this is the-beside-the-path-sowing.
this is the one having been sown beside the path.

οὗτός   this
dem pron: nom sg masc οὗτος "this"

ἐστιν   is
verb: pres act ind 3rd sg εἰμί "(he/she/it) is"

ὁ   the
article: nom sg masc ὁ "the"

παρὰ	beside
prep:	παρά "beside/alongside"

τὴν	the
article:	acc sg fem ὁ "the"

ὁδὸν	road/ path/ way
noun:	acc sg fem ὁδός "a road/path/way"

σπαρείς	one sowing
ptcp:	aor pass ptcp nom sg masc σπείρω "(one) having been sown"

Explanation. οὗτός is the subject, ἐστιν is the verb, and ὁ . . . σπαρείς is the predicate nominative. Verbs of being do not have direct objects.

ὁ παρὰ τὴν ὁδὸν σπαρείς is all the predicate nominative of the sentence. The article ὁ belongs with σπαρείς, "the one having been sown." Greek puts the prepositional phrase παρὰ τὴν ὁδὸν between the article and the participle to show that the phrase modifies the participle, to translate literally, "the having-been-sown-beside-the-road (one)."

20a ὁ δὲ ἐπὶ τὰ πετρώδη σπαρείς,
Lit. the but upon the rocky soil having been sown,
and the one having been sown on rocky soil—

ὁ	the
article:	nom sg masc ὁ "the"

δὲ	and
conj:	δέ "but/now"

ἐπὶ	upon
prep:	ἐπί "upon"

τὰ	the
article:	acc pl neut ὁ "the (ones)"

πετρώδη	rocky soil
adj:	acc pl neut πετρώδης "rocky (soils)"

σπαρείς	one having been sown
ptcp:	aor pass ptcp nom sg masc σπείρω "(one)-having-been-sown"

Explanation. δέ is second in the sentence because it is a post-positive, and always must be so.

The article ὁ belongs with the participle σπαρείς, "the one having been sown." The prepositional phrase ἐπὶ τὰ πετρώδη, between the article and the participle, shows that this phrase modifies the participle, literally "the upon-the-rocky-soil one having been sown."

20b οὗτός ἐστιν ὁ τὸν λόγον ἀκούων
Lit. this is the-hearing-the-word-one
this is the one hearing the word

οὗτός	this
dem pron:	nom sg masc οὗτος "this"

ἐστιν	is
verb:	pres act ind 3rd sg εἰμί "(he/she/it) is"

ὁ	the
article:	nom sg masc ὁ "the"

τὸν	the
article:	acc sg masc ὁ "the"

λόγον	word
noun:	acc sg masc λόγος "a word"

ἀκούων   the one hearing

ptcp: pres act ptcp nom sg masc ἀκούω "(one) hearing"

Explanation. The antecedent of οὗτός is ὁ . . . σπαρείς.

ὁ . . . ἀκούων is the predicate nominative, saying something about the subject οὗτός. The τὸν λόγον is nested between the article ὁ and the participle ἀκούων to show that it belongs to that construction, and being in the accusative case it is the direct object of the participle, translated "the one hearing the word." This "word" (λόγος) is used here as a summary of the message of the kingdom (see v. 19a).

20c καὶ εὐθὺς μετὰ χαρᾶς λαμβάνων αὐτόν,
Lit. and immediately with joy receiving it,
and immediately with joy receiving it,

καὶ   and
conj: καί "and"

εὐθὺς   immediately
adv: εὐθέως "immediately/next"

μετὰ   with
prep: μετά "with/after"

χαρᾶς   joy
noun: gen sg fem χαρά "of joy" "joy"

λαμβάνων   receiving
ptcp: pres act ptcp nom sg masc λαμβάνω "(one) taking/receiving"

αὐτόν   it
pers pron: acc sg masc αὐτός "him"

Explanation. It is probable that the article ὁ of the substantival participle ὁ . . . ἀκούων (v. 20b) carries over into 20c for λαμβάνων, to read in full, "the one . . . hearing . . . and receiving." The two participles likely share a definite article to make clear there is but one person who does both actions—hearing and receiving.

21a οὐκ ἔχει δὲ ῥίζαν ἐν ἑαυτῷ ἀλλὰ πρόσκαιρός ἐστιν,
Lit. not it has but root in itself but temporary it is,
but does not have a root in itself but is temporary,

οὐκ   not
neg particle: οὐ "no/not"

ἔχει   has
verb: pres act ind 3rd sg ἔχω "(he/she/it) has"

δὲ   and
conj: δέ "but/now"

ῥίζαν   root
noun: acc sg fem ῥίζα "a root"

ἐν   in
prep: ἐν "in/by/with"

ἑαυτῷ   itself
reflexive pron: 3rd dat sg masc ἑαυτοῦ "to himself"

ἀλλὰ   but
conj: ἀλλά "but"

πρόσκαιρός temporary
adj: nom sg masc πρόσκαιρος "temporary"

ἐστιν   is
verb: pres act ind 3rd sg εἰμί "(he/she/it) is"

Explanation. δέ is a very flexible conjunction, here used to show development of an idea rather than contrast.

The contrast is indicated by ἀλλά, and expresses the opposites in terms of not having a root in itself on the one hand and being temporary on the other. In other words, without a strong root the plant is temporary. And to be permanent it must have a strong root. This plant has no strong root in itself, and so it cannot endure.

πρόσκαιρος occurs only four times in the New Testament, including here and in the Markan parallel (Mark 4:17). It also occurs in 2 Cor 4:18: "... we look not at what can be seen but at what cannot be seen; for what can be seen is temporary (πρόσκαιρος), but what cannot be seen is eternal" (NRSV) and Hebrews 11:24-25: "By faith Moses, when he was grown up, refused to be called a son of Pharaoh's daughter, 25 choosing rather to share ill-treatment with the people of God than to enjoy the fleeting (πρόσκαιρος) pleasures of sin" (NRSV).

21b γενομένης δὲ θλίψεως ἢ διωγμοῦ διὰ τὸν λόγον εὐθὺς σκανδαλίζεται.
Lit. having occurred but tribulation or persecution through the word immediately it is caused to fall away.

and, when tribulation or persecution comes because of the word, immediately is caused to fall away.

γενομένης   when comes
ptcp: aor mid ptcp gen sg fem γίνομαι "of (her) having (for herself) become/occurred"

δὲ   and
conj: δέ "but/now"

θλίψεως   tribulation
noun: gen sg fem θλῖψις "of tribulation"

ἢ   or
particle: ἤ "or/than"

διωγμοῦ   persecution
noun: gen sg masc διωγμός "of a persecution"

διά	through/ because of/ on account of
prep:	διά "through/because of"

τὸν	the
article:	acc sg masc ὁ "the"

λόγον	word
noun:	acc sg masc λόγος "a word"

εὐθὺς	immediately
adv:	εὐθέως "immediately/next"

σκανδαλίζεται	is caused to fall away
verb:	pres pass ind 3rd sg σκανδαλίζω "(he/she/it) is made stumble"

Explanation. δέ is a very flexible conjunction, here used to show development of an idea rather than contrast.

γενομένης followed by the genitives θλίψεως and διωγμοῦ constitute a genitive absolute construction. This means that it is translated "when tribulation or persecution comes...."

διὰ τὸν λόγον indicates cause and requires that the persecution and tribulation under consideration is on account of or because "the word."

σκανδαλίζω is used in Matthew for causing to sin (Matt 5:29, 30; 18:6, 8, 9), causing offense (Matt 11:6; 13:57; 15:12; 17:27), even "fall away" from following Jesus as a disciple (Matt 24:10; 26:31, 33).

Tribulation (θλῖψις) and persecution are aspects of discipleship. Matthew does not say "if" they come, but "when." Disciples will be delivered up to such tribulations (θλῖψις, Matt 24:9), put to death, and hated by all nations on account of Jesus. Being a disciple of Jesus entails being prepared for these inevitable hardships, like he himself endured.

MATTHEW 13:3-9, 18-23

22a ὁ δὲ εἰς τὰς ἀκάνθας σπαρείς,
Lit. the-but-in-the -horns-sown-one,
and the one having been sown among the thorns—

ὁ	the
article:	nom sg masc ὁ "the"

δὲ	and
conj:	δέ "but/now"

εἰς	in/ into/ among
prep:	εἰς "into/for"

τὰς	the
article:	acc pl fem ὁ "the (ones)"

ἀκάνθας	thorns
noun:	acc pl fem ἄκανθα "thorns"

σπαρείς	having been sown,
ptcp:	aor pass ptcp nom sg masc σπείρω "(one) having been sown"

Explanation. δέ is second in the sentence because it is a post-positive, and always must be so.

The article ὁ belongs with the participle σπαρείς, "the one having been sown." The prepositional phrase εἰς τὰς ἀκάνθας, between the article and the participle, shows that this phrase modifies the participle and describes the location, literally "the among-the-thorns-having-been-sown-one."

22b οὗτός ἐστιν ὁ τὸν λόγον ἀκούων,
Lit. this is the-one-hearing-the-word,
this is the one hearing the word,

οὗτός	this (one)

dem pron: nom sg masc οὗτος "this"

ἐστιν	is

verb: pres act ind 3rd sg εἰμί "(he/she/it) is"

ὁ	the

article: nom sg masc ὁ "the"

τὸν	the

article: acc sg masc ὁ "the"

λόγον	word

noun: acc sg masc λόγος "a word"

ἀκούων	one hearing

ptcp: pres act ptcp nom sg masc ἀκούω "(one) hearing"

Explanation. This verse is identical to v. 20b.

The antecedent of οὗτός is ὁ . . . σπαρείς.

ὁ . . . ἀκούων is the predicate nominative, saying something about the subject οὗτός. The τὸν λόγον is nested between the article ὁ and the participle ἀκούων to show that it belongs to that construction, and being in the accusative case it is the direct object of the participle, translated "the one hearing the word."

22c καὶ ἡ μέριμνα τοῦ αἰῶνος καὶ ἡ ἀπάτη τοῦ πλούτου συνπνίγει τὸν λόγον

Lit. and the cares of the age and the deceit of wealth choke the word,
and yet the care of age and the deceit of wealth choke the word,

καί	and

conj: καί "and"

ἡ	the

article: nom sg fem ὁ "the"

MATTHEW 13:3-9, 18-23

μέριμνα anxiety/ care
noun: nom sg fem μέριμνα "anxiety/care"

τοῦ the
article: gen sg masc ὁ "of the"

αἰῶνος age
noun: gen sg masc αἰών "of an age/eternity/forever"

καὶ and
conj: καί "and"

ἡ the
article: nom sg fem ὁ "the"

ἀπάτη deceit
noun: nom sg fem ἀπάτη "deceit"

τοῦ the
article: gen sg masc ὁ "of the"

πλούτου of wealth
noun: gen sg masc πλοῦτος "of riches/wealth"

συνπνίγει crowd out/ choke
verb: pres act ind 3rd sg συμπνίγω "(he/she/it) crowds/chokes" "crowd/choke"

τὸν the
article: acc sg masc ὁ "the"

λόγον word
noun: acc sg masc λόγος "a word"

Explanation. μέριμνα is used by Paul in reference to the anxieties that come with cares and responsibilities (cf. 1 Cor 7:32, 33, 34; 2 Cor 11:28).

συμπνίγω is a compound word from σύν and πνίγω, meaning to "constrict by pressure," and so "choke."

τὸν λόγον is the direct object of συμπνίγω; it receives the action of choking as a direct result of the quality of the thorn-wrought soil in which the seed was sown.

The care of the age is very broadly understood, and can entail anything that distracts from attention to singular allegiance to the Kingdom of God (cf. Matt 6:33). The love of money has already been seen as a threat to discipleship (Matt 6:24) as dividing one's allegiance from God.

22d καὶ ἄκαρπος γίνεται.
Lit. and unfruitful it becomes.
and it becomes unfruitful.

καί	and
conj:	καί "and"

ἄκαρπος	unfruitful
adj:	nom sg masc ἄκαρπος "unfruitful"

γίνεται	becomes
verb:	pres mid/pass ind 3rd sg γίνομαι "(he/she/it) becomes/occurs"

Explanation. ἄκαρπος is an adjective, "unfruitful." It is a compound of the prefix ἄ, which negates the idea of the main word, and the word καρπος, meaning "fruit" or, as an adjective, "fruitful."

Becoming ἄκαρπος is a result of the choking done by the thorns (v. 22c). It is a condition imposed upon the word because of the setting in which it is sown. The fruit looked for is perseverance and endurance. While the same metaphor is used for ethical behavior of the Christian (Gal 5:22–24), here it is similar to the usage in Hebrews (Heb 6:7), where the author is looking for the reader to have a faith marked by perseverance through any hardships.

23a ὁ δὲ ἐπὶ τὴν καλὴν γῆν σπαρείς,
Lit. The-but-upon-the-good-soil-sown-ones,
But the one sown on the good soil,

ὁ	The
article:	nom sg masc ὁ "the"
δὲ	but
conj:	δέ "but/now"
ἐπὶ	upon
prep:	ἐπί "upon"
τὴν	the
article:	acc sg fem ὁ "the"
καλὴν	good
adj:	acc sg fem καλός "noble/good"
γῆν	earth/ land/ soil
noun:	acc sg fem γῆ "earth/land"
σπαρείς	having been sown
ptcp:	aor pass ptcp nom sg masc σπείρω "(one) having been sown"

Explanation. The article ὁ belongs with the participle σπαρείς, "the one having been sown." The prepositional phrase ἐπὶ τὴν καλὴν γῆν, between the article and the participle, shows that this phrase modifies the participle, literally "the having-been-sown-upon-the-good-soil one."

23b οὗτός ἐστιν ὁ τὸν λόγον ἀκούων καὶ συνιείς,
Lit. this is the-hearing-the-word-one and understands,
this is the one who hears the word and understand it,

οὗτός	this
dem pron:	nom sg masc οὗτος "this"

ἐστιν	is
verb:	pres act ind 3rd sg εἰμί "(he/she/it) is"

ὁ	the
article:	nom sg masc ὁ "the"

τὸν	the
article:	acc sg masc ὁ "the"

λόγον	word
noun:	acc sg masc λόγος "a word"

ἀκούων	hearing
ptcp:	pres act ptcp nom sg masc ἀκούω "(one) hearing"

καὶ	and
conj:	καί "and"

συνιείς	understanding
ptcp:	pres act ptcp nom sg masc συνίημι "(one) understanding"

Explanation. The antecedent of οὗτός is ὁ . . . σπαρείς.

ὁ . . . ἀκούων is the predicate nominative, saying something about the subject οὗτός. The τὸν λόγον is nested between the article ὁ and the participle ἀκούων to show that it belongs to that construction, and being in the accusative case it is the direct object of the participle, translated "the one hearing the word."

This verse is *nearly* identical to vv. 20b and 22b except for the addition of understanding (καὶ συνιείς).

Having ears to hear and eyes to see, but neither hearing or seeing is linked with rebellion against God (Ezek 12:2).

23c ὃς δὴ καρποφορεῖ καὶ ποιεῖ ὃ μὲν ἑκατὸν, ὃ δὲ ἑξήκοντα, ὃ δὲ τριάκοντα.

Lit. who indeed bears fruit and does one hundred, but sixty, but thirty.

who indeed bears fruit and produces, one a hundred, one sixty, and one thirty (times what was sown).

ὃς	who
rel pron:	nom sg masc ὅς "which"

δὴ	indeed
particle:	δή "indeed"

καρποφορεῖ	bears fruit
verb:	pres act ind 3rd sg καρποφορέω "(he/she/it) bears fruit"

καὶ	and
conj:	καί "and"

ποιεῖ	does/ makes/ produces
verb:	pres act ind 3rd sg ποιέω "(he/she/it) did/made"

ὃ	which/ some
rel pron:	nom sg neut ὅς "which"

μὲν	*untranslated*
particle:	μέν "indeed"

ἑκατὸν	one hundred
adj:	num ἑκατόν "one hundred"

ὃ	which/ some/ one
rel pron:	nom sg neut ὅς "which"

δὲ	and
conj:	δέ "but/now"

ἑξήκοντα   sixty
adj: num ἑξήκοντα "sixty"

ὃ   which/ some/ one
rel pron: acc sg neut ὅς "which"

δὲ   and
conj: δέ "but/now"

τριάκοντα   thirty
adj: num τριάκοντα "thirty"

Explanation. Like in v. 8b, ὃ is a relative pronoun that is translated like a pronoun, here "one."

μέν is simply a particle of anticipation, pointing forward to the progress of the narrative. It can be translated "indeed" or not translated at all.

The remainder of the sentence is unstated in Greek, but implied, and can be rendered in English: " . . . times what was sown."

Preaching the Text

1. **Main idea:** Jesus wants people to hear and understand the gospel message, and so bear multifold fruit.

2. **Tip for Preaching:** It is important to recognize when interpreting parables that there is typically one main point. Here we are helped in that Jesus interprets his own parable (vv. 18–23); the only difference between the soil that bears fruit and that which does not is the presence of *understanding the "word of the kingdom"* (v. 23). So, the main point could be summarized as follows: Jesus wants people to hear and understand the gospel message, and so bear multifold fruit. The notion of "understanding" is likely receptivity of it. Though Jesus does not define "bearing fruit" most think it refers to the ethical conduct laid out in the Sermon on the Mount (Matthew 5–7). Regardless, this is an important parable for explaining why the very same gospel message can yield genuine conversion to faith in Christ and a lifetime of God-honoring living to one person and have a very different effect on another person.

   Notice in the chart below how Jesus provides explanation for each symbol in the parable:

3. **From Text to Sermon: The Parable of the Sower and Its Interpretation**

    a. **Parable:** 13:4 "And as he sowed, some seeds fell on the path, and the birds came and ate them up." (NRSV)

      Interpretation: 13:19 "When anyone hears the word of the kingdom and does not understand it, the evil one comes and snatches away what is sown in the heart; this is what was sown on the path." (NRSV)

      Comment: This seems to refer to the gospel message coming to someone who never really accepts it. It is taken away before it begins to germinate in the person's heart.

    b. **Parable:** 13:5–6 "Other seeds fell on rocky ground, where they did not have much soil, and they sprang up quickly, since they had no depth of soil. But when the sun rose, they were scorched; and since they had no root, they withered away." (NRSV)

      Interpretation: 13:20–21 "As for what was sown on rocky ground, this is the one who hears the word and immediately receives it with joy; yet such a person has no root, but endures only for a while, and when trouble or persecution arises on account of the word, that person immediately falls away." (NRSV)

Comment: Note here that the trouble or persecution on account of the word is *not the problem*. The problem is that the gospel message does not have any root. It was received initially with joy, but the person lacked endurance *through* the hardships. In fact, the hardships serve to expose the fact that the roots simply are not deep.

c. **Parable:** 13:7 "Other seeds fell among thorns, and the thorns grew up and choked them." (NRSV)

Interpretation: 13:22 "As for what was sown among thorns, this is the one who hears the word, but the cares of the world and the lure of wealth choke the word, and it yields nothing." (NRSV)

Comment: The thorns are those things which "choke" the word. There is an implicit priority assessment made on the part of the person that permits and facilitates the message itself to be choked and so unable to bear fruit.

d. **Parable:** 13:8 "Other seeds fell on good soil and brought forth grain, some a hundredfold, some sixty, some thirty." (NRSV)

Interpretation: 13:23 "But as for what was sown on good soil, this is the one who hears the word and understands it, who indeed bears fruit and yields, in one case a hundredfold, in another sixty, and in another thirty." (NRSV)

Comment: Bearing fruit is always an outcome, and to some extent an indication of authentic understanding. But reception of the gospel message cannot be reduced to simple moral principles without theological foundations and content.

4. **Why parables?** The part skipped between the parable (Matt 13:1–8) and its explanation (Matt 13:17–23) is also important. Though it does not explain *this* parable, it does explain why Jesus teaches in parables at all (Matt 13:9–17). When the disciples ask Jesus why he speaks in parables (13:10), he answers that "To you it has been given to know the secrets of the kingdom of heaven" (13:11, NRSV). Then

he explains that the reason he speaks *to them* in parables is that "so that they might not look with their eyes, and listen with their ears, and understand with their heart and turn—and I would heal them" (Matt 13:15, NRSV). At first blush it *seems* like Jesus is saying he speaks in parables so that people do not understand him! But upon closer inspection, Jesus is citing Isaiah 6:9-10, which is a parable of judgment against unbelieving Israel. In other words, for *them*—unbelievers—parables pronounce judgment. The reason is that parables are "encounter mechanisms," meaning they land on people in different ways. For disciples—the primary audience for parables—the parables teach them something about the Kingdom. For the "crowds," parables often draw them to make a decision one way or another about Jesus, typically because they are interested in him enough to follow him and hear him, but not yet enough to be a disciple. But for unbelievers, the parables simply confirm their unbelief—it is an act of judgment. They do not *create* unbelief—Jesus' opponents already come with that. Rather, they confound the opponents and confirm them in their unbelief. What kind of soil is your heart? Is it resistant? Enthusiastic, but only to a degree? Or is it receptive, allowing the seed of the Good News to enter, penetrate, grow, thrive, and produced fruit? That is the kind of soil held out here as the ideal.

7
Matthew 16:13–23

What *Kind* of Savior?

This passage is all about definitions. Both Peter and Jesus refer to Jesus as "the Christ," but it becomes clear that they have *very different* understandings of what that title means? Peter, like other Jews at the time, surely had his own understanding of what "the Christ" was supposed to be. What about you? Do you have expectations about what Jesus, *the Christ*, is supposed to be? Peter learns—and so should we—that Jesus refuses to be defined by *any* definition but his own. That is the lesson of Matthew 16. But the context helps to bear this out even more clearly. When Jesus is asked by his opponents for a "sign from heaven" about who he is, he refuses with the single exception of the "sign of Jonah" (Matt 16:1–4). (Curiously, they seem to ignore that Jesus has just miraculously feed 4000 men, in addition to women and children [Matt 15:29–38]). The same thing occurs in Matthew 12, where Jesus explains that the sign of Jonah is that just as Jonah was three days and three nights in the belly of a fish, the Son of Man will be three days and nights in the heart of the earth (Matt 12:38–40). He is referring there—and here—to his death and resurrection. The point in this context is that his opponents ask for a sign from Jesus to prove who he is, and Jesus insists that his *death and resurrection* is "the" sign that points to his identity. But Jesus opponents do not get that, and their teaching is dangerous to Jesus' disciples (Matt 16:5–12). So, Jesus opens the question to his disciples with a "safe" question, asking about what *other people* say about Jesus (v. 13). Of course, they propound various theories in circulation (v. 14). But when Jesus turns to them to ask for their opinion (v. 15), Peter declares Jesus to be the "Messiah," the "son of the ling God" (v. 16). To this Jesus responds with well-known accolades and affirmations (vv. 17–19), before explaining that what this means is that Jesus is *must* suffer, be killed, and rise again (v. 21). Peter rebukes Jesus (v. 22) and Jesus in turn rebukes Peter, calling him "Satan" (v. 23). What has happened between Peter's lofty confession and Jesus' praise of it that caused the dialogue to turn so negative, even hostile? It is about definitions, and Jesus will only be defined by the purpose of the Father, not Peter's, nor yours, nor mine.

13a Ἐλθὼν δὲ ὁ Ἰησοῦς εἰς τὰ μέρη Καισαρείας τῆς Φιλίππου ἠρώτα τοὺς μαθητὰς αὐτοῦ λέγων

Lit. Having come but the Jesus into the district of Caesarea of Philip he was questioning the disciples of him saying

Now having come into the district of Caesarea of Philip, Jesus was questioning his disciples, saying,

Ἐλθὼν	having come
ptcp:	aor act ptcp nom sg masc ἔρχομαι "(he) having come"
δὲ	now
conj:	δέ "but/now"
ὁ	the
article:	nom sg masc ὁ "the"
Ἰησοῦς	Jesus
noun:	nom sg masc Ἰησοῦς "Jesus"
εἰς	into
prep:	εἰς "into/for"
τὰ	the
article:	acc pl neut ὁ "the (ones)"
μέρη	parts/ portions/ regions/ districts
noun:	acc pl neut μέρος "parts/portions"

Καισαρείας of Caesarea
noun: gen sg fem Καισάρεια "of Caesarea"

τῆς the
article: gen sg fem ὁ "of the"

Φιλίππου of Philip
noun: gen sg masc Φίλιππος "of Philip"

ἠρώτα was asking/ inquiring/ questioning
verb: impf act ind 3rd sg ἐρωτάω "(he/she/it) continually asked/inquired"

τοὺς the
article: acc pl masc ὁ "the (ones)"

μαθητὰς disciples
noun: acc pl masc μαθητής "disciples"

αὐτοῦ of him/ his
pers pron: gen sg masc αὐτός "of him/it"

λέγων saying
ptcp: pres act ptcp nom sg masc λέγω "(one) saying"

Explanation. ἠρώτα is an imperfect verb, indicating a continuous past action of "asking." The questioning was ongoing and probably concurrent to the action of entering the region of Caesarea Philippi.

Caesarea Philippi, known in antiquity as Paneas, is located in the northern regions of Israel at the foothills of Mount Hermon and at one of the headwaters of the Jordan River. It was an administrative center for Herod Philip, son of Herod the Great, who renamed the town Caesarea after "Caesar." It is called "Caesarea Philip" to distinguish it from another Caesarea, "Caesarea Maritima," on the Mediterranean coast, constructed by Herod the Great.

13b τίνα λέγουσιν οἱ ἄνθρωποι εἶναι τὸν υἱὸν τοῦ ἀνθρώπου;
Lit. "Who they say the people to be the son of person?
"Who do people say that the Son of Man is?"

τίνα	who?
interr pron:	acc sg masc τίς "whom?/what?"

λέγουσιν	they say
verb:	pres act ind 3rd pl λέγω "(they) say"

οἱ	the
article:	nom pl masc ὁ "the (ones)"

ἄνθρωποι	people
noun:	nom pl masc ἄνθρωπος "men"

εἶναι	to be
verb:	pres act inf εἰμί "to be"

τὸν	the
article:	acc sg masc ὁ "the"

υἱὸν	son
noun:	acc sg masc υἱός "a son"

τοῦ	of
article:	gen sg masc ὁ "of the"

ἀνθρώπου	man
noun:	gen sg masc ἄνθρωπος "of a man"

Explanation. λέγουσιν . . . εἶναι literally translates "they say . . . to be." The infinitive εἶναι introduces an indirect discourse, meaning something other people are saying.

ἄνθρωπος means "person" and is sometimes gender-specific as "man." Here the word is masculine as part of a title, "son of Man" (ὁ υἱὸς τοῦ ἀνθρώπου).

The title ὁ υἱὸς τοῦ ἀνθρώπου is often used by Jesus in reference to himself. It evokes a vision by the prophet Daniel: "As the visions during the night continued, I saw coming with the clouds of heaven One like a son of man. When he reached the Ancient of Days and was presented before him, He received dominion, splendor, and kingship; all nations, peoples and tongues will serve him. His dominion is an everlasting dominion that shall not pass away, his kingship, one that shall not be destroyed" (Daniel 7:13-14 NAB). Throughout the Matthew Jesus identifies himself as the Son of Man. It is partly a statement of his humanity, but also his deity; Jesus is the one who receives dominion, splendor, and kingship from the Ancient of Days. Later, when Jesus claims that all authority on heaven and earth is given to him (Matt 28:18), he is alluding to this passage in Daniel and himself as that Son of Man.

14a οἱ δὲ εἶπαν·

Lit. The's but they said,

And they said,

οἱ	They
article:	nom pl masc ὁ "the (ones)"

δὲ	and
conj:	δέ "but/now"

εἶπαν	said
verb:	aor act ind 3rd pl λέγω "they said"

Explanation. Οἱ is acting here like a personal pronoun, αὐτοί, "they."

14b οἱ μὲν Ἰωάννην τὸν βαπτιστήν,

Lit. The's John the baptizer,

"They say John the Baptizer,

οἱ	the
article:	nom pl masc ὁ "the (ones)"

MATTHEW 16:13-23

μὲν   untranslated
particle: μέν "indeed"

Ἰωάννην   John
noun: acc sg masc Ἰωάννης "John"

τὸν   the
article: acc sg masc ὁ "the"

βαπτιστήν   Baptizer
noun: acc sg masc βαπτιστής "a baptist/baptizer"

Explanation. Οἱ is acting here like a personal pronoun, αὐτοί, "they."

There is no verb in this sentence, but since Jesus asks what people "say" it is easily deduced that the implied verb is "they say . . . to be" (λέγουσιν . . . εἶναι, see v. 13b).

μέν indicates progression and is untranslated.

βαπτιστής is a means of distinguishing John from others by that name, and uses his function, "baptizer."

By this time John the Baptist had already been in prison (Matt 11:2) and subsequently executed (Matt 14:3–12). Herod the tetrarch previously confused Jesus with John the Baptist, raised from the dead (Matt 14:1–2).

14c ἄλλοι δὲ Ἠλίαν,
Lit. others but Elijah,
but others (say) Elijah,

     ἄλλοι   others
     adj: nom pl masc ἄλλος "other (ones)"

     δὲ   but/ and
     conj: δέ "but/now"

’Ηλίαν   Elijah
noun: acc sg masc Ἡλίας "Elijah"

Explanation. According to Malachi 4:5, God will send Elijah the prophet "before the great and terrible day of the Lord comes" (NRSV). Matthew explicitly identifies this Elijah with John the Baptist (Matt 11:13). So, in their confusion here people think that Jesus is the forerunner to the coming of the Lord, rather than the Lord himself.

14d ἕτεροι δὲ Ἰερεμίαν ἢ ἕνα τῶν προφητῶν.
Lit. others but Jeremiah or one of the prophets."
but others (say) Jeremiah or one of the prophets."

ἕτεροι   others
adj: nom pl masc ἕτερος "other/different (ones)"

δὲ   but
conj: δέ "but/now"

Ἰερεμίαν   Jeremiah
noun: acc sg masc Ἰερεμίας "Jeremiah"

ἢ   or
particle: ἢ "or/than"

ἕνα   one
adj: acc sg masc εἷς "one"

τῶν   the
article: gen pl masc ὁ "of the (ones)"

προφητῶν   prophets
noun: gen pl masc προφήτης "of prophets"

Explanation. ἕνα is an adjective from εἷς, "one."

προφητῶν is plural. These people do not know which prophet from the Old Testament Jesus may be, but speculate he must be one of them.

15 λέγει αὐτοῖς· ὑμεῖς δὲ τίνα με λέγετε εἶναι;
Lit. He said to them, "You but who me you say to be?"
He said to them, "But you, who do you say that I am?"

λέγει	said
verb:	pres act ind 3rd sg λέγω "(he/she/it) says"

αὐτοῖς	to them
pers pron: dat pl masc αὐτός "to them"	

ὑμεῖς	you (pl)
pers pron: 2nd nom pl σύ "you (pl)"	

δὲ	but
conj:	δέ "but/now"

τίνα	who?
interr pron: acc sg masc τίς "whom?/what?"	

με	me
pers pron: 1st acc sg ἐγώ "me"	

λέγετε	you say
verb:	pres act ind 2nd pl λέγω "(you [pl]) say"

εἶναι	to be
verb:	pres act inf εἰμί "to be"

Explanation. λέγει is a present tense verb occurring in a narration of a past event, so it is a "historical present" translated "he said."

The word ὑμεῖς is placed at the front of the quotation for emphasis. The pronoun is also redundant, since it is implied in the verb λέγετε. This too is for emphasis. Having asked what others think about him, Jesus asks the disciples pointedly what they think. The δὲ is contrastive.

ὑμεῖς δὲ τίνα με λέγετε εἶναι is literally, "But you who me you say to be?" The placement of "you" is emphatic. It is now *their* turn to offer an opinion of who Jesus is.

Notice Jesus turns from referring to himself in the third person as "son of Man," to referring to himself as "me" (με). Here he clearly identifies himself as the son of man.

This is a pivotal moment in the scene. The conversation changes from speculations of others to the opinions of Jesus' very own disciples. As will be seen, they have a sense of who Jesus is, but a very distorted notion of what that entails.

16a ἀποκριθεὶς δὲ Σίμων Πέτρος εἶπεν·

Lit. Answering but Simon Peter he said,

And, answering, Simon Peter said,

ἀποκριθεὶς	answering
ptcp:	aor pass ptcp nom sg masc ἀποκρίνομαι "(he) having been answered"
δὲ	and
conj:	δέ "but/now/and"
Σίμων	Simon
noun:	nom sg masc Σίμων "Simon"
Πέτρος	Peter
noun:	nom sg masc Πέτρος "Peter"
εἶπεν	said
verb:	aor act ind 3rd sg λέγω "he/she/it said"

Explanation. Matthew commonly begins a sentence with a participle that modifies a finite verb that follows it.

The inclusion of the verb from ἀποκρίνομαι is unnecessary in this context. Surely whatever Peter says next is an answer. But by including it Matthew underscores that what Peter is about to say is a direct and explicit answer to the question about who exactly he thinks Jesus is. Peter here likely speaks for the group, as a leader among the disciples.

16b σὺ εἶ ὁ χριστὸς ὁ υἱὸς τοῦ θεοῦ τοῦ ζῶντος.
Lit. "You are the Christ the son of God of the living."
"You are the Messiah, the Son of the living God."

σὺ   you
pers pron: 2nd nom sg σύ "you"

εἶ   are
verb: pres act ind 2nd sg εἰμί "(you) are"

ὁ   the
article: nom sg masc ὁ "the"

χριστὸς   Christ
noun: nom sg masc Χριστός "Christ"

ὁ   the
article: nom sg masc ὁ "the"

υἱὸς   son
noun: nom sg masc υἱός "a son"

τοῦ   the
article: gen sg masc ὁ "of the"

θεοῦ   of God
noun: gen sg masc θεός "of God/a god"

τοῦ	the
article:	gen sg masc ὁ "of the"

ζῶντος	living
ptcp:	pres act ptcp gen sg masc ζάω "of (one) living"

Explanation. The placement of σύ is emphatic.

Χριστός means "anointed" or "anointed one" and is the common Greek word corresponding to the Hebrew מָשִׁיחַ. It is used as a designation for someone "anointed" for a particular sacred task. The Old Testament speaks of the "anointed priest" (ὁ ἱερεὺς ὁ χριστὸς, הַכֹּהֵן הַמָּשִׁיחַ; Lev 4:5, 16; 6:15) upon whose head is poured the "oil of anointment" (τό ἐλαίον τοῦ χριστου, שֶׁמֶן הַמִּשְׁחָה; Lev 21:10, 12), and a designation for kings as "his anointed" (χριστοῦ αὐτοῦ, מְשִׁיחוֹ; 1 Sam 2:10, 35; 12:3, 5; Pss 2:2; 20:6 [19:7 LXX]; 28:8 [27:8 LXX]; 84:9 [83:10 LXX]; 89:38 [88:39 LXX]; 89:51 [88:52 LXX]; 132:10; Hab 3:13; Sir 46:19; Amos 4:14 LXX; Dan 9:26) or "the anointed of the Lord" (κυρίου χριστὸς αὐτοῦ, יְהוָה מְשִׁיחוֹ; 1 Sam 16:6; 24:7, 11; 26:9, 11, 16, 23; 2 Sam 1:14, 16; 2:5 [LXX]; 19:22; Lam 4:20; cf. 2 Sam 23:1; 2 Chron 6:42).

17a Ἀποκριθεὶς δὲ ὁ Ἰησοῦς εἶπεν αὐτῷ·
Lit. Answering but Jesus said to him,
And, answering, Jesus said to him,

Ἀποκριθεὶς	answering
ptcp:	aor pass ptcp nom sg masc ἀποκρίνομαι "(he) having been answered"

δὲ	and
conj:	δέ "but/now"

ὁ	the
article:	nom sg masc ὁ "the"

Ἰησοῦς   Jesus
noun: nom sg masc Ἰησοῦς "Jesus"

εἶπεν   said
verb: aor act ind 3rd sg λέγω "he/she/it said"

αὐτῷ   to him
pers pron: dat sg masc αὐτός "to him"

Explanation. αὐτῷ is in the dative case and so the indirect object of the verb εἶπεν. Jesus' answer is directed to Peter.

17b μακάριος εἶ, Σίμων Βαριωνᾶ,
Lit. *"Blessed are you, Simon Bariōna,*
"Blessed are you, Simon, son of Jonah,

μακάριος Blessed
adj: nom sg masc μακάριος "blessed/happy"

εἶ   you are
verb: pres act ind 2nd sg εἰμί "(you) are"

Σίμων   Simon
noun: voc sg masc Σίμων "O Simon!" "

Βαριωνᾶ Bar-Jonah/ son of Jonah
noun: indecl Βαριωνᾶ "Bar-Jonah"

Explanation. The meanings and translations of μακάριος are many. It is most often translated "blessed," but also "fortunate," "happy" or even "privileged." The term suggests that the one upon whom it is pronounced is in a very favorable situation. See Matt 5:3.

Βαριωνᾶ is a Greek transliteration of the Aramaic בַּר יוֹנָה, "son of Jonah."

17c ὅτι σὰρξ καὶ αἷμα οὐκ ἀπεκάλυψέν σοι
Lit. because flesh and blood not revealed to you
because flesh and blood did not reveal this to you

ὅτι	because
conj:	ὅτι "because/that"

σὰρξ	flesh
noun:	nom sg fem σάρξ "flesh"

καὶ	and
conj:	καί "and"

αἷμα	blood
noun:	nom sg neut αἷμα "a blood"

οὐκ	not
neg particle:	οὐ "no/not"

ἀπεκάλυψέν	revealed
verb:	aor act ind 3rd sg ἀποκαλύπτω "he/she/it revealed"

σοι	to you
pers pron:	2nd dat sg σύ "to you"

Explanation. vv. 17c-d give the reason (ὅτι) Simon is "blessed."

Matthew's use of σὰρξ καὶ αἷμα means natural means, especially by a person. Peter's recognition of the identity of Jesus was not the result of natural means—the testimony of others, his witnessing of miraculous events, or even living with Jesus for a time.

Matthew uses ἀποκαλύπτω to show the source of Peter's recognition of Jesus. That is from a divine revelation is underscored by this word and the source indicated in v. 17d, namely the heavenly Father.

MATTHEW 16:13-23

17d ἀλλ' ὁ πατήρ μου ὁ ἐν τοῖς οὐρανοῖς.
Lit. but the father of me the in the heavens.
but my Father, who is in the heavens.

ἀλλ'	but
conj:	ἀλλά "but"

ὁ	the
article:	nom sg masc ὁ "the"

πατήρ	father
noun:	nom sg masc πατήρ "a father"

μου	my/ of me
pers pron:	1st gen sg ἐγώ "of me/my"

ὁ	the
article:	nom sg masc ὁ "the"

ἐν	in
prep:	ἐν "in/by/with"

τοῖς	the
article:	dat pl masc ὁ "to the (ones)"

οὐρανοῖς	heavens
noun:	dat pl masc οὐρανός "to heavens"

Explanation. ἀλλ' is a contraction from ἀλλά. Greek does this when the following word begins with a vowel so as to aid in pronunciation.

Note that the one revealing the identity of Jesus is Jesus' own father. It is the Father, by supernatural means, that has made known Jesus' identity to Peter.

ὁ is a definite article: without a noun. It likely functions to render the prepositional phrase ἐν τοῖς οὐρανοῖς into an adjective or else like a relative pronoun, "which."

18a κἀγὼ δέ σοι λέγω ὅτι
Lit. *and I but to you say that*
and I also say to you that

κἀγώ   I also
pers pron: 1st nom sg κἀγώ "and/also I"

δέ   but
conj: δέ "but/now"

σοι   to you
pers pron: 2nd dat sg σύ "to you"

λέγω   I say
verb: pres act ind 1st sg λέγω "(I) say"

ὅτι   that
conj: ὅτι "because/that"

Explanation. κἀγώ is a contraction (crasis) of the words καί and ἐγώ. Notice the smooth breathing is retained over the alpha. The καί typically functions like a conjunction, but that place is already taken by δέ. So here the καί must be translated like the adverb "also."

ὅτι introduces the complement, the content of what it is that is said.

18b σὺ εἶ Πέτρος,
Lit. *you are Peter,*
you are Peter,

σύ   you
pers pron: 2nd nom sg σύ "you"

εἶ   are
verb: pres act ind 2nd sg εἰμί "(you) are"

Πέτρος   Peter
noun: nom sg masc Πέτρος "Peter"

18c καὶ ἐπὶ ταύτῃ τῇ πέτρᾳ οἰκοδομήσω μου τὴν ἐκκλησίαν
Lit. and upon to this to the rock I will build of me the church
and upon this rock I will build my church

    καὶ   and
    conj: καί "and"

    ἐπὶ   upon
    prep: ἐπί "upon"

    ταύτῃ   this
    dem pron: dat sg fem οὗτος "to this"

    τῇ   the
    article: dat sg fem ὁ "to the"

    πέτρᾳ   rock
    noun: dat sg fem πέτρα "to a rock"

    οἰκοδομήσω   I will build
    verb: fut act ind 1st sg οἰκοδομέω "(I) will build"

    μου   my/ of me
    pers pron: 1st gen sg ἐγώ "of me/my"

    τὴν   the
    article: acc sg fem ὁ "the"

    ἐκκλησίαν   church
    noun: acc sg fem ἐκκλησία "a church/assembly"

Explanation. The antecedent of ταύτῃ is debated. Some regard it as the statement by Peter regarding the identity of Jesus. Others regard it as Peter himself.

οἰκοδομήσω is a first singular verb. Jesus himself is the one who builds the church, which he calls "my church" (μου τὴν ἐκκλησίαν).

The word πέτρα, "rock," is a wordplay on the name Πέτρος, "Peter." This is among the most debated passages in Matthew, or perhaps the entire New Testament. Does Jesus intend to build his church upon the "rock" of Peter, or of what Peter said. The most natural way to read it is that that Peter is in view. Traditionally Roman Catholics view this as the establishment of the successive papacy, and Protestants attempt to remove Peter from the center of the interpretation because of the papal interpretation. Yet the passage most clearly indicates Peter, and nothing of a successive papacy is indicated in the immediate context. Rather, it is a reciprocal declaration on the part of Jesus: Peter says something about Jesus, and Jesus in turn says something about Peter, which begins to be realized in the book of Acts. In Acts the apostle Peter takes a leading role when the church encompassed only about one hundred and twenty people (Acts 1:15). It is he that calls for the replacement of Judas among the Twelve (Acts 1:16–22), and explains the coming of the Spirit at Pentecost (Acts 2:14–36). Indeed, he remains the primary apostle for the first half of the book of Acts until the appearance of Paul (Acts 13)

18d καὶ πύλαι ᾅδου οὐ κατισχύσουσιν αὐτῆς.

Lit. and gates of death not overpower of it.

and the gates of death will not overpower it.

καί	and
conj:	καί "and"

πύλαι	gates
noun:	nom pl fem πύλη "gates"

ᾅδου   hades/ death
noun: gen sg masc ᾅδης "of Hades"

οὐ   not
neg particle: οὐ "no/not"

κατισχύσουσιν   overcome/ overpower
verb: fut act ind 3rd pl κατισχύω "(they) will overcome"

αὐτῆς   it
pers pron: gen sg fem αὐτός "of her"

Explanation. ᾅδης, often transliterated "Hades," is the entry point to the realm of the dead.

The antecedent of αὐτῆς is the church (ἐκκλησία). It is the church that will endure, even through the martyrdom of many of her apostles.

"Hades" is likely a reference to the grave, indicating that death will not overcome the church. Or, put another way, Christ has overcome death. As Paul boasts, "Where, O death, is your victory? Where, O death, is your sting?" [56] The sting of death is sin, and the power of sin is the law. [57] But thanks be to God! He gives us the victory through our Lord Jesus Christ" (1 Cor. 15:55-57 NIV)

19a δώσω σοι τὰς κλεῖδας τῆς βασιλείας τῶν οὐρανῶν,
Lit. I will give to you the keys of the kingdom of the heavens,
I will give you the keys of the kingdom of the heavens,

δώσω   I will give
verb: fut act ind 1st sg δίδωμι "(I) will give"

σοι   to you (sg)
pers pron: 2nd dat sg σύ "to you"

τὰς   the
article: acc pl fem ὁ "the (ones)"

κλεῖδας	keys
noun:	acc pl fem κλείς "keys"

τῆς	of the
article:	gen sg fem ὁ "of the"

βασιλείας	kingdom
noun:	gen sg fem βασιλεία "of a kingdom"

τῶν	of the
article:	gen pl masc ὁ "of the (ones)"

οὐρανῶν	heavens
noun:	gen pl masc οὐρανός "of heavens"

Explanation. Keys of the Kingdom implies a certain kind of authority (cf. Rev 1:18) which Jesus has and extends to Peter and is defined below (Matt 16:19b).

19b καὶ ὃ ἐὰν δήσῃς ἐπὶ τῆς γῆς ἔσται δεδεμένον ἐν τοῖς οὐρανοῖς,

Lit. and that which if you should bind upon the earth will be bound in the heavens,

and whatever you may bind upon earth will be bound in the heavens,

καὶ	and
conj:	καί "and"

ὃ	which/ that which
rel pron:	acc sg neut ὅς "which"

ἐὰν	if
conditional:	ἐάν "if"

δήσῃς	you may bind
verb:	aor act subj 2nd sg δέω "you should begin to bind"

MATTHEW 16:13–23

ἐπὶ   on/ upon
prep: ἐπί "upon"

τῆς   the
article: gen sg fem ὁ "of the"

γῆς   earth
noun: gen sg fem γῆ "of earth/land"

ἔσται   it will be
verb: fut mid ind 3rd sg εἰμί "(he/she/it) will (for oneself) be"

δεδεμένον   having been bound
ptcp: perf pass ptcp nom sg neut δέω "(one) having been bound"

ἐν   in
prep: ἐν "in/by/with"

τοῖς   the
article: dat pl masc ὁ "to the (ones)"

οὐρανοῖς   heavens
noun: dat pl masc οὐρανός "to heavens"

Explanation. ὃ ἐὰν δήσῃς is literally "which if you should bind." But the ὃ ἐάν is here the direct object of the verb δήσῃς, the subject of which is "you" (singular). Idiomatically it translates "whatever you may bind."

Binding and loosing is a role of determining admittance to the kingdom. But this is not a role as a gate-keeper, with the right to determine the legitimacy of one's conversion and suitability for genuine salvation. Rather the "keys" for "binding and loosing" pertains to the proclamation of the saving gospel of Jesus Christ. They are determining factors in one's salvation by virtue of their charge to proclaim the gospel message. The disciples, in a sense, because custodians of the teachings of Jesus.

19c καὶ ὃ ἐὰν λύσῃς ἐπὶ τῆς γῆς ἔσται λελυμένον ἐν τοῖς οὐρανοῖς.

Lit. and that which if you should loose upon the earth will be loosed in the heavens.

and whatever you may loose upon earth will be loosed in the heavens."

καὶ	and
conj:	καί "and"

ὃ	which/ that which
rel pron:	acc sg neut ὅς "which"

ἐὰν	if
conditional:	ἐάν "if"

λύσῃς	you (sg) may loose
verb:	aor act subj 2nd sg λύω "you should begin to loose/annul/break"

ἐπὶ	upon
prep:	ἐπί "upon"

τῆς	the
article:	gen sg fem ὁ "of the"

γῆς	earth
noun:	gen sg fem γῆ "of earth/land"

ἔσται	it will be
verb:	fut mid ind 3rd sg εἰμί "(he/she/it) will (for oneself) be"

λελυμένον	having been loosed
ptcp:	perf pass ptcp nom sg neut λύω "(one) having been loosed/annulled/broken"

ἐν	in
prep:	ἐν "in/by/with"

τοῖς	the
article:	dat pl masc ὁ "to the (ones)"

οὐρανοῖς	heavens
noun:	dat pl masc οὐρανός "to heavens"

Explanation. ὃ ἐὰν λύσῃς is literally "which if you should loose." But the ὃ ἐάν is here the direct object of the verb λύσῃς, the subject of which is "you" (singular). Idiomatically it translates "whatever you may loose."

20a Τότε ἐπετίμησεν τοῖς μαθηταῖς
Lit. Then he strictly warned to the disciples
Then he strictly warned the disciples

Τότε	then
adv:	τότε "then"

ἐπετίμησεν	he strictly warned
verb:	aor act ind 3rd sg ἐπιτιμάω "he/she/it rebuked"

τοῖς	the
article:	dat pl masc ὁ "to the (ones)"

μαθηταῖς	disciples
noun:	dat pl masc μαθητής "to disciples"

Explanation. Jesus' strict warning (ἐπιτιμάω) occurs only here in Matthew. It regards them telling no one that Jesus is the Christ (v. 20b). Why Jesus does not want them to tell others about what he surely wants them to know becomes clear in Peter's response to Jesus' imminent suffering. The ideas and roles of the "messiah" of Peter's understanding is far from those of Jesus' own.

20b ἵνα μηδενὶ εἴπωσιν ὅτι αὐτός ἐστιν ὁ χριστός.
Lit. that to no one they should say that he is the Christ.
that they should say to no one that he is the Messiah.

ἵνα	that/ in order that
conj:	ἵνα "in order that"
μηδενὶ	to no one
adj:	dat sg masc μηδείς "to no (one)"
εἴπωσιν	they should say/ tell
verb:	aor act subj 3rd pl λέγω "they should begin to say"
ὅτι	that
conj:	ὅτι "because/that"
αὐτός	he
pers pron:	nom sg masc αὐτός "he"
ἐστιν	is
verb:	pres act ind 3rd sg εἰμί "(he/she/it) is"
ὁ	the
article:	nom sg masc ὁ "the"
χριστός	Christ/ Messiah
noun:	nom sg masc Χριστός "Christ"

Explanation. ἵνα indicates purpose. μηδενί is an indirect object, indicating to whom something should be said; no one. The εἴπωσιν is a subjunctive third plural verb, in which the implied subject is "they," meaning the disciples. So, it translates "that they should say to no one..." ὅτι indicates the content of what should be said to no one: αὐτός ἐστιν ὁ χριστός.

MATTHEW 16:13-23

21a Ἀπὸ τότε ἤρξατο ὁ Ἰησοῦς δεικνύειν τοῖς μαθηταῖς αὐτοῦ ὅτι

Lit. From then he began Jesus Christ to show to the disciples of him that

From then Jesus Christ began to show his disciples that

Ἀπὸ	From
prep:	ἀπό "(away) from"
τότε	then
adv:	τότε "then"
ἤρξατο	he began
verb:	aor mid ind 3rd sg ἄρχομαι "(one oneself) began"
ὁ	the
article:	nom sg masc ὁ "the"
Ἰησοῦς	Jesus
noun:	nom sg masc Ἰησοῦς "Jesus"
δεικνύειν	to show
verb:	pres act inf δεικνύω "to show"
τοῖς	the
article:	dat pl masc ὁ "to the (ones)"
μαθηταῖς	to disciples
noun:	dat pl masc μαθητής "to disciples"
αὐτοῦ	his/ of him
pers pron:	gen sg masc αὐτός "of him/it"
ὅτι	that
conj:	ὅτι "because/that"

Explanation. Ἀπὸ τότε ἤρξατο means that Jesus began to do something at this point that he had not done before, and that his doing it

AN EXPOSITOR'S HANDBOOK TO THE GREEK TEXT OF MATTHEW

was an ongoing basis. The occasion of Peter using the word "messiah" prompts Jesus to define it right away. Jesus' notion of his own messiahship pertains to the necessity (δεῖ) of Jesus' travel to Jerusalem (21b), suffering many things (21c), being killed and raised on the third day (21d).

21b δεῖ αὐτὸν εἰς Ἱεροσόλυμα ἀπελθεῖν
Lit. it was necessary him into Jerusalem to go
it was necessary for him to go to Jerusalem

 δεῖ it is necessary
 verb: pres act ind 3rd sg δεῖ "(he/she/it) is necessary"

 αὐτὸν him
 pers pron: acc sg masc αὐτός "him"

 εἰς into
 prep: εἰς "into/for"

 Ἱεροσόλυμα Jerusalem
 noun: acc sg fem Ἱεροσόλυμα "Jerusalem"

 ἀπελθεῖν to go/ go away
 verb: aor act inf ἀπέρχομαι "to begin to come/go away"

Explanation. δεῖ αὐτὸν, literally "it is necessary him" translates idiomatically "it is necessary for him."

δεῖ is typically followed by a complementary infinitive, in this case ἀπελθεῖν. But there are other infinitives (below) that are equally necessary.

21c καὶ πολλὰ παθεῖν ἀπὸ τῶν πρεσβυτέρων καὶ ἀρχιερέων καὶ γραμματέων
Lit. and many to suffer from the elders and chief priests and scribes
and to suffer many things from the elders and chief priests and scribes

MATTHEW 16:13-23

καὶ   and
conj: καί "and"

πολλὰ   many
adj: acc pl neut πολύς "many (ones)"

παθεῖν   to suffer
verb: aor act inf πάσχω "to begin to suffer"

ἀπὸ   from
prep: ἀπό "(away) from"

τῶν   the
article: gen pl masc ὁ "of the (ones)"

πρεσβυτέρων   elders
adj: gen pl masc πρεσβύτερος "of eldest (ones)"

καὶ   and
conj: καί "and"

ἀρχιερέων   chief priests
noun: gen pl masc ἀρχιερεύς "of high/chief priests"

καὶ   and
conj: καί "and"

γραμματέων   scribes
noun: gen pl masc γραμματεύς "of scribes"

Explanation. Jesus does not disclose what he will suffer (παθεῖν) from the elders and chief priests and scribes, only that it is necessary (δεῖ) and there is much of it (πολλά).

21d καὶ ἀποκτανθῆναι καὶ τῇ τρίτῃ ἡμέρᾳ ἐγερθῆναι.
Lit. and to be killed and to the third day to be raised.
and to be killed and on the third day to be raised.

καί	and
conj:	καί "and"

ἀποκτανθῆναι to be killed
verb: aor pass inf ἀποκτείνω "to begin to be killed"

καί   and
conj: καί "and"

τῇ   the
article: dat sg fem ὁ "to the"

τρίτῃ   third
adj: dat sg fem τρίτος "to a third"

ἡμέρᾳ   day
noun: dat sg fem ἡμέρα "to a day"

ἐγερθῆναι will be raised
verb: aor pass inf ἐγείρω "to begin to be raised up"

Explanation. All the verbs here are complementary infinitives describing the verb δεῖ (v. 21b)–it is necessary for these things to occur.

All the verbs here are in the passive voice, indicating someone else will be doing them to Jesus—killing him and raising him.

τῇ τρίτῃ ἡμέρᾳ is in the dative case, indicating when he will be raised (ἐγερθῆναι).

22a καὶ προσλαβόμενος αὐτὸν ὁ Πέτρος ἤρξατο ἐπιτιμᾶν αὐτῷ λέγων·
Lit. And taking to himself him Peter began to rebuke to him saying,
And taking him to himself, Peter began to rebuke him, saying,

MATTHEW 16:13-23

καὶ   and
conj: καί "and"

προσλαβόμενος   taking to himself
ptcp: aor mid ptcp nom sg masc προσλαμβάνω "(he) having (for himself) received towards"

αὐτὸν   him
pers pron: acc sg masc αὐτός "him"

ὁ   the
article: nom sg masc ὁ "the"

Πέτρος   Peter
noun: nom sg masc Πέτρος "Peter"

ἤρξατο   began
verb: aor mid ind 3rd sg ἄρχομαι "(one oneself) began"

ἐπιτιμᾶν   to rebuke
verb: pres act inf ἐπιτιμάω "to rebuke"

αὐτῷ   him
pers pron: dat sg masc αὐτός "to him"

λέγων   saying
ptcp: pres act ptcp nom sg masc λέγω "(one) saying"

Explanation. προσλαβόμενος, "taking to himself," means that Peter means for the discussion to be private.

ἤρξατο is the verb but makes no sense by itself; it requires a complementary infinitive. Here ἐπιτιμᾶν means "to rebuke," and so the sentence reads "he began to rebuke."

λέγων introduces the content of Peter's rebuke, which constitute vv. 22b and 22c.

22b ἵλεώς σοι, κύριε·

Lit. merciful to you, Lord;

"merciful to you, Lord!

ἵλεώς	merciful
adj:	nom sg masc ἵλεως "merciful"

σοι	to you (sg)
pers pron: 2nd dat sg σύ "to you"	

κύριε	Lord
noun:	voc sg masc κύριος "O Lord!"

Explanation. ἵλεώς σοι is an idiom, literally "merciful to you" in the sense of "May God be merciful to you in not letting this happen!" It is an emphatic expression, comparable to the English "God forbid!" It occurs only here in the New Testament, but variations of it occur a few times in the LXX (2 Sam 20:20; 23:17; 1 Chron 11:19; 1 Macc 2:21).

κύριε is in the vocative, a case of direct address. The exclamation is made to Jesus.

22c οὐ μὴ ἔσται σοι τοῦτο.

Lit. No not will be to you this.

This will never be to you."

οὐ	no/ not
neg particle: οὐ "no/not"	

μή	no/ not
neg particle: μή "no/not (stop)"	

ἔσται	it will be
verb:	fut mid ind 3rd sg εἰμί "(he/she/it) will (for oneself) be"

MATTHEW 16:13-23

σοι   to you
pers pron: 2nd dat sg σύ "to you"

τοῦτο   this
dem pron: nom sg neut οὗτος "this"

Explanation. οὐ μή is a double-negative, which compounds in Greek to mean "never." Each word in this sentence is emphatic, and one can almost imagine the vehemence with which the impetuous and strong-willed Peter utters them to Jesus.

The antecedent of τοῦτο is all the hardships experienced in the infinitives above.

23a ὁ δὲ στραφεὶς εἶπεν τῷ Πέτρῳ·
Lit. The but turning he said to Peter,
But, turning, he said to Peter,

    ὁ   the
    article: nom sg masc ὁ "the"

    δὲ   but
    conj: δέ "but/now"

    στραφείς turning
    ptcp: aor pass ptcp nom sg masc στρέφω "(one) having been turned"

    εἶπεν   he said
    verb: aor act ind 3rd sg λέγω "he/she/it said"

    τῷ   the
    article: dat sg masc ὁ "to the"

    Πέτρῳ   Peter
    noun: dat sg masc Πέτρος "to Peter"

Explanation. στραφείς may indicate he is now facing Peter directly, or it may indicate the private conversation is now made available to the other disciples as well.

23b ὕπαγε ὀπίσω μου, σατανᾶ·
Lit. Get behind me, Satan;
"Get behind me, Satan!

ὕπαγε	Go/ depart
verb:	pres act imv 2nd sg ὑπάγω "depart/go forth (you)"

ὀπίσω	behind
adv:	ὀπίσω "behind/back"

μου	of me
pers pron:	1st gen sg ἐγώ "of me/my"

σατανᾶ	Satan
noun:	voc sg masc Σατανᾶς "O Satan!"

Explanation. It is possible that the exhortation to get ὀπίσω μου is a renewed call to discipleship for Peter in addition to a rebuke (Matt 4:19; 10:38; 16:24).

σατανᾶ is in the vocative case, meaning it is a direct address to Peter.

23c σκάνδαλον εἶ ἐμοῦ,
Lit. Stumbling block you are of me,
You are a stumbling bock to me,

σκάνδαλον	stumbling block
noun:	nom sg neut σκάνδαλον "a stumbling block"

εἶ	you are
verb:	pres act ind 2nd sg εἰμί "(you) are"

ἐμοῦ   of me
pers pron: 1st gen sg ἐγώ "of me/my"

Explanation. σκάνδαλον is used here to mean something that obstructs one's purpose or direction; perhaps even a trap, enticement, or temptation (cf. Matt 13:41; 18:7). Jesus calls Peter Satan not because he identifies him directly with the tempter himself, but because like in the temptation narrative (Matt 4:1–11) there is an implicit attempt to detail Jesus' determined purpose to the cross. Whereas Satan wanted to grant Jesus the rewards of his messiahship without the hardships of the cross, Peter simply denies that the cross and its accompanying hardships are even part of what it means to be the messiah. But Jesus said these things are necessary (δεῖ), as he is bent on the will of the Father (cf. Matt 7:21; 12:50).

23d ὅτι οὐ φρονεῖς τὰ τοῦ θεοῦ ἀλλὰ τὰ τῶν ἀνθρώπων.
Lit. *because not you are thinking the of God but the of people.*
because you are not thinking the things of God but the things of humans."

ὅτι   because
conj: ὅτι "because/that"

οὐ   not
neg particle: οὐ "no/not"

φρονεῖς   thinking/ intending
verb: pres act ind 2nd sg φρονέω "(you) think/ purpose/intend"

τὰ   the (things)
article: acc pl neut ὁ "the (ones)"

τοῦ   the
article: gen sg masc ὁ "of the"

θεοῦ	of God
noun:	gen sg masc θεός "of God/a god"

ἀλλά	but
conj:	ἀλλά "but"

τά	the (things)
article:	acc pl neut ὁ "the (ones)"

τῶν	the
article:	gen pl masc ὁ "of the (ones)"

ἀνθρώπων	of people/ of humans
noun:	gen pl masc ἄνθρωπος "of men"

Explanation. τά is an article with no noun, best rendered "the things."

There is a sharp contrast here, recognized by Jesus, in Peter's thinking, where human affairs are taking priority over those of God. Jesus is clearly rebuking Peter for embracing the former over the latter.

Preaching the Text

1. **Main idea:** Jesus' primary role as Savior is to suffer and die for sins.
2. **Text to Sermon:**
   a. Notice how Jesus goes from asking his disciples about rumors other people have about Jesus (vv. 13–15) to what *they* think about Jesus (v. 16). Everyone has some opinion about Jesus, that he is something more than just, well, Jesus. He surely must be some special figure in Israel's history. In a sense, they're all right. But in another sense, they're all wrong, especially Peter. True, Jesus is "the Messiah" and the "Son of the Living God." Peter gets the label correct, and Jesus affirms this in no uncertain terms. In fact, Jesus pronounces a blessing upon Peter as the recipient of a special revelation from God—this truth that Jesus is the Messiah, was revealed to him from the Heavenly Father. That is a tremendous encouragement; recognition of the truth about who Jesus is comes not from smarts or heritage or experience. Those can be factors, but ultimately it is an act of God (see also John 6:44, 65; cf. Heb 12:2).
   b. There is much debate between interpreters of all theological backgrounds centered around vv. 18–19, especially around a few points: first, what is the "rock" on which Christ will build his church? And, second, what does it mean for Peter to have the keys to the kingdom, with power to bind and loose? Regardless of one's understanding of these difficult questions, it is clear that Jesus is affirming that the church endures and the identification of Jesus as the Christ is tied to it.
   c. If acknowledging Jesus is the Christ is such a big deal, why does Jesus tell the disciples not to tell anyone (v. 20)? Matthew does not explicitly say, but it is a pretty safe guess that the disciples know only part of the story. As we will see (vv. 21–23), Peter knows *who* the Christ is, but he does not know *what* the Christ is. Something has happened between Peter acknowledging that Jesus is the Christ (v. 16) and Peter rebuking Jesus (v. 22). What is it? Let us follow the narrative closely. First, notice that Matthew says "from that time on, Jesus began to . . . " This means that Jesus is *now* doing something he had *not done before*. That is, he is *now defining what the*

Christ is. That is, once Peter has used the "Christ" term for Jesus, Jesus is going to define it. And this is how he defines it, in terms of necessity (v. 21) to (1) go to Jerusalem, (2) suffer greatly, (3) be killed, and (4) be raised. This is Jesus' mission as the Messiah. And, this is what troubles Peter, who *rebukes* Jesus. In other words, for Peter Jesus is the Messiah, but he is not *that* kind of a messiah. And this Jesus sternly rebukes: calling Peter Satan. Elsewhere in Matthew Jesus calls his opponents many less-than-flattering things, such as "hypocrites" (Matt 23:13, 15, 23, 25, 27, 29), "blind guides" (23:16), "fools" (23:17), and whitewashed tombs (23:27), but nothing so harsh as this! Why? Jesus says "You are a stumbling block to me; for you are setting your mind not on divine things but on human things" (v. 23, NRSV). This can only be pertaining to Peter's understanding of the Christ. It is not enough to know that Jesus is the Messiah, it is essential to know what *kind of Messiah* he is.

3. **Tip for Preaching:** The very key to this text is that Peter know that Jesus was *the* Savior, the Messiah. The problem comes about when Jesus explains precisely *what kind that means.* Peter was sure Jesus *was* the Messiah, but obviously, whatever Peter thought that meant, it did not, in his mind, involve Jesus being handed over, suffering, and being killed. This is no small thing, and Jesus will not have even Peter understand what He, Jesus, is about in any other way. He calls him "Satan" not to identify him explicitly as the devil, but here Matthew gives us an indication of precisely how serious it is to regard Jesus' mission as anything less than to follow precisely the will of the Father in suffering, being killed, and rising on the third day. Jesus is many more things to us, but He is no less than the Savior who dies for sins, who gives His life as the ransom for many (Matt 20:28).

8

Matthew 19:16–22

What Do I Still Lack?

This is a story about an unnamed person; he could be you. You may not be a rich young man, but there may be something—anything—in your life that would keep you from following Jesus. That is what this account is about. By now, in chapter 19, readers of Matthew know a lot about Jesus. They know all they need to know to make a decision—follow or not. This passage is a message about discipleship. The person is unnamed because it really does not matter who he is or what exactly happens to him. The gospel author leaves that part deliberately blank, allowing readers to fill in the blank with his or her own name, and his or her own outcome. Initially the man is just called "someone" (εἷς) who asks Jesus what he must "do" to have eternal life (Matt 19:16). Rather than directly answering the question, surprisingly, Jesus asks the man why he would ask Jesus about this, only to then answer the man's original question before he could respond: keep the commandments (Matt 19:17). When Jesus explains to him which commands (vv. 18–19), the man says he has kept them all (v. 20a). He presumes he is still lacking something to gain eternal life, and asks Jesus what that may be (v. 20b). Jesus' answer does not explicitly come from the Ten Commandments but implicitly suggests them by placing God, in the person of Jesus (Matt 1:23), at the forefront (cf. Exod 20:3–7). Jesus' instructions also undermine the very heart of murder, adultery, theft, and covetousness (Exod 20:13–17). In short, Jesus commands him to give up everything, gain treasure in heaven, and follow him (v. 21). This good news for the young man is bad news; he already has treasure, and he will not give it up to follow Jesus (v. 22).

16a Καὶ ἰδοὺ εἷς προσελθὼν αὐτῷ εἶπεν· διδάσκαλε,
Lit. And behold one coming to him said "Teacher,
And, behold, one (person), approaching him, said, "Teacher,

Καὶ	and
conj:	καί "and"

ἰδοὺ	behold
verb:	aor mid imv 2nd sg ὁράω "begin (you for yourself) to see"

εἷς	one (person)
adj:	nom sg masc εἷς "one"

προσελθὼν	coming to/ approaching
ptcp:	aor act ptcp nom sg masc προσέρχομαι "(he) having come toward"

αὐτῷ	him

pers pron: dat sg masc αὐτός "to him"

εἶπεν	he said
verb:	aor act ind 3rd sg λέγω "he/she/it said"

διδάσκαλε	teacher
noun:	voc sg masc διδάσκαλος "O teacher!"

Explanation. εἷς is an adjective, with nothing to modify. So it is acting substantivally (like a noun), and translated "one (person)," with the "(person)" being implied.

διδάσκαλε is in the vocative case, indicating direct address to Jesus. Jesus is regularly addressed by people as teacher in the vocative case in Matthew (Matt 8:19; 12:38; 22:16, 24, 36). Presumably the man asking recognizes that Jesus will give an authoritative answer to his question in 16b.

16b τί ἀγαθὸν ποιήσω ἵνα σχῶ ζωὴν αἰώνιον;
Lit. what good I will do in order that I will have life eternal?"
what good thing must I do that I may have eternal life?"

τί	what
interr pron:	acc sg neut τίς "whom?/what?"

ἀγαθὸν	good
adj:	acc sg neut ἀγαθός "good"

ποιήσω	I should do
verb:	aor act subj 1st sg ποιέω "I should begin to do/make"

ἵνα	that
conj:	ἵνα "in order that"

σχῶ	I should have/ I may have
verb:	aor act subj 1st sg ἔχω "I should begin to have"

ζωὴν	life
noun:	acc sg fem ζωή "a life"

αἰώνιον	eternal
adj:	acc sg fem αἰώνιος "age long/eternal"

Explanation. τί is an interrogative pronoun, meaning it asks a question. It is in the accusative case from τίς and is the direct object of ποιήσω.

ἀγαθόν is an adjective acting substantivally, and so translated "good thing."

The verbs ποιήσω and σχῶ are in the subjunctive mood, indicating the hypothetical nature of the actions. Notice the man's question uses verbs that entail having something (ἔχω) as a result of doing something (ποιέω).

17a ὁ δὲ εἶπεν αὐτῷ·
Lit. *The but he said to him,*
And he said to him,

ὁ	the
article:	nom sg masc ὁ "the"

δὲ	and
conj:	δέ "but/now"

εἶπεν	he said
verb:	aor act ind 3rd sg λέγω "he/she/it said"

αὐτῷ	to him
pers pron: dat sg masc αὐτός "to him"	

ὁ is an article acting like a subject, probably inferring ὁ Ἰησοῦς. This is the subject of the verb εἶπεν. The αὐτῷ is in the dative case and so is the indirect object, indicating that what Jesus said was directed to the young man.

17b τί με ἐρωτᾷς περὶ τοῦ ἀγαθοῦ;
Lit. *"Why me you ask concerning of good?*
"Why do you ask me about what is good?

τί	why?
interr pron: acc sg neut τίς "whom?/what?"	

με	me
pers pron: 1st acc sg ἐγώ "me"	

ἐρωτᾷς	you ask
verb:	pres act ind 2nd sg ἐρωτάω "(you) ask/inquire"

περὶ	concerning
prep:	περί "concerning/around"

τοῦ	the
article:	gen sg neut ὁ "of the"

ἀγαθοῦ	of good
adj:	gen sg neut ἀγαθός "of a good"

Explanation. The interrogative τί looks for a reason.

The placement of με toward the front of the sentence is emphatic. "Why do you ask *me* about what is good?"

τοῦ ἀγαθοῦ is in the genitive case only because it is preceded by περί. The meaning of a preposition is determined by the case of its object. So Matthew, wanting περί to mean "concerning" or "about," had to put τοῦ ἀγαθοῦ in the genitive case to get that meaning from the preposition περί. The question raises for the young man—and the reader—that the identity of Jesus is somehow involved in this issue. Of everyone who could be asked about "good," why come to Jesus? How the man regards Jesus and what Jesus has to offer is determinative of how the man responds.

17c εἷς ἐστὶν ὁ ἀγαθός·
Lit. One is the good;
There is one who is good;

εἷς	One
adj:	nom sg masc εἷς "one"

ἐστὶν	is
verb:	pres act ind 3rd sg εἰμί "(he/she/it) is"

ὁ	the
article:	nom sg masc ὁ "the"

ἀγαθός	good
adj:	nom sg masc ἀγαθός "good"

Explanation. εἷς is the nominative subject of the verb ἐστίν and placed in front for emphasis.

The statement is subtle but very important to understanding this passage: Jesus has already indicated that his own identity is tied to the young man's question, and now he says that the subject of "good" really belongs to God. Hadn't you better ask him? Or do you understand that Jesus *is* God?

17d εἰ δὲ θέλεις εἰς τὴν ζωὴν εἰσελθεῖν,
Lit. If but you desire into life to enter,
But if you wish to enter into life,

εἰ	if
conditional:	εἰ "if"
δὲ	but
conj:	δέ "but/now"
θέλεις	you desire
verb:	pres act ind 2nd sg θέλω "(you) will"
εἰς	into
prep:	εἰς "into/for" "into/for"
τὴν	the
article:	acc sg fem ὁ "the"
ζωὴν	life
noun:	acc sg fem ζωή "a life"
εἰσελθεῖν	to enter
verb:	aor act inf εἰσέρχομαι "to begin to come in/enter"

Explanation. εἰσελθεῖν is a complementary infinitive, describing θέλεις.

The young man wants to "inherit" eternal life; Jesus here speaks of "entering" eternal life. It is unlikely that there is any difference in meaning.

17e τήρησον τὰς ἐντολάς.
Lit. keep the commandments."
keep the commandments."

τήρησον	keep/ observe
verb:	aor act imv 2nd sg τηρέω "keep/observe (you)"

τὰς	the
article:	acc pl fem ὁ "the (ones)"

ἐντολάς	commands/ commandments
noun:	acc pl fem ἐντολή "commands"

Explanation. εἰ introduces an "if-then" structure; εἰ means "if," but there is no Greek word for the English "then." It is implied even when not translated.

Here Jesus simply instructs the young man, not that keeping the commandments is the means to eternal life, but as a means of determining how far the young man is willing to go with this. As we will see, he has been willing to go so far that he has obeyed the commandments Jesus lays out for him since his youth, but he also recognizes that he lacks something yet. Jesus then raises the final step to truly see how far the young man is willing to go to get what he seeks.

18a Λέγει αὐτῷ· ποίας;
Lit. He said to him, "Which?"
He said to him, "Which?"

Λέγει	he said
verb:	pres act ind 3rd sg λέγω "(he/she/it) says"

αὐτῷ   to him
pers pron: dat sg masc αὐτός "to him"

ποίας   Which?
interr pron: acc pl fem ποῖος "what sort?"

Explanation. λέγει is a present tense verb which, in this context, is a historical present, "he said."

Ποίας infers Ποίας ἐντολάς τηρήσω, "Which commandments (shall) I keep?"

18b ὁ δὲ Ἰησοῦς εἶπεν·
Lit. The but Jesus said,
Jesus said,

ὁ   the
article: nom sg masc ὁ "the"

δὲ   indicates progression is not translated
conj: δέ "but/now"

Ἰησοῦς   Jesus
noun: nom sg masc Ἰησοῦς "Jesus"

εἶπεν   said
verb: aor act ind 3rd sg λέγω "(he/she/it) said"

18c τό οὐ φονεύσεις,
Lit. The not you shall murder;
"You shall never murder;

τό   the
article: acc sg neut ὁ "the"

οὐ   not
neg particle: οὐ "no/not"

φονεύσεις   you (sg) will not murder
verb: fut act ind 2nd sg φονεύω "(you) will murder"

Explanation. Τό the article here acts like a noun, idiomatically inferring, "The command you should keep is . . . "

οὐ φονεύσεις is taken directly from the LXX of Exod 20:15 (//Deut 5:18). It is common for the LXX to render the Hebrew negation (לֹא) and qal imperfect (here, תִּרְצָח) with οὐ and a future tense verb. The connotation in Hebrew is an emphatic imperative negation, which can get lost in Greek: "you shall never . . . ."

18d οὐ μοιχεύσεις,

Lit. Not you shall commit adultery,
you shall never commit adultery,

οὐ   not
neg particle: οὐ "no/not"

μοιχεύσεις   you (sg) will commit adultery
verb: fut act ind 2nd sg μοιχεύω "(you) will commit adultery"

Explanation. Οὐ μοιχεύσεις is verbatim from Exod 20:13 (//Deut 5:17).

It is common for the LXX to render the Hebrew negation (לֹא) and qal imperfect (here, תִּנְאָף) with οὐ and a future tense verb.

18e οὐ κλέψεις,

Lit. Not you shall steal,
you shall never steal,

οὐ   not
neg particle: οὐ "no/not"

κλέψεις   you will steal
verb: fut act ind 2nd sg κλέπτω "(you) will steal"

Explanation. Οὐ κλέψεις is from Exod 20:14 (//Deut 5:19), the corresponding Hebrew reads לֹא תִּגְנֹב.

18f οὐ ψευδομαρτυρήσεις,
Lit. not you shall witness-falsely,
you shall never bear false witness,

οὐ   no/ not
neg particle: οὐ "no/not"

ψευδομαρτυρήσεις   bear false witness
verb: fut act ind 2nd sg ψευδομαρτυρέω "(you) will falsely witness"

Explanation. Οὐ ψευδομαρτυρήσεις is from LXX Exod 20:16 (// Deut 5:20). The corresponding Hebrew reads לֹא־תַעֲנֶה בְרֵעֲךָ עֵד שָׁקֶר, literally "you shall not answer against your neighbor a false-witness."

ψευδομαρτυρέω is a compound verb from ψευδο, "false," and μαρτυρέω, "I bear witness."

19a τίμα τὸν πατέρα καὶ τὴν μητέρα,
Lit. Honor the father and the mother,
Honor the father and the mother;

τίμα   honor
verb: pres act imv 2nd sg τιμάω "honor/value (you)"

τὸν   the
article: acc sg masc ὁ "the"

πατέρα   father
noun: acc sg masc πατήρ "a father"

καὶ	and
conj:	καί "and"

τὴν	the
article:	acc sg fem ὁ "the"

μητέρα	mother
noun:	acc sg fem μήτηρ "a mother"

Explanation. There is no personal pronoun "your" (σου) here, though surely it can be inferred.

The command τίμα is a singular imperative, indicating a command to individuals.

This command comes from LXX Exod 20:12 (// Deut 5:16). The Hebrew reads כַּבֵּד אֶת־אָבִיךָ וְאֶת־אִמֶּךָ.

19b καὶ ἀγαπήσεις τὸν πλησίον σου ὡς σεαυτόν.
Lit. and You shall love the neighbor of you as yourself."
And, you shall love your neighbor as yourself."

καί	and
conj:	καί "and"

ἀγαπήσεις	you (sg) will love
verb:	fut act ind 2nd sg ἀγαπάω "(you) will love"

τὸν	the
article:	acc sg masc ὁ "the"

πλησίον	neighbor
adv:	πλησίον "neighbor"

σου	of you/ your
pers pron:	2nd gen sg σύ "of you"

ὡς   as
adv: ὡς "as"

σεαυτόν   yourself
reflexive pron: 2nd acc sg masc σεαυτοῦ "yourself"

Explanation. ὡς σεαυτόν implies a verb "love" to infer "as you love yourself."

This command comes from LXX Lev 19:18.

20a λέγει αὐτῷ ὁ νεανίσκος·
Lit. *He said to him the young man*
The young man said to him,

λέγει   he said
verb: pres act ind 3rd sg λέγω "(he/she/it) says"

αὐτῷ   to him
pers pron: dat sg masc αὐτός "to him"

ὁ   the
article: nom sg masc ὁ "the"

νεανίσκος   young man
noun: nom sg masc νεανίσκος "a young man"

Explanation. λέγει is a present tense verb but in this context is a historical present

20b πάντα ταῦτα ἐφύλαξα· τί ἔτι ὑστερῶ;
Lit. *"All these I have observed; what still I lack?"*
"All these things I have observed. What do I still lack?"

πάντα   all
adj: acc pl neut πᾶς "all (ones)"

ταῦτα	these (things)
dem pron:	acc pl neut οὗτος "these"

ἐφύλαξα	I have kept/ observed
verb:	aor act ind 1st sg φυλάσσω "I guarded/kept"

τί	what?
interr pron:	acc sg neut τίς "whom?/what?"

ἔτι	yet/ still
adv:	ἔτι "yet/still"

ὑστερῶ	I lack/ I am lacking
verb:	pres act ind 1st sg ὑστερέω "(I) have lack"

Explanation. Ταῦτα πάντα is likely in an emphatic position.

ὑστερῶ is a present tense verb, likely indicating a state of being rather than a continuous action.

The young man has been obedient to the Law, and Jesus nowhere questions that. It is the young man himself who recognizes there is something lacking (v. 20b).

21a ἔφη αὐτῷ ὁ Ἰησοῦς·

Lit. he was saying to him Jesus

Jesus was saying to him,

ἔφη	was saying
verb:	impf act ind 3rd sg φημί "(he/she/it) continually stated/claimed"

αὐτῷ	to him
pers pron:	dat sg masc αὐτός "to him"

ὁ	the
article:	nom sg masc ὁ "the"

Ἰησοῦς   Jesus
noun: nom sg masc Ἰησοῦς "Jesus"

Explanation. ἔφη is an imperfect verb, suggesting a continuous past action which may infer some explanation took place.

21b εἰ θέλεις τέλειος εἶναι,
Lit. If you desire mature to be,
"If you wish to be mature,"

εἰ   if
conditional: εἰ "if"

θέλεις   you (sg) wish/ will/ desire
verb: pres act ind 2nd sg θέλω "(you) will"

τέλειος   mature/ complete
adj: nom sg masc τέλειος "mature/complete"

εἶναι   to be
verb: pres act inf εἰμί "to be"

Explanation. εἰ introduces the beginning (protasis) of a conditional statement, anticipating an implied "then" (apodosis)

The subject is an implied "you (sg)," found in the verb θέλεις. εἶναι is a complementary infinitive, describing the verb ("you desire *to be* ... "). τέλειος is the predicate nominative of the infinitive. It is in the nominative case because it is a predicate nominative, and verbs of being (εἶναι) cannot take direct objects (in the accusative or any other case).

τέλειος is sometimes translated "perfect," but this is misleading. It is much more likely a statement of maturity or wholeness (cf. James 1:4) exhibited by the requested behavior (vv. 21c-f). Notice that Jesus equates being τέλειος with the young man's request about acquiring eternal life.

MATTHEW 19:16–22

21c ὕπαγε πώλησόν σου τὰ ὑπάρχοντα καὶ
Lit. go sell of you the belongings and
go, sell your possessions, and

ὕπαγε	Go!
verb:	pres act imv 2nd sg ὑπάγω "depart/go forth (you)"

πώλησόν	sell
verb:	aor act imv 2nd sg πωλέω "begin (you) to sell/barter"

σου	of you/ your
pers pron:	2nd gen sg σύ "of you"

τὰ	the
article:	acc pl neut ὁ "the (ones)"

ὑπάρχοντα	belongings
ptcp:	pres act ptcp acc pl neut ὑπάρχω "(those) existing/subsisting"

καὶ	and
conj:	καί "and"

Explanation. τὰ ὑπάρχοντα is a substantival participle in reference to the things which belong to a person, or possessions.

21d δὸς τοῖς πτωχοῖς,
Lit. give to the poor,
give to the poor (people),

δὸς	give
verb:	aor act imv 2nd sg δίδωμι "begin (you) to give"

τοῖς	the
article:	dat pl masc ὁ "to the (ones)"

πτωχοῖς   to the poor
adj: dat pl masc πτωχός "to poor (ones)"

Explanation. πτωχοῖς is an adjective which, with its definitive article τοῖς, is acting substantivally and so translated like a noun, "the poor (people)."

21e καὶ ἕξεις θησαυρὸν ἐν οὐρανοῖς,
Lit. and you will have treasures in the heavens,
and you will have treasure in the heavens,

καὶ   and
conj: καί "and"

ἕξεις   you will have
verb: fut act ind 2nd sg ἔχω "(you) will have"

θησαυρὸν   treasure
noun: acc sg masc θησαυρός "a treasury"

ἐν   in
prep: ἐν "in/by/with"

οὐρανοῖς   the heavens
noun: dat pl masc οὐρανός "to heavens"

Explanation. Jesus has already taught his disciples to seek treasures in the heavens (Matt 6:19–21), and to seek first the kingdom of heaven (6:33). Now the young man is asked to exchange one set of treasures for another, his earthly for heavenly.

21f καὶ δεῦρο ἀκολούθει μοι.
Lit. and come follow me."
and come follow me."

MATTHEW 19:16–22

καί	and
conj:	καί "and"

δεῦρο	come
verb:	pres act imv 2nd sg δεῦρο "come here (you)"

ἀκολούθει	follow
verb:	pres act imv 2nd sg ἀκολουθέω "follow (you)"

μοι	me
pers pron:	1st dat sg ἐγώ "to me"

Explanation. The two imperative verbs δεῦρο and ἀκολούθει are put in immediate succession with no conjunction or subordinating action.

The final step is to "follow" Jesus. The term (ἀκολουθέω) is commonly used in Matthew for following Jesus both literally and metaphorically, and connotes discipleship (see especially Matt 10:38; cf. also Matt 4:20, 22, 25; 8:1, 10, 19, 22-23; 9:9; 12:15; 14:13; 16:24; 19:2, 27-28; 20:29, 34; 21:9; 26:58).

22a ἀκούσας δὲ ὁ νεανίσκος τὸν λόγον ἀπῆλθεν λυπούμενος·
Lit. having heard but the young man the word he went away grieving,
But having heard the word the young man he went away grieving,

ἀκούσας	having heard
ptcp:	aor act ptcp nom sg masc ἀκούω "(he) having heard"

δέ	But
conj:	δέ "but/now"

ὁ	the
article:	nom sg masc ὁ "the"

νεανίσκος	young man
noun:	nom sg masc νεανίσκος "a young man"

τὸν	the
article:	acc sg masc ὁ "the"

λόγον	word
noun:	acc sg masc λόγος "a word"

ἀπῆλθεν	he went away
verb:	aor act ind 3rd sg ἀπέρχομαι "he/she/it came/went away"

λυπούμενος	grieving/ sorrowful
ptcp:	pres pass ptcp nom sg masc λυπέω "(one) being made sorry/grieved"

Explanation. λόγον here refers to the teaching of Jesus making the specific request of v. 21.

ἀπῆλθεν is the verb, saying that he departed. That is, he did not do as Jesus requested in v. 21. The participle λυπούμενος is adverbial, describing the manner in which he departed.

Jesus told the man to go and sell his possessions. He leaves, but not to sell things. Instead, he leaves despondent because he is unwilling to exchange his earthly treasures for heavenly ones.

22b ἦν γὰρ ἔχων κτήματα πολλά.

Lit. there was having possessions much.

for he had many possessions.

ἦν	he was being
verb:	impf act ind 3rd sg εἰμί "(he/she/it) continually was"

γὰρ	for
conj:	γάρ "for/because"

ἔχων   one having
ptcp: pres act ptcp nom sg masc ἔχω "(one) having"

κτήματα   possessions
noun: acc pl neut κτῆμα "possessions"

πολλά   much/ many
adj: acc pl neut πολύς "many (ones)"

Explanation. γάρ explains v. 21b, meaning the reason he departs grieving is his great wealth. It is naturally inferred that the offer of treasure in heaven did not in his estimation entice him to give up his great wealth on earth.

ἦν . . . ἔχων is a periphrastic construction, literally "he was having . . . ."

κτῆμα generally refers to possessions, but in the LXX can refer specifically to property (LXX Hos 2:17; Joel 1:11).

Preaching the Text

1. **Main idea:** Christians must be willing to give up *everything* to follow Jesus.

2. **Text to Sermon:**

    a. This kind of story is called "words on discipleship." It differs from stories like "call narratives," in which a named person is told to follow Jesus. Call narratives name the person, describe Jesus calling them specifically, and their immediate response of obedience. The call of Matthew is a "call narrative" (Matt 9:9). But "words on discipleship" are different—they do not name the person or tell the readers anything about them. The point is not how one person responded, like in a call narrative. The point instead is on what anyone can expect from being a disciple of Jesus. So even though you may be neither rich, nor young, nor a man, you can put yourself in this person's place and ask yourself some hard questions.

    b. There are several preaching points that can be elucidated from these verses: Readers of Matthew know enough about Jesus to know he is someone to go to to ask about gaining eternal life. Notice the man refers to Jesus as "teacher," and so presumes he has something to say. He also presumes that doing some "good deed" (ἀγαθὸν ποιήσω) is required in order to get eternal life (ἵνα σχῶ ζωὴν αἰώνιον, v. 16). Surprisingly, answers the man's question with a question of his own: "Why do you ask me about what is good? There is only one who is good" (v. 17). Of course, Jesus is referring to God; the Lord is good (Ps 134:3; Lam 3:25). The question is probably emphatic: "Why do you ask *me* about what is good?" The one who is the pinnacle of goodness is God. Jesus never gives the man the opportunity to answer the question, but implicitly it is profound: you should ask *God*, why do you come to *me*? The question asks the young man how he regards Jesus' relationship to God, at least as a prophetic voice and surely, in Matthew's narrative, God incarnate. In other words, the entire outcome of the passage is determined by how the young man regards Jesus.

    c. When Jesus tells him to keep the commands, he lists a selection from the Ten Commandments (Exod 20:12–16) and the "love command" (Lev 19:18; Matt 19:18-19). It is perhaps surprising that since the man has done all these things he does not presume he has eternal life; rather he presumes he still lacks something.

d. Jesus answers the question of lacking (v. 21) in terms of "perfection," and this state of "perfection" is presumably demonstrated by the requested behavior. Jesus answers in terms of commands: (1) go, (2) sell your possessions, (3) give the money to the poor, and you will have treasure in heaven; then (4) come, follow me. Young man followed those commands, but not Jesus' commands. Instead (v. 22) he went, but not with Jesus. Instead, he went grieving. The reason (v. 22) he had many possessions. Presumably the offer of treasure in the heavens (θησαυρὸν ἐν οὐρανοῖς, v. 21) could not induce him to give up his many possessions (κτήματα πολλά).

e. A few words need to be said about the following context (vv. 23-26). Here Jesus explains that it is hard for a rich person to enter the kingdom of heaven (v. 23), and illustrates that it is easier for a camel to go through the "eye of a needle" than a rich person to enter the kingdom of God (v. 24). This astounds the disciples, presumably because they presume that the wealthy receive God's favor (v. 25). It is often conjectured that the "eye of a needle" is a gate in Jerusalem that a camel can pass through only if it is unloaded of its burdens. This is fictitious; there is no such gate nor was there, and such an understanding contradicts the plain sense of the passage. When Jesus gives this illustration (v. 24) readers are to think of a very large mammal passing through a very tiny hole. If you think, "That's impossible!" then you get the point, as Jesus explains: for people it is impossible, "but for God all things are possible" (Matt 19:26).

3. **Tip for Preaching:** The main concern here is obviously about money, and its hindrance and the difficulty wealth produces for entry into the kingdom. But more broadly the obstacle can be any number of things; there may be any number of things that Jesus may say to you or to me to get rid of, and follow him. Would you do it? Or, perhaps a better way of asking this is: is there anything in your life that you would not give up for Jesus? If Jesus came up to you and asked you to get rid of

something and follow him, what would it be? Would you give it up gladly? Or, like this man, turn away sad?

9

Matthew 21:1–11

Behold, Your King!

Jesus and his disciples approach Jerusalem from the east, coming to the town of Bethphage which likely sat atop the Mount of Olives (Matt 21:1). The latter is a very large hill that overlooks Jerusalem with the Kidron Valley between. From it one can see the temple structure, which lies on the east side of the city adjacent the Kidron Valley. From this vantage point Jesus sends two disciples into the village (probably Bethphage) to acquire a donkey and a colt (v. 2) which Jesus intends to ride in fulfillment of scripture (Matt 21:3–7). The scripture cited is from Zechariah (9:9) in which the prophet announces the coming of Israel's humble king. This is the key to the whole passage: Jesus is the messianic king coming into Jerusalem, and the crowds hail his entry with cloaks and branches along the road (21:8). To give point to their welcome the crowds shouted praises to Jesus as the "son of David" who comes in the name of the Lord (v. 9). The uproar could not go unnoticed, and the crowds explain that this is the prophet, Jesus from Nazareth (Matt 21:10–11). This king is a prophet.

1a   Καὶ ὅτε ἤγγισαν εἰς Ἱεροσόλυμα καὶ
     Lit. And when they drew near into Jerusalem and
     And when they drew near to Jerusalem and

   Καὶ   and
   conj: καί "and"

ὅτε	when
adv:	ὅτε "when"

ἤγγισαν	the drew near
verb:	aor act ind 3rd pl ἐγγίζω "they came near"

εἰς	into
prep:	εἰς "into/for"

Ἱεροσόλυμα	Jerusalem
noun:	acc sg fem Ἱεροσόλυμα "Jerusalem"

καὶ	and
conj:	καί "and"

Explanation. Typically, the Bible describes people going "up" to Jerusalem, since it sits on a hill—Mount Zion. But here Jesus and his disciples are on an adjacent hill, the Mount of Olives, to the east of Jerusalem across the Kidron Valley.

1b ἦλθον εἰς Βηθφαγὴ εἰς τὸ ὄρος τῶν ἐλαιῶν,
Lit. they came into Bethphage into the Mount of Olives,
came to Bethphage, to the Mount of Olives,

ἦλθον	they came
verb:	aor act ind 3rd pl ἔρχομαι "they came"

εἰς	into
prep:	εἰς "into/for"

Βηθφαγὴ	Bethphage
noun: indecl Βηθφαγή "Bethphage"	

εἰς	into
prep:	εἰς "into/for"

τὸ   the
article: acc sg neut ὁ "the"

ὄρος   Mount
noun: acc sg neut ὄρος "a mountain"

τῶν   the
article: gen pl fem ὁ "of the (ones)"

ἐλαιῶν   of Olives
noun: gen pl fem ἐλαία "of olives/olive trees"

Explanation. Zechariah prophesied that the Lord will come in the last day and stand upon the Mount of Olives: "Then the LORD will go forth and fight against those nations as when he fights on a day of battle. On that day his feet shall stand on the Mount of Olives, which lies before Jerusalem on the east; and the Mount of Olives shall be split in two from east to west by a very wide valley; so that one half of the Mount shall withdraw northward, and the other half southward." (Zech 14:3-4 NRSV)

The Mount of Olives is about 2700 feet in elevation. The Kidron Valley originates near Jerusalem and separates the Mount of Olives to the east from Jerusalem and the Temple Mount to the west, and extends about twenty miles south-east to the Dead Sea. It is from the Mount of Olives that Jesus ascends to heaven (cf. Luke 24:50–51; Acts 1:11–12).

Matthew identifies only Bethphage (Matt 21:1), whereas both Mark (11:1) and Luke (19:29) have both Bethphage and Bethany. The latter appears more often in the gospels (Matt 21:17; 26:6; Mark 11:1, 11-12; 14:3; Luke 19:29; 24:50; John 1:28; 11:1, 18; 12:1).

Outside the New Testament and later Christian sources, "Bethphage" is sparsely mentioned (cf. m. Menaḥot 11:2). Its name is thought to derive from an Aramaic expression for "house of early/unripe figs," and lay on the road from Jericho to Jerusalem.

1c–2a τότε Ἰησοῦς ἀπέστειλεν δύο μαθητὰς λέγων αὐτοῖς·
Lit. then Jesus sent two disciples, saying to them,
then Jesus sent two disciples, saying to them,

τότε   then
adv: τότε "then"

Ἰησοῦς   Jesus
noun: nom sg masc Ἰησοῦς "Jesus"

ἀπέστειλεν sent/ sent forth
verb: aor act ind 3rd sg ἀποστέλλω "he/she/it sent forth"

δύο   two
adj: num δύο "two"

μαθητὰς   disciples
noun: acc pl masc μαθητής "disciples"

λέγων   saying
ptcp: pres act ptcp nom sg masc λέγω "(one) saying"

αὐτοῖς   to them
pers pron: dat pl masc αὐτός "to them"

λέγων is a present participle describing ἀπέστειλεν.

2b πορεύεσθε εἰς τὴν κώμην τὴν κατέναντι ὑμῶν,
Lit. "Go into the village which (is) ahead of you (pl),
"Go into the village ahead of you,

Πορεύεσθε   God
verb: pres mid/pass imv 2nd pl πορεύομαι "go/proceed (you [pl])"

εἰς	into
prep:	εἰς "into/for"

τὴν	the
article:	acc sg fem ὁ "the"

κώμην	village
noun:	acc sg fem κώμη "a village"

τὴν	the
article:	acc sg fem ὁ "the"

κατέναντι	opposite
adv:	κατέναντι "opposite"

ὑμῶν	you (pl)
pers pron:	2nd gen pl σύ "of you (pl)"

Explanation. The τὴν before κατέναντι ὑμῶν likely intends the entire phrase to be read not as an adverb, which κατέναντι alone is, but as an adjective phrase describing the village (τὴν κώμην). Which village? The village opposite you. Presumably the disciples know which villages Jesus had in mind.

2c καὶ εὐθέως εὑρήσετε ὄνον δεδεμένην
Lit. and immediately you will find a donkey having been tied up
and immediately you will find a donkey having been tied up

καί	and
conj:	καί "and"

εὐθέως	immediately
adv:	εὐθέως "immediately/next"

εὑρήσετε	you will find
verb:	fut act ind 2nd pl εὑρίσκω "(you [pl]) will find"

ὄνον   donkey
noun: acc sg fem ὄνος "a donkey"

δεδεμένην   having been tied up/ bound
ptcp: perf pass ptcp acc sg fem δέω "(one) having been bound"

Explanation. εὐθύς probably suggests immediately upon entering the village.

The future tense εὑρήσετε may be prophetic, or it may indicate something Jesus already arranged. Regardless, the event is purposeful and highly symbolic, as will become evident below.

δεδεμένην is an adjectival participle describing ὄνον, the donkey.

2d   καὶ πῶλον μετ' αὐτῆς·
Lit. and a colt with it;
and a colt with it;

καί   and
conj: καί "and"

πῶλον   a colt
noun: acc sg masc πῶλος "a foal/colt"

μετ'   with
prep: μετά "with/after"

αὐτῆς   it
pers pron: gen sg fem αὐτός "of her"

Explanation. μετ' αὐτῆς is a contraction from μετα αὐτῆς to aid in pronunciation (elision).

αὐτῆς in the feminine does not indicate the gender of the animal but rather because it shares the gender of its antecedent ὄνος, which is also feminine.

2e λύσαντες ἀγάγετέ μοι.
Lit. *untying bring to me.*
untying them, bring them to me.

λύσαντες   loosing/ untying
ptcp: aor act ptcp nom pl masc λύω "(they) having loosed/ annulled/broken"

ἀγάγετέ   bring/ lead
verb: aor act imv 2nd pl ἄγω "begin (you [pl]) to lead/bring"

μοι   to me
pers pron: 1st dat sg ἐγώ "to me"

Explanation. λύσαντες literally means "loosing," but since it is clear that the animal is tied up (δεδεμένην, v. 2c) the manner of loosing is surely untying.

The verb ἀγάγετέ does not have a stated direct object, but it is implied "them" (αὐτούς). The μοι is the indirect object. The animals (αὐτούς) are what is brought. Jesus (μοι) is the one to whom they are brought.

3a καὶ ἐάν τις ὑμῖν εἴπῃ τι,
Lit. *And if anyone to you (pl) should say anything,*
And if anyone should anything to you,

καί   and
conj: καί "and"

ἐάν   if
conditional: ἐάν "if"

τις   anyone
indef pron: nom sg masc τίς "whom/what"

ὑμῖν   to you (pl)
pers pron: 2nd dat pl σύ "to you (pl)"

εἴπῃ   should say
verb: aor act subj 3rd sg λέγω "he/she/it should begin to say"

τι   anything
indef pron: acc sg neut τίς "whom/what"

Explanation. ἐάν . . . εἴπῃ here Jesus anticipates potential objection by anyone observing the disciples taking the animals.

τίς is an indefinite pronoun from τίς, "anyone" or "someone." Here it is the nominative singular masculine and is the subject of the verb εἴπῃ.

τι is also an indefinite pronoun from τίς, here in the accusative singular neuter and the direct object of the verb εἴπῃ, "anything."

3b ἐρεῖτε ὅτι ὁ κύριος αὐτῶν χρείαν ἔχει·
Lit. you will say that, "The Lord of them need he has";
you shall say that "The Lord has need of them."

ἐρεῖτε   you (pl) will say
verb: fut act ind 2nd pl ἐρέω "(you [pl]) will say"

ὅτι   that
conj: ὅτι "because/that"

ὁ   the
article: nom sg masc ὁ "the"

κύριος   lord
noun: nom sg masc κύριος "Lord/a lord"

αὐτῶν   them/ of them
pers pron: gen pl masc αὐτός "of them"

χρείαν   need
noun: acc sg fem χρεία "need"

ἔχει   he has
verb: pres act ind 3rd sg ἔχω "(he/she/it) has"

Explanation. ἐρεῖτε is a future tense verb acting like a command, called an imperatival future.

χρείαν is a noun, "need," and the direct object of ἔχει. It is modified by αὐτῶν, "of them."

3c εὐθὺς δὲ ἀποστελεῖ αὐτούς.
    Lit. Immediately but he will send them."
    And immediately he will send them."

εὐθὺς   immediately
adv: εὐθέως "immediately/next"

δὲ   and
conj: δέ "but/now"

ἀποστελεῖ   he will send
verb: fut act ind 3rd sg ἀποστέλλω "(he/she/it) will send forth"

αὐτούς   them
pers pron: acc pl masc αὐτός "them"

Explanation. εὐθύς connotes immediate yielding of the animals to Jesus, whether it is because it is arranged this way or because they mention the need of the Lord (κύριος) is not stated.

The implied subject of ἀποστελεῖ is an unstated αὐτός, the antecedent of which is the τις, "anyone" (v. 3a).

4 τοῦτο δὲ γέγονεν ἵνα πληρωθῇ τὸ ῥηθὲν διὰ τοῦ προφήτου λέγοντος·

Lit. This but happened in order that it may be fulfilled that which was spoke through the prophet saying

Now this happened in order that what was spoken through the prophet might be fulfilled, saying,

Τοῦτο	this
dem pron:	nom sg neut οὗτος "this"

δὲ	but/ now
conj:	δέ "but/now"

γέγονεν	occurred/ came about/ happened
verb:	perf act ind 3rd sg γίνομαι "(he/she/it) has become/occurred"

ἵνα	in order that
conj:	ἵνα "in order that"

πληρωθῇ	it may be fulfilled
verb:	aor pass subj 3rd sg πληρόω "(he/she/it) should begin to be filled/fulfilled"

τὸ	the
article:	nom sg neut ὁ "the"

ῥηθὲν	which was said
ptcp:	aor pass ptcp nom sg neut ἐρέω "(it) having been said"

διὰ	through/ by means of
prep:	διά "through/because of"

τοῦ	the
article:	gen sg masc ὁ "of the"

προφήτου	prophet
noun:	gen sg masc προφήτης "of a prophet"

MATTHEW 21:1–11

λέγοντος	saying
ptcp:	pres act ptcp gen sg masc λέγω "of (one) saying"

Explanation. Τοῦτο is the nominative subject of the verb γέγονεν. Its antecedent, which becomes clear in v. 5b, is the acquisition and use of the animals. This acquisition occurred in fulfillment of scripture (v. 5a).

τὸ ῥηθὲν is an adjectival participle. The article shows that it is functioning like a noun (substantivally), "that which was said."

5a εἴπατε τῇ θυγατρὶ Σιών· ἰδοὺ ὁ βασιλεύς σου ἔρχεταί σοι
Lit. Say to the daughter of Siōn Behold the king of you comes to you
Say to the daughter of Zion, 'Behold, your king is coming to you

εἴπατε	Say
verb:	aor act imv 2nd pl λέγω "begin (you [pl]) to say"

τῇ	to the
article:	dat sg fem ὁ "to the"

θυγατρὶ	daughter
noun:	dat sg fem θυγάτηρ "to a daughter"

Σιών	of Zion
noun:	indecl Σιών "Zion"

ἰδοὺ	Behold!
verb:	aor mid imv 2nd sg ὁράω "begin (you for yourself) to see"

ὁ	the
article:	nom sg masc ὁ "the"

βασιλεύς	king
noun:	nom sg masc βασιλεύς "a king"

σου   of you/ your
pers pron: 2nd gen sg σύ "of you"

ἔρχεταί   comes
verb: pres mid/pass ind 3rd sg ἔρχομαι "(he/she/it) comes"

σοι   to you
pers pron: 2nd dat sg σύ "to you"

Explanation. The citation comes from Isaiah 62:11 and Zech 9:9. The former reads: "The Lord has proclaimed to the end of the earth: Say to daughter Zion, 'See, your salvation comes; his reward is with him, and his recompense before him.' They shall be called, 'The Holy People, The Redeemed of the Lord'; and you shall be called, 'Sought Out, A City Not Forsaken.'" (Isa 62:11-12 NRSV)

In Zechariah 9, the context is a prophecy against Israel's enemies (Zech 9:1–3), with a promise to take away their possessions and destroy her by fire (9:4). Other nations will also face judgment (9:5–7) while the Lord himself encamps at his temple to guard it from oppressors (9:8). This launches into an exhortation to praise: "Rejoice greatly, Daughter Zion! Shout, Daughter Jerusalem! See, your king comes to you, righteous and victorious, lowly and riding on a donkey, on a colt, the foal of a donkey" (Zech 9:9 NIV). This is followed by promises of peace, restoration, and salvation for God's people (Zech 9:10–16). He will free them "because of the blood of my covenant" (9:11) and "will save his people on that day as a shepherd saves his flock" (Zech 9:16 NIV).

The beginning, Εἴπατε τῇ θυγατρὶ Σιών (Matt 21:5) is *verbatim* from Isaiah 62:11 (εἴπατε τῇ θυγατρὶ Σιων LXX). But the content of what is said, Ἰδοὺ ὁ βασιλεύς σου ἔρχεταί σοι, comes *verbatim* from Zechariah 9:9: ἰδοὺ ὁ βασιλεύς σου ἔρχεταί σοι (LXX).

5b   πραῢς καὶ ἐπιβεβηκὼς ἐπὶ ὄνον
Lit. gentle and having been mounted upon a donkey
gentle and having been mounted upon a donkey

MATTHEW 21:1–11

πραΰς	gentle
adj:	nom sg masc πραΰς "meek/ gentle"

καὶ	and
conj:	καί "and"

ἐπιβεβηκὼς	having been mounted
ptcp:	perf act ptcp nom sg masc ἐπιβαίνω "(one) having gone onto/ mounted/ embarked"

ἐπὶ	upon
prep:	ἐπί "upon"

ὄνον	a donkey
noun:	acc sg fem ὄνος "a donkey"

Explanation. The citation comes from Zech 9:9 (see below).

Matthew omits Zechariah's δίκαιος καὶ σῴζων αὐτός ("just and salvific is he," NETS). MT: צַדִּיק וְנוֹשָׁע הוּא.

Matthew reads ὄνον for LXX Zechariah's ὑποζύγιον (חֲמוֹר), which he moves to the end of the verse (5c). Both words can mean "donkey," though ὑποζύγιον is more generally a pack animal.

5c καὶ ἐπὶ πῶλον υἱὸν ὑποζυγίου.
Lit. and upon a colt, son of a pack animal."
and upon a colt, the son of a pack animal.'"

καὶ	and
conj:	καί "and"

ἐπὶ	upon
prep:	ἐπί "upon"

πῶλον	a colt
noun:	acc sg masc πῶλος "a foal/colt"

υἱὸν   son
noun: acc sg masc υἱός "a son"

ὑποζυγίου   of a donkey/ pack animal
noun: gen sg neut ὑποζύγιον "of a donkey"

Explanation. The context of Zech 9:9 (see below).

Matthew retains Zechariah's πῶλον ("foal," or "colt") but calls it a "son of a pack animal" (υἱὸν ὑποζυγίου), following the MT's בֶּן־אֲתֹנוֹת ("the son of a female donkey") rather than LXX Zechariah's simple "young" (νέον, Zech 9:9 LXX).

6–7a   πορευθέντες δὲ οἱ μαθηταὶ καὶ ποιήσαντες καθὼς συνέταξεν αὐτοῖς ὁ Ἰησοῦς ἤγαγον τὴν ὄνον καὶ τὸν πῶλον

Lit. Going but the disciples and doing just as he commanded to them Jesus they brought the donkey and the colt,

So going and doing just as Jesus had instructed them, the disciples brought the donkey and the colt,

πορευθέντες   going
ptcp: aor pass ptcp nom pl masc πορεύομαι "(those) having been gone/proceeded"

δὲ   indicates development/ so
conj: δέ "but/now"

οἱ   the
article: nom pl masc ὁ "the (ones)"

μαθηταὶ   disciples
noun: nom pl masc μαθητής "disciples"

καὶ   and
conj: καί "and"

ποιήσαντες doing
ptcp: aor act ptcp nom pl masc ποιέω "(they) having done/made"

καθὼς   just as
adv: καθώς "just as"

συνέταξεν   he commanded
verb: aor act ind 3rd sg συντάσσω "he/she/it arranged together/directed"

αὐτοῖς them
pers pron: dat pl masc αὐτός "to them"

ὁ   the
article: nom sg masc ὁ "the"

Ἰησοῦς Jesus
noun: nom sg masc Ἰησοῦς "Jesus"

ἤγαγον they led/ brought
verb: aor act ind 3rd pl ἄγω "they led/brought"

τὴν the
article: acc sg fem ὁ "the"

ὄνον   donkey
noun: acc sg fem ὄνος "a donkey"

καὶ and
conj: καί "and"

τὸν the
article: acc sg masc ὁ "the"

πῶλον   colt
noun: acc sg masc πῶλος "a foal/colt"

Explanation. Matthew often begins a sentence with a participle followed by the verb it modifies. Here there are two participles followed by the verb: Πορευθέντες . . . ποιήσαντες . . . συνέταξεν.

καθὼς συνέταξεν αὐτοῖς ὁ Ἰησοῦς is an adverbial phrase, modifying ποιήσαντες ("doing"). This phrase, however, itself has a subject and verb. The disciples are doing just as (καθώς) Jesus commanded them. The language suggests following the instructions closely in obedience. The verb is συνέταξεν, the subject of which is ὁ Ἰησοῦς. Jesus is the one doing the commanding. The αὐτοῖς is the indirect object in reference to the disciples. They are the ones being commanded, and they obey exactly.

7b καὶ ἐπέθηκαν ἐπ' αὐτῶν τὰ ἱμάτια,
Lit. and they placed upon them the garments,
and they placed the garments on them,

καί	and
conj:	καί "and"

ἐπέθηκαν	they placed
verb:	aor act ind 3rd pl ἐπιτίθημι "they placed upon"

ἐπ'	upon
prep:	ἐπί "upon"

αὐτῶν	them
pers pron:	gen pl masc αὐτός "of them"

τά	the
article:	acc pl neut ὁ "the (ones)"

ἱμάτια	garments
noun:	acc pl neut ἱμάτιον "(outer) garments"

Explanation. ἐπιτίθημι is a compound verb from the preposition ἐπί ("on" or "upon") and the verb τίθημι ("I put" or "I place") to mean "I put upon" or "I place upon."

ἐπ' αὐτῶν is a contraction from ἐπί αὐτῶν called elision, commonly done to aid in pronunciation.

7c   καὶ ἐπεκάθισεν ἐπάνω αὐτῶν.
Lit. And he sat above of them.
and he sat upon above them.

καί	and
conj:	καί "and"

ἐπεκάθισεν	he sat upon
verb:	aor act ind 3rd sg ἐπικαθίζω "he/she/it sat/got on"

ἐπάνω	above
adv:	ἐπάνω "above"

αὐτῶν   them
pers pron: gen pl masc αὐτός "of them"

Explanation. The antecedent of αὐτῶν is likely the garments (plural), or perhaps the garments *and* the animal, which would also warrant a plural. Readers are not to understand this to mean Jesus sat upon two animals.

The language of ἐπεκάθισεν ἐπάνω is somewhat redundant. The verb ἐπικαθίζω is a compound verb from ἐπί ("on" or "upon") and καθίζω ("I sit") to mean ἐπικαθίζω, "I sit upon." The ἐπάνω is an adverb meaning "above." So Jesus sat upon the garments above them. It is now clear how else he could have sat upon them.

8a ὁ δὲ πλεῖστος ὄχλος ἔστρωσαν ἑαυτῶν τὰ ἱμάτια ἐν τῇ ὁδῷ,

Lit. The but very large crowd spread of their own the garments in the road,

And a very large crowd spread out their own garments on the road,

ὁ	the
article:	nom sg masc ὁ "the"

δὲ	and
conj:	δέ "but/now"

πλεῖστος	very large
adj:	nom sg masc πολύς "much"

ὄχλος	crowd
noun:	nom sg masc ὄχλος "a crowd"

ἔστρωσαν	spread out
verb:	aor act ind 3rd pl στρώννυμι "they did spread out"

ἑαυτῶν	of themselves
reflexive pron:	3rd gen pl masc ἑαυτοῦ "of themselves/ (yourselves)"

τὰ	the
article:	acc pl neut ὁ "the (ones)"

ἱμάτια	garments
noun:	acc pl neut ἱμάτιον "(outer) garments"

ἐν	in
prep:	ἐν "in/by/with"

τῇ	the
article:	dat sg fem ὁ "to the"

ὁδῷ	way/ path/ road
noun:	dat sg fem ὁδός "to a road/path/way"

Explanation. πλεῖστος is a superlative form of πολύς, which is here placed at the front of the sentence for emphasis.

Why Matthew says they spread "their own" (ἑαυτῶν) garments rather than simply "garments" is not clear.

Matthew uses a plural verb, ἔστρωσαν, even though the subject is a grammatical singular (ὄχλος) because it is a "collective singular," meaning it is a grammatical singular noun but represents a concept that incorporates more than one person.

8b ἄλλοι δὲ ἔκοπτον κλάδους ἀπὸ τῶν δένδρων
Lit. *others but cutting branches from of the trees*
and others were cutting branches from the trees

ἄλλοι	others
adj:	nom pl masc ἄλλος "other (ones)"
δὲ	but/ and
conj:	δέ "but/now"
ἔκοπτον	were cutting
verb:	impf act ind 3rd pl κόπτω "(they) continually mourned/ lamented/beat the breast"
κλάδους	branches
noun:	acc pl masc κλάδος "branches"
ἀπὸ	from
prep:	ἀπό "(away) from"
τῶν	the
article:	gen pl neut ὁ "of the (ones)"

δένδρων   trees
noun: gen pl neut δένδρον "of trees"

Explanation. ἄλλοι is an adjective acting substantivally in reference to "other people" distinct from those laying down garments (v. 8a).

ἔκοπτον is an imperfect verb indicating a continuous past action. The verb κόπτω in the active means to cut by means of a sharp-edged tool, whereas in the middle voice it is used for mourning. There is no connection to be made between the two concepts.

8c   καὶ ἐστρώννυον ἐν τῇ ὁδῷ.
     Lit. and spreading in the road.
     and spreading (them) on the road.

καὶ   and
conj: καί "and"

ἐστρώννυον   they were spreading
verb: impf act ind 3rd pl στρώννυμι "(they) continually spread out"

ἐν   in
prep: ἐν "in/by/with"

τῇ   the
article: dat sg fem ὁ "to the"

ὁδῷ   road/ way/ path
noun: dat sg fem ὁδός "to a road/path/way"

Explanation. ἐστρώννυον is an imperfect verb indicating a continuous past action.

9a οἱ δὲ ὄχλοι οἱ προάγοντες αὐτὸν
Lit. The but crowd the going before him
And the crowds going in front of him

οἱ	the
article:	nom pl masc ὁ "the (ones)"

δὲ	and
conj:	δέ "but/now"

ὄχλοι	crowds
noun:	nom pl masc ὄχλος "crowds"

οἱ	the
article:	nom pl masc ὁ "the (ones)"

προάγοντες	going before
ptcp:	pres act ptcp nom pl masc προάγω "(those) leading before/preceding"

αὐτὸν	him
pers pron:	acc sg masc αὐτός "him"

Explanation. The verb in this sentence is ἔκραζον (v. 9b). οἱ ὄχλοι is the subject, and the articular participle οἱ προάγοντες describes the subject. The αὐτόν is the object of the participle, and so all of v. 9a is the first of a two-part compound subject "The crowd going ahead of him."

προάγω is a compound verb from προ, "before" and ἄγω, "I go" or "I lead."

The crowds going ahead of Jesus and behind him (v. 9b) indicates a kingly procession into his conquered and liberated city.

9b καὶ οἱ ἀκολουθοῦντες ἔκραζον λέγοντες·
Lit. and the following were crying out saying
and following (him) were crying out, saying,

καί	and
conj:	καί "and"

οἱ	the
article:	nom pl masc ὁ "the (ones)"

ἀκολουθοῦντες	ones following
ptcp:	pres act ptcp nom pl masc ἀκολουθέω "(those) following"

ἔκραζον	were crying out
verb:	impf act ind 3rd pl κράζω "(they) continually cried out/shouted"

λέγοντες	saying
ptcp:	pres act ptcp nom pl masc λέγω "(those) saying"

Explanation. οἱ ἀκολουθοῦντες is the second part of the compound subject (from v. 9a) for the verb ἔκραζον. ἀκολουθοῦντες has no stated direct object, but it is inferred that it is the same αὐτὸν, "him," from v. 9a.

ἔκραζον is an imperfect verb connoting a continuous past action.

λέγοντες introduces the content of what they were crying out (ἔκραζον).

9c ὡσαννὰ τῷ υἱῷ Δαυίδ·
Lit. "Hosanna to the son of David!"
"Hosanna to the Son of David!"

ὡσαννὰ	Hosanna
Hebrew:	ὡσαννά "Hosanna (cause salvation)!"

τῷ	to the
article:	dat sg masc ὁ "to the"

υἱῷ   son of
noun: dat sg masc υἱός "to a son"

Δαυίδ   David
noun: indecl Δαυίδ "David"

Explanation. Ὡσαννὰ is not a Greek word, but an Aramaic word of praise (Aramaic הוֹשַׁע נָא [*hôšaʿ nāʾ*]) rendered into Greek letters. It means "O save!" which is referenced in the LXX as "save now!" (σῶσον δή; Ps 118:25 [117:25 LXX])

υἱός Δαυίδ is an important title for Jesus' kingship, like in Matt 1:20. It draws originally from 2 Sam 7, where the Lord through the prophet Nathan promises David that he will have a son to sit on the throne of his kingdom forever (2 Sam 7:12–17). In Matthew Jesus is said to be from David's line (1:1, 6, 17, 20), and the title "son of David" is used in association with Jesus' healings (Matt 9:27; 12:23; 15:22; 20:30–31) and even his divinity (Matt 22:42–45). A few decades before this time, a Jewish author wrote a series of psalms that speak, among other things, about what they anticipate in a "son of David." This writing, called the Psalms of Solomon, depicts a militant, even violent "son of David" who will come into Jerusalem and destroy unrighteous rulers (Pss Sol 17). *This* son of David is not entering Jerusalem as a violent warrior but as a humble king.

9d   εὐλογημένος ὁ ἐρχόμενος ἐν ὀνόματι κυρίου·
      Lit. Blessed the one coming in the name of the Lord;
      Blessed is the one who coming in the name of the Lord;

εὐλογημένος having been blessed
ptcp: perf pass ptcp nom sg masc εὐλογέω "(one) having been blessed"

ὁ   the
article: nom sg masc ὁ "the"

ἐρχόμενος	one coming
ptcp:	pres mid/pass ptcp nom sg masc ἔρχομαι "(one) coming"

ἐν	in
prep:	ἐν "in/by/with"

ὀνόματι	name
noun:	dat sg neut ὄνομα "to a name"

κυρίου	of the Lord
noun:	gen sg masc κύριος "of the Lord/a lord"

Explanation. Verse 9d is verbatim from the LXX of Ps 118:26 (εὐλογημένος ὁ ἐρχόμενος ἐν ὀνόματι κυρίου (MT: בָּרוּךְ הַבָּא בְּשֵׁם יְהוָה).

Psalm 118 is a jubilant psalm of thanksgiving (Ps 118:1), likely of a king celebrating victory. It acclaims the steadfast love (חֶסֶד) of the Lord (118:2–4); the Lord's presence with the Psalmist (vv. 6–7) as a refuge (vv. 8–13), salvation (v. 14), and preservation of the Psalmist's life (vv. 15–18). The psalmist appeals to open gates of the temple's forecourt to give thanks to the Lord (vv. 19–21). The temple's priests bless the king, who is the psalmist, as one who comes in the name of the Lord (v. 26). So the quotation is taken from a priestly blessing upon a king who comes to the temple to praise the Lord for the king's victory. This seems to suggest that Jesus is the king, coming to the temple to praise the Lord for the anticipated victory he will achieve in Jerusalem.

9e ὡσαννὰ ἐν τοῖς ὑψίστοις.

Lit. Hosanna in the highest.

Hosanna in the highest!"

ὡσαννὰ	Hosanna
Hebrew:	ὡσαννά "Hosanna (cause salvation)!"

ἐν   in
prep: ἐν "in/by/with"

τοῖς   the
article: dat pl neut ὁ "to the (ones)"

ὑψίστοις   highest
adj: dat pl neut ὕψιστος "to most high/highest (ones)"

Explanation. ὕψιστος is a superlative adjective, "highest."

10a Καὶ εἰσελθόντος αὐτοῦ εἰς Ἱεροσόλυμα ἐσείσθη πᾶσα ἡ πόλις λέγουσα·

Lit. And entering of him into Jerusalem and was shaken all the city saying,

And when he entered into Jerusalem, the whole city was shaken, saying,

Καὶ   and
conj: καί "and"

εἰσελθόντος   having entered
ptcp: aor act ptcp gen sg masc εἰσέρχομαι "of (him) having come in/entered"

αὐτοῦ   of him
pers pron: gen sg masc αὐτός "of him/it"

εἰς   into
prep: εἰς "into/for"

Ἱεροσόλυμα   Jerusalem
noun: acc sg fem Ἱεροσόλυμα "Jerusalem"

ἐσείσθη   was shaken
verb: aor pass ind 3rd sg σείω "(he/she/it) was shaken/rocked"

πᾶσα	all
adj:	nom sg fem πᾶς "all"

ἡ	the
article:	nom sg fem ὁ "the"

πόλις	city
noun:	nom sg fem πόλις "a city"

λέγουσα	saying
ptcp:	pres act ptcp nom sg fem λέγω "(one) saying"

Explanation. εἰσελθόντος αὐτοῦ is a genitive absolute, "when he entered."

ἐσείσθη πᾶσα ἡ πόλις recalls the statement about all Jerusalem being troubled (ἐταράχθη) in Matt 2:3.

τίς ἐστιν οὗτος;
10b τίς ἐστιν οὗτος;
Lit. "Who is this?"
"Who is this?"

τίς	who
interr pron:	nom sg masc τίς "who?/what?"

ἐστιν	is
verb:	pres act ind 3rd sg εἰμί "(he/she/it) is"

οὗτος	this
dem pron:	nom sg masc οὗτος "this"

Explanation. Τίς is an interrogative pronoun, nominative singular masculine. It is either the subject or the predicate nominative. οὗτος is a demonstrative pronoun nominative singular masculine. It is either the subject or the predicate nominative. The word order emphasizes the interrogative, "Who is this?"

11a οἱ δὲ ὄχλοι ἔλεγον·
Lit. The but crowds were saying,
And the crowds were saying,

    οἱ   the
    article: nom pl masc ὁ "the (ones)"

    δὲ   and
    conj: δέ "but/now"

    ὄχλοι   crowds
    noun: nom pl masc ὄχλος "crowds"

    ἔλεγον   were saying
    verb: impf act ind 3rd pl λέγω "(they) continually said"

Explanation. v. 11 is the answer to v. 10b.

ἔλεγον is an imperfect verb connoting a continuous past action.

11b οὗτός ἐστιν ὁ προφήτης Ἰησοῦς ὁ ἀπὸ Ναζαρὲθ τῆς Γαλιλαίας.
Lit. "This is the prophet Jesus the from Nazareth of Galilee."
"This is the prophet Jesus from Nazareth in Galilee."

    οὗτος   This
    dem pron: nom sg masc οὗτος "this"

    ἐστιν   is
    verb: pres act ind 3rd sg εἰμί "(he/she/it) is"

    ὁ   the
    article: nom sg masc ὁ "the"

    προφήτης prophet
    noun: nom sg masc προφήτης "a prophet"

Ἰησοῦς	Jesus
noun:	nom sg masc Ἰησοῦς "Jesus"

ὁ	the
article:	nom sg masc ὁ "the"

ἀπὸ	from
prep:	ἀπό "(away) from"

Ναζαρὲθ	Nazareth
noun:	indecl Ναζαρέθ "Nazareth"

τῆς	of the
article:	gen sg fem ὁ "of the"

Γαλιλαίας	Galilee
noun:	gen sg fem Γαλιλαία "of Galilee"

Explanation. Οὗτός is a direct answer to the question, "who is this (Οὗτός)?"

Preaching the Text

1. **Main idea:** The identity of Jesus is the central question of this passage.

2. **Text to Sermon:**
    a. This chapter begins the "Passion Narrative" in Matthew (chapter 21–28). The word "Passion" comes from a Latin term meaning "suffering." Ironically, the sufferings of Jesus begin with his entry into Jerusalem as a triumphant messianic king. But all that comes about here is leading directly to the crucifixion; Jesus is the crucified messianic king, the son of David. The importance of the Passion Narrative in Matthew can be seen by how the evangelist devotes so much attention to it. One can see that the first part of his gospel (chapters 1–3) covers the birth up to adulthood, about 30 years. The main portion of the gospel (chapters 4–20) cover the majority of his public ministry, about three years. Then at the Passion Narrative (chapters 21–28) things slow down into a slow-motion account of the final week—seven days—of Jesus' life. This is a literary device used to cause the reader to slow down. Focus. Ponder and reflect.

    b. At the outset (Matt 21:1–7) the narrative is presented with a two-fold focus: First, Jesus is about to suffer but he is entirely in control. The ensuing narrative—whether pre-arranged by Jesus or supernaturally orchestrated—is well-known to Jesus and indeed is his deliberate plan. What occurs here is no accident. Second, what occurs here is part of the fulfillment of the Divine plan of scripture. Both are fronted in this narrative so that the reader sees from the outset that whatever transpires from here on out—from 21:1 through 28:20—is all part of a purposeful work of Jesus in accord with the scriptural plan of the Father.

    c. There is no lofty ceremony by Jesus for his entry into Jerusalem, but he enters as a messianic king. The pomp comes from the reception he receives as the son of David. He is hailed and welcomed by the crowd (ὄχλος, v. 8), though soon that crowd (ὄχλος) will participate in his arrest (Matt 26:47). They praise him as coming in the name of the Lord and as the Son of David (21:9). His entry into Jerusalem raises a turmoil, which centers on the question of his identity: "Who is this?" (v. 10). Previously his disciples asked, "What sort of man is this, that even the winds and the sea obey him?" (Matt 8:27 NRSV). Later Peter will boldly assert to Jesus: "You are the Messiah, the Son of the living God" (Matt 16:16 NRSV). Now the city is faced with the same question, to which the crowd (ὄχλος) responds: "This is the prophet Jesus from Nazareth in Galilee" (Matt 21:11, NRSV).

d. The citation in Matt 21:5 is a conflation of Isaiah 62:11 and Zechariah 9:9. The former regards Israel's restoration after the completion of the Babylonian and Assyrian exiles (Isa 62:1–10), where the Lord proclaims to his people that their "savior" (יִשְׁעֵךְ, or "salvation") is coming (62:11). This deliverer will bring his reward and recompense with him (Isa 62:12), seemingly indicating an eschatological messianic figure. Zechariah's context pertains to the coming of Zion's king (Zech 9:9–13) who announces the coming of the Lord, who will himself restore splendor of Israel (Zech 9:14–17). This is all heralded by the arrival of this king (מֶלֶךְ) who comes to establish peace (Zech 9:9–10). Both contexts indicate a predication of God's intervention on behalf of the redemption of his people, which Matthew ascribes to Jesus in this context. His entry, though violent to himself by his crucifixion, is a humble one in which, ultimately, he establishes peace by saving his people from their sins (Matt 1:21).

e. There is also an allusion in Matt 21:9 to Psalm 119 (118 LXX), a psalm of thanksgiving centered around the enduring steadfast love of the Lord (Ps 119:1, 29 [118:1, 29 LXX]). In it the psalmist finds refuge in the Lord's deliverance from his distress (Ps 119:5-28 [118:5-28 LXX]). Matthew's citation regards Jesus as one coming *in the name of* the Lord, being blessed by the crowds in thanksgiving.

3. **Tip for Preaching:** Here Jesus is the rightful king entering into Jerusalem, acclaimed as the Son of David. But His crown will be a crown of thorns (Matt 27:29), because His Kingdom is one in which the first will be last and the last first (Matt 19:30), the meek inherit the earth (Matt 5:5), and whoever wants to be first among those of His kingdom must be their slave (Matt 20:27), following the example of their master

(Matt 20:28). This King is not an ordinary King, nor is His Kingdom an ordinary Kingdom.

10
Matthew 21:23–27
Jesus' Authority

This passage shouts out that Jesus is God. But it does so in a whisper. The word "God" is not even here, and yet a careful reading shows the subtle yet strategic way in which Matthew shapes this account to make it stand out with unmistakable clarity. Jesus is in the temple teaching when he is approached by the chief priests and elders, who ask him two questions: First, by what authority is he doing these things? And, second, who gave him this authority (Matt 21:23). Jesus turns the situation around and immediately puts them on the defensive: He will answer their question, if they first answer his (v. 24). No mention is made of their acquiescence to this arrangement, rather Jesus begins with his question (v. 25). Where does John's baptism come from? And here Jesus gives them two options: heaven or human? (v. 25). Readers are given insight into the thought processes of their answer (vv. 25–26). Their response that they do not know is not satisfactory to Jesus (v. 27), yet as we will see there is more to it.

23a   Καὶ ἐλθόντος αὐτοῦ εἰς τὸ ἱερὸν
      Lit. And after entering of him into the temple
      And after he entered the temple,

      Καὶ   and
      conj: καί "and"

MATTHEW 21:23-27

ἐλθόντος	after entering
ptcp:	aor act ptcp gen sg masc ἔρχομαι "of (him) having come"

αὐτοῦ	of him
pers pron:	gen sg masc αὐτός "of him/it"

εἰς	into
prep:	εἰς "into/for"

τὸ	the
article:	acc sg neut ὁ "the"

ἱερὸν	temple
noun:	acc sg neut ἱερόν "a temple"

Explanation. ἐλθόντος αὐτοῦ is a genitive absolute construction

ἱερόν refers to the temple courts, not the actual sanctuary where sacrifices were performed.

23b προσῆλθαν αὐτῷ διδάσκοντι οἱ ἀρχιερεῖς καὶ οἱ πρεσβύτεροι τοῦ λαοῦ λέγοντες·

Lit. they came toward him while teaching the chief priests and the elders of the people saying

the chief priests and elders of the people approached him as he was teaching, saying,

προσῆλθαν	they came toward/ approached
verb:	aor act ind 3rd pl προσέρχομαι "they came toward"

αὐτῷ	to him
pers pron:	dat sg masc αὐτός "to him"

διδάσκοντι	to the one teaching/ while teaching
ptcp:	pres act ptcp dat sg masc διδάσκω "to (one) teaching"

οἱ	the
article:	nom pl masc ὁ "the (ones)"

ἀρχιερεῖς	chief priests
noun:	nom pl masc ἀρχιερεύς "high/chief priests"

καί	and
conj:	καί "and"

οἱ	the
article:	nom pl masc ὁ "the (ones)"

πρεσβύτεροι	elders
adj:	nom pl masc πρεσβύτερος "eldest (ones)"

τοῦ	of the
article:	gen sg masc ὁ "of the"

λαοῦ	people
noun:	gen sg masc λαός "of a people"

λέγοντες	saying
ptcp:	pres act ptcp nom pl masc λέγω "(those) saying"

Explanation. προσῆλθαν is the verb, αὐτῷ is the direct object. Typically, direct objects are in the accusative case, but some verbs take their direct objects in the dative, as here.

ἀρχιερεύς refers to the "chief priests" or "principal priests." These were prominent figures in the priesthood, often standing alone as leading figures in the Sanhedrin (e.g., Josephus, *Jewish War* 2.5.3 §322; 2.16.3 §342; 5.1.5 §36; 6.9.3 §42). The chief priests (ἀρχιερεύς) in Matthew are almost always paired with another group, notably the "scribes" (γραμματεῖς; 2:4; 16:21; 20:15, 18, 23; 26:3–4) or the elders (πρεσβύτεροι; Matt 26:47; 27:1, 12, 20, 41).

πρεσβύτερος is generally a lay (non-priestly) member of the governing Sanhedrin, typically from important and influential families. In Matthew they are noted for their traditions pertaining to hand-washing (Matt 15:2) and are paired with chief priests when plotting against Jesus (Matt 26:3, 47, 57; 27:1, 3, 12, 20; 28:12), or with both chief priests and scribes for the same purpose (Matt 16:21; 27:41).

23c ἐν ποίᾳ ἐξουσίᾳ ταῦτα ποιεῖς;
Lit. "By what authority these things you do?"
"By what authority are you doing these things?

ἐν	by/with
prep:	ἐν "in/by/with"

ποίᾳ	what sort of?/ what kind of?
interr pron: dat sg fem ποῖος "to what sort?"	

ἐξουσίᾳ	authority
noun:	dat sg fem ἐξουσία "to an authority"

ταῦτα	these (things)
dem pron: acc pl neut οὗτος "these"	

ποιεῖς	you (sg) do
verb:	pres act ind 2nd sg ποιέω "(you) do/make"

Explanation. ταῦτα is a plural demonstrative pronoun, here acting as the direct object meaning "these" with an implied "these (things)." Since the only thing Jesus is doing is teaching, their question pertains to the authority of his teaching.

ἐν ποίᾳ ἐξουσίᾳ asks which or what authority is here being used. Below (23b) they will ask for the personal origin of that authority.

23d καὶ τίς σοι ἔδωκεν τὴν ἐξουσίαν ταύτην;
Lit. "And who to you gave the authority this?"
"And who gave you this authority?"

καί and
conj: καί "and"

τίς who
interr pron: nom sg masc τίς "who?/what?"

σοι to you (sg)
pers pron: 2nd dat sg σύ "to you"

ἔδωκεν gave
verb: aor act ind 3rd sg δίδωμι "he/she/it gave"

τὴν the
article: acc sg fem ὁ "the"

ἐξουσίαν authority
noun: acc sg fem ἐξουσία "an authority"

ταύτην this
dem pron: acc sg fem οὗτος "this"

Explanation. τίς is an interrogative pronoun asking for the personal origin of the reception of this authority. The presumption seems to be that the authority is derived by Jesus from someone else, rather than innate to him. But from whom? Precisely what they were looking for is not entirely clear. Perhaps they are seeking the approbation of a recognized or authoritative teacher under whose tutelage Jesus learned, as Paul had done under rabbi Gamaliel (Acts 22:3).

The placement of σοι suggests emphasis.

The ταύτην describes τὴν ἐξουσίαν and clarifies it is the same "authority" mentioned before.

24a ἀποκριθεὶς δὲ ὁ Ἰησοῦς εἶπεν αὐτοῖς·
Lit. *Answering but the Jesus said to them*
And, answering, Jesus said to them,

MATTHEW 21:23-27

ἀποκριθεὶς	answering
ptcp:	aor pass ptcp nom sg masc ἀποκρίνομαι "(he) having been answered"

δὲ	and
conj:	δέ "but/now"

ὁ	the
article:	nom sg masc ὁ "the"

Ἰησοῦς	Jesus
noun:	nom sg masc Ἰησοῦς "Jesus"

εἶπεν	said
verb:	aor act ind 3rd sg λέγω "he/she/it said"

αὐτοῖς	to them
pers pron:	dat pl masc αὐτός "to them"

Explanation. Matthew commonly uses a participle ahead of the verb it modifies, here ἀποκριθείς and εἶπεν.

24b ἐρωτήσω ὑμᾶς κἀγὼ λόγον ἕνα,
Lit. I will ask you also I word one,
"I also will ask you one word,

ἐρωτήσω	I will ask
verb:	fut act ind 1st sg ἐρωτάω "(I) will ask/inquire"

ὑμᾶς	you (pl)
pers pron:	2nd acc pl σύ "you (pl)"

κἀγὼ	also I
pers pron:	1st nom sg κἀγώ "and/also I"

λόγον   word
noun: acc sg masc λόγος "a word"

ἕνα   one
adj: acc sg masc εἷς "one"

Explanation. κἀγώ is a contraction of καί, "and/ also" and ἐγώ, "I." ἕνα is an adjective modifying λόγον.

24c ὃν ἐὰν εἴπητέ μοι κἀγὼ ὑμῖν ἐρῶ ἐν ποίᾳ ἐξουσίᾳ ταῦτα ποιῶ·
Lit. That which if you should say to me and I to you (pl) I will say in what authority these I do;

which, if you should tell me, I also will tell you by what authority I do these (things);

ὃν   Which/ that which/
rel pron: acc sg masc ὅς "which"

ἐὰν   if
conditional: ἐάν "if"

εἴπητέ   you (pl) should say
verb: aor act subj 2nd pl λέγω "you (pl) should begin to say"

μοι   to me/ me
pers pron: 1st dat sg ἐγώ "to me"

κἀγώ   and I/ also I
pers pron: 1st nom sg κἀγώ "and/also I"

ὑμῖν   to you (pl)
pers pron: 2nd dat pl σύ "to you (pl)"

ἐρῶ   I will say
verb: fut act ind 1st sg ἐρέω "(I) will say"

MATTHEW 21:23-27

ἐν   in/ by
prep: ἐν "in/by/with"

ποίᾳ   what sort of/ what kind of
interr pron: dat sg fem ποῖος "to what sort?"

ἐξουσίᾳ   authority
noun: dat sg fem ἐξουσία "to an authority"

ταῦτα   these (things)
dem pron: acc pl neut οὗτος "these"

ποιῶ   I do
verb: pres act ind 1st sg ποιέω "(I) do/make"

Explanation. ἐὰν εἴπητέ is a conditional statement using a subjunctive verb. If they should answer him, he will then answer them.

The language of ἐν ποίᾳ ἐξουσίᾳ mirrors exactly the opponents' question. Jesus is willing to answer the precise question they pose, but there is a condition: he first poses a simple question to them. If they answer his question, he will answer theirs. Later Jesus' implicit claim here is made explicit, where he asserts that all authority (πᾶσα ἐξουσία) on heaven and on earth has been given to him (Matt 28:18).

25a τὸ βάπτισμα τὸ Ἰωάννου πόθεν ἦν;
Lit. the baptism the of John where it was?
The baptism of John, where was it from?

τὸ   the
article: nom sg neut ὁ "the"

βάπτισμα   baptism
noun: nom sg neut βάπτισμα "a baptism"

τό	the
article:	nom sg neut ὁ "the"

Ἰωάννου	of John
noun:	gen sg masc Ἰωάννης "of John"

πόθεν	from where
interr adv:	πόθεν "from where?"

ἦν	it was
verb:	impf act ind 3rd sg εἰμί "(he/she/it) continually was"

Explanation. τό before Ἰωάννου likely functions to change the noun to function like an adjective, like "the Johannine baptism" or the "John-baptism."

πόθεν is an interrogative adverb of place, asking the location of its origins.

25b ἐξ οὐρανοῦ ἢ ἐξ ἀνθρώπων;
Lit. of heaven or of humans?
from heaven or from humans?"

ἐξ	from/ out of
prep:	ἐκ "from/out of"

οὐρανοῦ	of heaven
noun:	gen sg masc οὐρανός "of the heaven"

ἤ	or
particle:	ἤ "or/than"

ἐξ	from/ out of
prep:	ἐκ "from/out of"

ἀνθρώπων	of people
noun:	gen pl masc ἄνθρωπος "of men"

Explanation. Jesus gives only two options, contrasted by ἤ.

Readers know unequivocally that John's baptism is from heaven. Jesus identifies him as the one who is more than a prophet, the one coming in the spirit and power of Elijah (Matt 11:7–13; 17:12–13).

25c Οἱ δὲ διελογίζοντο ἐν ἑαυτοῖς λέγοντες·
Lit. the's but were discussing in themselves saying
And they were discussing this among themselves, saying,

οἱ	the
article:	nom pl masc ὁ "the (ones)"

δὲ	and
conj:	δέ "but/now"

διελογίζοντο	they were reasoning/ discussing/ dialoguing
verb:	impf mid/pass ind 3rd pl διαλογίζομαι "(they) continually reasoned/considered"

ἐν	in
prep:	ἐν "in/by/with"

ἑαυτοῖς   to themselves
reflexive pron: 3rd dat pl masc ἑαυτοῦ "to themselves/(yourselves)"

λέγοντες	saying
ptcp:	pres act ptcp nom pl masc λέγω "(those) saying"

Explanation. διελογίζοντο is an imperfect verb indicating continuous past action.

ἐν ἑαυτοῖς, literally "in themselves" means "among themselves." This is a private dialogue among the opponents. Yet Jesus is aware of it and what they are deliberating and, more importantly, their motives.

26a ἐὰν εἴπωμεν· ἐξ οὐρανοῦ,
Lit. If we should say, "From heaven,
"If we say, 'From heaven,'

ἐὰν	if
conditional: ἐάν "if"	

εἴπωμεν	we say/ we should say
verb:	aor act subj 1st pl λέγω "we should begin to say"

ἐξ	from/ out of
prep:	ἐκ "from/out of"

οὐρανοῦ	heaven
noun:	gen sg masc οὐρανός "of the heaven"

Explanation. ἐάν introduces a conditional sentence, followed by a subjunctive verb εἴπωμεν, "if we should say." It raises the condition of saying something, namely answering Jesus' question that John's baptism comes from heaven. This is the first part—the protasis—of a conditional, if/then, statement.

26b ἐρεῖ ἡμῖν· διὰ τί οὖν οὐκ ἐπιστεύσατε αὐτῷ;
Lit. he will say to us, "Through why then not you believed to him?"
he will say to us, 'Why, then, did you not believe him?'

ἐρεῖ	he will say
verb:	fut act ind 3rd sg ἐρέω "(he/she/it) will say"

ἡμῖν	to us
pers pron: 1st dat pl ἐγώ "to us"	

διὰ	through
prep:	διά "through/because of"

τί   what?
interr pron: acc sg neut τίς "whom?/what?"

οὖν   then
conj: οὖν "therefore"

οὐκ   not
neg particle: οὐ "no/not"

ἐπιστεύσατε you (pl) believe
verb: aor act ind 2nd pl πιστεύω "you (pl) believed"

αὐτῷ   him
pers pron: dat sg masc αὐτός "to him"

Explanation. This is the apodoses, or "then" portion of an "if/then" statement. For the "if" Greek typically uses ἐάν and a subjunctive verb. For the apodosis, "then" portion, there is no word or formula in Greek.

ἐρεῖ is a future tense verb used because Jesus' opponents anticipate what Jesus will—in the future—say in response to their answer.

διά τί is an idiom meaning "why?"

οὖν, "then" or "therefore" indicates an inference, based on their answer.

Curiously, it never occurs to these men that if he was sent from heaven, they should have believed him. Their concern is not with gaining the truth about John or even learning from God's message through him, but with saving face in the argument with Jesus. This option does not work for them not because they do not believe it or because it is not true, but because they anticipate how Jesus can respond. They lose the argument.

26c ἐὰν δὲ εἴπωμεν· ἐξ ἀνθρώπων,
    Lit. *If but we should say, 'from humans,'*
    But if we should say, 'From humans,'

ἐάν   if
conditional: ἐάν "if"

δέ   but
conj: δέ "but/now/and"

εἴπωμεν   we should say
verb: aor act subj 1st pl λέγω "we should begin to say"

ἐξ   from
prep: ἐκ "from/out of"

ἀνθρώπων   humans
noun: gen pl masc ἄνθρωπος "of men/people/ humans"

Explanation. ἐάν introduces a conditional sentence, followed by a subjunctive verb εἴπωμεν, "if we should say." It raises the condition of saying something, namely answering Jesus' question that John's baptism comes from humans. This is the first part—the protasis—of a conditional, if/then, statement.

ἄνθρωπος is sometimes translated with the gender-specific, "man" but more commonly is general and inclusive "human."

26d φοβούμεθα τὸν ὄχλον,
Lit. we fear the crowd,
we fear the crowd,

φοβούμεθα   we fear/ are afraid
verb: pres mid/pass ind 1st pl φοβέω "(we) fear/are afraid"

τὸν   the
article: acc sg masc ὁ "the"

ὄχλον   crowd
noun: acc sg masc ὄχλος "a crowd"

MATTHEW 21:23–27

Explanation. The statement φοβούμεθα τὸν ὄχλον indicates their concern for repercussions to them from the crowd.

26e πάντες γὰρ ὡς προφήτην ἔχουσιν τὸν Ἰωάννην.
Lit. all for as prophet they held the John.
for (they) all as a prophet have John.

πάντες	all (pl)
adj:	nom pl masc πᾶς "all (ones)"
γὰρ	for
conj:	γάρ "for/because"
ὡς	as
adv:	ὡς "as"
προφήτην	prophet
noun:	acc sg masc προφήτης "a prophet"
ἔχουσιν	they have/ are having
verb:	pres act ind 3rd pl ἔχω "(they) have"
τὸν	the
article:	acc sg masc ὁ "the"
Ἰωάνην	John
noun:	acc sg masc Ἰωάννης "John"

Explanation. γάρ indicates the reason they feared the crowd.

πάντες is an adjective functioning like a noun with nothing to modify. In English it could be simple "all" or "everyone." The point is that this opinion of John was widely held, regardless of what they personally may believe.

ὡς προφήτην ἔχουσιν, literally "as a prophet they have" simply means that they regard or consider him to be a prophet.

Again, their consideration about whether John's ministry is of human origin does not deal with whether or not that is true, but instead it concerns how they will be perceived by the crowds.

27a καὶ ἀποκριθέντες τῷ Ἰησοῦ εἶπαν,
Lit. and answering to Jesus they said,
And, answering Jesus, they said,

καί	and
conj:	καί "and"

ἀποκριθέντες	answering
ptcp:	aor pass ptcp nom pl masc ἀποκρίνομαι "(those) having been answered"

τῷ	the
article:	dat sg masc ὁ "to the"

Ἰησοῦ	to Jesus
noun:	dat sg masc Ἰησοῦς "to Jesus"

εἶπαν	they said
verb:	aor act ind 3rd pl λέγω "they said"

Explanation. Ἰησοῦ looks exactly like a genitive form of Ἰησοῦς, but the definite article τῷ clarifies that it is a dative. The dative singular and genitive singular of Ἰησοῦς look the same, Ἰησοῦ.

The familiar participle (ἀποκριθέντες) and finite verb (εἶπαν) together indicate that this is taken as a direct answer to Jesus either/or question. It was not an option given, but it exposes something about them. Do they really not know? Or, at least, have an opinion?

27b οὐκ οἴδαμεν.
Lit. "Not we know."
"We do not know."

οὐκ   not
neg particle: οὐ "no/not"

οἴδαμεν   we have known
verb: perf act ind 1st pl εἰδώ "(we) have known"

Explanation. The answer is brief and terse, not to say duplicitous. Jesus sees through their lie. He does not offer to inform them; they know, or at least think they know. Jesus' response, instead, indicates what is really happening with their response.

27c ἔφη αὐτοῖς καὶ αὐτός·
Lit. He said to them and he,
He also was saying to them,

ἔφη   he was saying
verb: impf act ind 3rd sg φημί "(he/she/it) continually stated/claimed"

αὐτοῖς   to them
pers pron: dat pl masc αὐτός "to them"

καὶ   also
conj: καί "and"

αὐτός   he
pers pron: nom sg masc αὐτός "he"

Explanation. The presence of more than one form of αὐτός can be confusing. It is important to always look to the verb first. Here the verb is ἔφη, which being a third singular verb requires a nominative singular subject. Here this is αὐτός. The αὐτοῖς is a dative plural, and so is the indirect object, "to them." The word καί is a conjunction or an adverb. Context will help determine which makes most sense in English, which here is clearly an adverb.

27d οὐδὲ ἐγὼ λέγω ὑμῖν ἐν ποίᾳ ἐξουσίᾳ ταῦτα ποιῶ.
Lit. "Neither I say to you (pl) in what to power these I do."
"Neither will I tell you by what authority I am doing these things."

οὐδὲ   nor/ neither
neg conj: οὐδέ "nor/not even"

ἐγὼ   I
pers pron: 1st nom sg ἐγώ "I"

λέγω   say/ tell
verb: pres act ind 1st sg λέγω "(I) say"

ὑμῖν   to you (pl)
pers pron: 2nd dat pl σύ "to you (pl)"

ἐν   by
prep: ἐν "in/by/with"

ποίᾳ   what sort of/ what
interr pron: dat sg fem ποῖος "to what sort?"

ἐξουσίᾳ   authority
noun: dat sg fem ἐξουσία "to an authority"

ταῦτα   these (things)
dem pron: acc pl neut οὗτος "these"

ποιῶ   I do/ I am doing
verb: pres act ind 1st sg ποιέω "(I) do/make"

Explanation. οὐδέ is important since "neither" indicates that *his* answer is in a sense like *their* answer. That is, he *neither* "will not tell" them means that he realizes that they *do* know, or at least have an opinion, but are simply *refusing to tell him*. They are lying, and Jesus sees through it. Moreover, because they are concealing their true opinions, Jesus refuses to answer their simple question.

The language ἐγὼ λέγω ὑμῖν is emphatic. Essentially: *You* will not tell *me*, so neither will *I* tell *you*.

The matter in question is again repeated: ἐν ποίᾳ ἐξουσίᾳ ταῦτα ποιῶ.

Preaching the Text

1. **Main idea:** Jesus has the authority of God

2. **Text to Sermon:**

   a. This passage is a controversy story, or a controversy narrative. These are familiar in the gospels and typically depict several features. First, there is a question given to Jesus by an opponent. Typically, as one can imagine, Jesus' opponents do not ask questions to gain information. Their questions are not *real* questions, but rather intended points of arguments or even traps. The second part of a controversy story is a counter-question by Jesus. This results, third, in an answer by the opponent in which they expose a particular weakness *about themselves*. Finally, fourth, there is a rejection of the original question by Jesus because of the inadequacies of their responses. Here we can see how each of these plays out and helps to understand this passage in its narrative context.

   b. At the outset Matthew describes the scene of Jesus teaching in the temple when he is questioned by the chief priests and elders, asking (1) by what authority he is doing these things—presumably teaching, and (2) who gave him this authority (21:23). This is the question by the opponents. Jesus responds by setting rules for engagement: he will answer their question on the condition that they answer his (v. 24). The question he puts to them pertains to the origins of John's baptism, whether it was of human or heaven origin (v. 25a). Here (vv. 25b–26) we see internal deliberation by the opponents, weighing either option and how it would bear out in their argument with Jesus. First, they consider whether they said if it was from heaven, they anticipate Jesus would ask why they did not believe him. (Nothing is said about any remorse or regret for failing to believe a man sent from heaven!). Second, they consider whether his authority comes from humans (v. 26a), this would contradict the crowds who regarded John as a prophet (v. 26b). But neither of these two options are vocalized, so they effectively attempt to avoid the question by telling Jesus "We do not know" (v. 27a). But they are lying, and Jesus knows it. He responds "Neither will I tell you...," which means that Jesus recognizes that they are simply refusing to tell their view. The word *neither* makes that abundantly clear. They surely have an opinion, but refuse to answer it presumably because of the fear of losing an argument to Jesus on the one hand and the fear of the crowd on the other. Now, the controversy stories contain answers by the opponent that expose their weaknesses—here duplicity and deceit. Then Jesus rejects the original question not because he does not have an answer but because of their own inadequacies and inability to answer his simple question. Now, here is the key to the whole thing: if they answer *Jesus'* question correctly—John's baptism is from heaven—they answer *their own* question correctly—Jesus' authority is from heaven (God). Jesus first wants them to be able to answer the easier question, about John, before they can answer the more profound question, about himself. It is like a young runner learning to do the hurdles. The coach starts out with short hurtles and then gradually increases their height. Here Jesus is starting with the simpler test, and they get tripped up by it. But the reader is left with no doubt as to the answer to their question to Jesus: Ἐν ποίᾳ ἐξουσίᾳ ταῦτα ποιεῖς. The answer is: God's.

3. **Tip for Preaching:** In preaching this passage, it is important to follow the strategic thrust and parry by Jesus in this discussion to expose what is really going on. This is outlined above, but be sure to draw attention to the moves Jesus makes and make it clear to your listeners—what is the answer to Jesus' opponents' question? What is the answer to Jesus' question? Why does Jesus refuse to answer their original question? All of this strategic discussion moves the story forward. And, the beautiful thing about it is that although it never actually says so, this passage *screams out* that Jesus has the authority of God! That is how gospels work.

11
Matthew 26:26–29
Lord's Supper

This familiar passage is about Jesus explaining the significance of his death on the cross *before* it occurs. The context is one in which he is celebrating the Passover with his disciples (Matt 26:17). This was a festival celebrated first in Egypt, where the enslaved Israelites sacrificed a lamb, spread its blood on the doorposts and lintels of their home. They roasted the animal and ate it; what remained uneaten was to be burned as a sacrifice (Exod 12). They were to eat it with sandals on their feet and a staff in their hand to indicate the haste with which they will depart Egypt (Exod 12:11). The Lord then went through Egypt and killed the firstborn of every household, but those with the blood on the doorposts and lintels were passed over by this plague (Exod 12:12–13). Here Jesus anticipates his own death; his body is not *yet* broken, yet he symbolically breaks the bread, which is his body, and gives it to his disciples (Matt 26:26). His blood is not *yet* shed, yet he symbolically pours the wine, which is his blood, and gives that too to his disciples (Matt 26:27–28). But this is blood *of the covenant* that is poured out *for the forgiveness of sins* (v. 28). That is the very heart of what is soon to occur at his crucifixion, after which he will drink anew with his disciples in his Father's kingdom (v. 29).

 26a Ἐσθιόντων δὲ αὐτῶν λαβὼν ὁ Ἰησοῦς ἄρτον
  Lit. While eating but of them taking the Jesus bread
  And as they were eating, Jesus, taking bread

MATTHEW 26:26–29

Ἐσθιόντων while eating
ptcp: pres act ptcp gen pl masc ἐσθίω "of (those) eating"

δὲ and
conj: δέ "but/now/and"

αὐτῶν of them
pers pron: gen pl masc αὐτός "of them"

λαβὼν taking
ptcp: aor act ptcp nom sg masc λαμβάνω "(he) having taken/received"

ὁ the
article: nom sg masc ὁ "the"

Ἰησοῦς Jesus
noun: nom sg masc Ἰησοῦς "Jesus"

ἄρτον bread
noun: acc sg masc ἄρτος "a bread/loaf"

Explanation. Ἐσθιόντων . . . αὐτῶν is a genitive absolute. The "Last Supper" was not itself a meal, but occurred *during* a meal.

ἄρτον is the direct object of the participle λαβών. It is also the implied direct object of ἔκλασεν, δούς, λάβετε and φάγετε.

26b καὶ εὐλογήσας ἔκλασεν

Lit. And having blessed he broke

and having blessed (it), broke (it)

καὶ and
conj: καί "and"

εὐλογήσας having blessed
ptcp: aor act ptcp nom sg masc εὐλογέω "(he) having blessed"

ἔκλασεν he broke
verb: aor act ind 3rd sg κλάω "he/she/it broke (bread)"

Explanation. Both the participle εὐλογήσας and the verb ἔκλασεν imply a direct object. The blessing may be directed to God or the bread. The object of ἔκλασεν is an implied ἄρτον ("bread"). The blessings is likely an equivalent of saying grace before a meal.

26c καὶ δοὺς τοῖς μαθηταῖς εἶπεν·
Lit. and giving to the disciples he said,
and, giving (it) to the disciples, said,

καὶ and
conj: καί "and"

δοὺς giving
ptcp: aor act ptcp nom sg masc δίδωμι "(he) having given"

τοῖς to the
article: dat pl masc ὁ "to the (ones)"

μαθηταῖς disciples
noun: dat pl masc μαθητής "to disciples"

εἶπεν he said
verb: aor act ind 3rd sg λέγω "he/she/it said"

Explanation. The participle δούς implies a direct object, αὐτόν, in reference to the bread (ἄρτον).

The indirect object is τοῖς μαθηταῖς, the bread is given "to the disciples."

26d λάβετε φάγετε,
Lit. Take eat,
"Take, eat,

λάβετε	take
verb:	aor act imv 2nd pl λαμβάνω "begin (you [pl]) to take/receive"

φάγετε	eat
verb:	aor act imv 2nd pl ἐσθίω "begin (you [pl]) to eat"

Explanation. Both verbs are imperative second plurals, directed to the disciples.

26e τοῦτό ἐστιν τὸ σῶμά μου.
Lit. this is the body of me."
this is my body."

τοῦτό	this
dem pron: nom sg neut οὗτος "this"	

ἐστιν	is
verb:	pres act ind 3rd sg εἰμί "(he/she/it) is"

τὸ	the
article:	nom sg neut ὁ "the"

σῶμά	body
noun:	nom sg neut σῶμα "a body"

μου	of me/ my
pers pron: 1st gen sg ἐγώ "of me/my"	

Explanation. The antecedent of τοῦτό is the bread ἄρτον. Here it is the subject of ἐστιν.

27a καὶ λαβὼν ποτήριον καὶ εὐχαριστήσας
Lit. And taking a cup and giving thanks
And, taking a cup and giving thanks,

καὶ	and
conj:	καί "and"

λαβών	taking
ptcp:	aor act ptcp nom sg masc λαμβάνω "(he) having taken/received"

ποτήριον	cup
noun:	acc sg neut ποτήριον "a cup"

καὶ	and
conj:	καί "and"

εὐχαριστήσας	giving thanks
ptcp:	aor act ptcp nom sg masc εὐχαριστέω "(he) having given thanks"

Explanation. A tradition, attested in some rabbinic sources subsequent to the New Testament, claims that the Passover was celebrated with four cups, one for each promise made to Israel in Exodus (Exod 6:6–7). Some think this may be the third cup, the "cup of blessing" (cf. 1 Cor 10:16).

27b ἔδωκεν αὐτοῖς λέγων·

Lit. he gave to them saying

he gave (it) to them, saying,

ἔδωκεν	he gave
verb:	aor act ind 3rd sg δίδωμι "he/she/it gave"

αὐτοῖς	to them
pers pron:	dat pl masc αὐτός "to them"

λέγων	saying
ptcp:	pres act ptcp nom sg masc λέγω "(one) saying"

Explanation. The direct object of the verb ἔδωκεν is not stated, but is an implied "it" in reference to the bread. The indirect object is αὐτοῖς, "to them."

27c πίετε ἐξ αὐτοῦ πάντες,
Lit. *Drink of you all,*
"Drink from (it), all (of you),

πίετε	Drink
verb:	aor act imv 2nd pl πίνω "begin (you [pl]) to drink"

ἐξ	from/ out of
prep:	ἐκ "from/out of"

αὐτοῦ	of it
pers pron:	gen sg neut αὐτός "of him/it"

πάντες	all
adj:	nom pl masc πᾶς "all (ones)"

Explanation. The verb πίετε is a second person plural, meaning "you (pl) drink. The prepositional phrase ἐξ αὐτοῦ is an adverb, meaning to drink "from it." πάντες is a vocative verb, addressed to all those present.

28a τοῦτο γάρ ἐστιν τὸ αἷμά μου τῆς διαθήκης
Lit. *this for is the blood of me of the covenant*
for this is my blood of the covenant,

τοῦτο	this
dem pron: nom sg neut οὗτος "this"	

γάρ	for
conj:	γάρ "for/because"

ἐστιν   is
verb: pres act ind 3rd sg εἰμί "(he/she/it) is"

τό   the
article: nom sg neut ὁ "the"

αἷμά   blood
noun: nom sg neut αἷμα "a blood"

μου   of me/ my
pers pron: 1st gen sg ἐγώ "of me/my"

τῆς   the
article: gen sg fem ὁ "of the"

διαθήκης of covenant
noun: gen sg fem διαθήκη "of a covenant"

Explanation. The γάρ is explanatory, indicating why they are all to drink from the cup. That reason is that "this" (τοῦτο)—in reference to the cup—is "my blood of the covenant" (τὸ αἷμά μου τῆς διαθήκης).

The phrase τὸ αἷμά μου τῆς διαθήκης derives directly from the LXX of Exod 24:8. Here Moses receives the "Book of the Covenant" and reads it to the people. They respond, "We will do everything the LORD has said; we will obey" (Exod 24:7 NIV). This is followed by an act of covenant ratification. Moses takes blood, sprinkles it on the people, and declares, "This is the blood of the covenant that the LORD has made with you in accordance with all these words" (Exod 24:8 NIV). Jesus is here instituting the new covenant (Jer 31:31; cf. Luke 22:20; 1 Cor 11:25; Heb 8:6, 8) of which Christ is the mediator (Heb 9:15; 12:24) and Paul is a minister (2 Cor 3:6).

The placement of τοῦτο is emphatic.

28b τὸ περὶ πολλῶν ἐκχυννόμενον
Lit. the which many is poured out
which is poured out for many,

τὸ	the
article:	nom sg neut ὁ "the"

περὶ	concerning/ for
prep:	περί "concerning/around"

πολλῶν	many
adj:	gen pl masc πολύς "of many (ones)"

ἐκχυννόμενον	being poured out
ptcp:	pres pass ptcp nom sg neut ἐκχέω "(one) being poured out"

Explanation. The definite article τό belongs with the present participle ἐκχυννόμενον, literally "the one being poured out." The prepositional phrase περί πολλῶν describes the participle.

ἐκχυννόμενον is from the verb ἐκχέω, a verb commonly used in the LXX for pouring sacrificial blood (Exod 29:12; Lev 4:7, 18, 25, 30).

The phrase περί πολλῶν may have been influenced by the Isaianic account of the suffering servant (Isa 53:1–12, esp. vv. 4, 10). There the servant takes up "our pain" and "our suffering" (Isa 53:4), being pierced for "our transgressions" and crushed for "our iniquities" (53:5). The punishment that was on him brought "us peace" and "we are healed" by his wounds (53:5). Our iniquity is laid upon him (53:6). In his sufferings he bears the iniquities of others, "will justify many" (53:11), and "bore the sin of many" (53:12).

28c εἰς ἄφεσιν ἁμαρτιῶν.
Lit. for forgiveness of sins.
for the forgiveness of sins.

εἰς   into / for
prep: εἰς "into/for"

ἄφεσιν   remission/ forgiveness
noun: acc sg fem ἄφεσις "remission/release"

ἁμαρτιῶν of sins
noun: gen pl fem ἁμαρτία "of sins"

Explanation. εἰς ἄφεσιν indicates purpose.

εἰς ἄφεσιν ἁμαρτιῶν occurs at the baptism scene in both Mark (Mark 1:4) and Luke (Luke 3:3; cf. Acts 2:38).

Here is the Matthean outcome of the one who will save his people from their sins (1:21), suffer at the hands of the wicked to the point of death and be raised again (Matt 16), and offering his life as a ransom for many (Matt 20:28). He will accomplish the forgiveness of sins.

29a λέγω δὲ ὑμῖν,

Lit. I say but to you (pl),

And I say to you,

λέγω   I say
verb: pres act ind 1st sg λέγω "(I) say"

δὲ   and
conj: δέ "but/now/and"

ὑμῖν   to you (pl)
pers pron: 2nd dat pl σύ "to you (pl)"

29b οὐ μὴ πίω ἀπ' ἄρτι ἐκ τούτου τοῦ γενήματος τῆς ἀμπέλου

Lit. no not I will drink from now from this of fruit of the vine

by no means will I drink from now from this fruit of the vine

MATTHEW 26:26–29

οὐ   not
neg particle: οὐ "no/not"

μὴ   not
neg particle: μή "no/not (stop)"

πίω   I drink/ I should drink
verb: aor act subj 1st sg πίνω "I should begin to drink"

ἀπ'   from
prep: ἀπό "(away) from"

ἄρτι   now
adv: ἄρτι "just now"

ἐκ   from
prep: ἐκ "from/out of"

τούτου   this
dem pron: gen sg neut οὗτος "of this"

τοῦ   the
article: gen sg neut ὁ "of the"

γενήματος   fruit
noun: gen sg neut γένημα "of a crop/fruit"

τῆς   the
article: gen sg fem ὁ "of the"

ἀμπέλου   of vine
noun: gen sg fem ἄμπελος "of a vine"

Explanation. οὐ μή is a double-negative, which in Greek compounds the negation, "by no means."

ἀπ' ἄρτι is a contraction from ἀπό ἄρτι called "elision" used to aid pronunciation. Literally it means "from now" and idiomatically in English "from now on." The termination point (ἕως . . .) occurs in 29c.

29c ἕως τῆς ἡμέρας ἐκείνης ὅταν αὐτὸ πίνω μεθ' ὑμῶν καινὸν ἐν τῇ βασιλείᾳ τοῦ πατρός μου.
Lit. until of the day that when it I drink with of you new in to the kingdom of father my."
until that day when I drink it with you, new, in the kingdom of my Father."

ἕως	until
adv:	ἕως "until/while"
τῆς	the
article:	gen sg fem ὁ "of the"
ἡμέρας	day
noun:	gen sg fem ἡμέρα "of a day"
ἐκείνης	that
dem pron:	gen sg fem ἐκεῖνος "of that"
ὅταν	when
conj:	ὅταν "when/whenever"
αὐτὸ	it
pers pron:	acc sg neut αὐτός "it"
πίνω	I drink/ I may drink
verb:	pres act subj 1st sg πίνω "(I) should drink"
μεθ'	with
prep:	μετά "with/after"
ὑμῶν	you (pl)
pers pron:	2nd gen pl σύ "of you (pl)"

MATTHEW 26:26–29

καινὸν   new
adj: acc sg neut καινός "new quality"

ἐν   in
prep: ἐν "in/by/with"

τῇ   the
article: dat sg fem ὁ "to the"

βασιλείᾳ   kingdom
noun: dat sg fem βασιλεία "to a kingdom"

τοῦ   of the
article: gen sg masc ὁ "of the"

πατρός   father
noun: gen sg masc πατήρ "of a father"

μου   of me/ my
pers pron: 1st gen sg ἐγώ "of me/my"

Explanation: μεθ' ὑμῶν is a contraction from μετά ὑμῶν called "elision," used to aid pronunciation.

The word καινόν is an adjective that functions here as an adverb.

Preaching the Text

1. **Main idea:** The New Covenant in Jesus
2. **Text to Sermon:**
   a. This familiar passage is rich in profound symbolism. The bread is Jesus' body, the wine his blood—both distributed freely to those who receive it. But Jesus' exhortation explains that the wine is not just his blood, but his blood of the covenant (τὸ αἷμά μου τῆς διαθήκης, Matt 26:28).

   b. This language recalls the activities of Moses *after* the giving of the Ten Commandments. It is a covenant ratification process in which "Moses took the blood and dashed it on the people, and said, "See the blood of the covenant (τὸ αἷμα τῆς διαθήκης; דַם־הַבְּרִית) that the LORD has made with you in accordance with all these words" (Exod 24:8 NRSV). The difference from the OT context is small but profound: the blood is *Jesus'* blood - τὸ αἷμά μου. This is blood of the "New Covenant" which comes not from sacrificial animals but from the Son of God (see Jer 31:31).

   c. The Apostle Paul, writing his first letter to the Corinthians perhaps twenty years earlier than Matthew, recounts that in this setting Jesus announces "the new covenant in my blood" (1 Cor 11:25 NRSV).

   d. Another important statement included here is the purpose of the blood being poured out: εἰς ἄφεσιν ἁμαρτιῶν–for the remission of sins (Matt 26:28). Mark and Luke both place this phrase at John's baptism (Mark 1:4; Luke 3:3). The phrase is found elsewhere in Luke's record of Jesus' teaching toward the end of his gospel: "Thus it is written, that the Messiah is to suffer and to rise from the dead on the third day, and that repentance and forgiveness of sins is to be proclaimed in his name to all nations, beginning from Jerusalem" (Luke 24:46-47 NRSV; cf. also Acts 2:38).

   e. Finally, in v. 29, Jesus anticipates that he will indeed drink of the fruit of the vine again, but not until he does so *with his disciples* in his Father's kingdom.

3. **Tip for Preaching:** This passage is very familiar to most people in our churches, but makes most sense theologically when read in light of

the Old Testament passages cited above, both Exodus 24 and Jeremiah 31. So, it is worth taking some time to bring our congregations back to those contexts in the OT. It is also worth taking some time to explain how Paul expounds on this topic of the New Covenant in 1 Cor 11:25, reminding our congregations that this scene is what Paul is talking about and Paul, some years after the Lord's Supper, but before Matthew wrote his account, is explaining for his own readers, more explicitly what its significance is for us as Christians.

12
Mathew 27:32–50

(Mostly) True Accusations and Their Effects: The Death of Jesus

Most of us know the unsettling feeling of a *false* accusation; we get accused of doing something we really did not do. Jesus, however, was accused of something of which he really was "guilty." The center of this passage is the charge and the accusations against Jesus which come at him and the reader with rapid-fire effect. This passage is the climax of the entire gospel. Jesus has been discussing his suffering and death since he was first recognized by his disciples as "the Messiah, the Son of the living God" (Matt 16:16 NRSV). Indeed, being killed is one of the defining facets of Jesus' messianic mission (Matt 16:21), despite the confusion this creates for his disciples (Matt 16:22). Yet what was previously mentioned briefly, albeit strategically, now becomes center-stage (Matt 27:32–50). The evangelist takes readers through the slow and deliberate processes of the appearance of Simon of Cyrene to the arrival at Golgotha (27:32–33). Surprisingly, Matthew does not describe the crucifixion in any detail. Instead, he mentions the crucifixion as a temporal indicator of when those keeping watch cast lots (27:34–36). Then comes the barrage of accusations, first with a placard above his head: "This is Jesus, the King of the Jews" (Matt 27:37), then the description of his punishment with criminals (v. 28) followed by the disparaging comments of passers-by. Crucifixion was a public spectacle, used by the Romans as a crime deterrent. So Jesus, like others crucified by the Romans in antiquity, would have been hung on his cross alongside a major thoroughfare. So the deriding comments are hurled at him, chiding him for claiming to destroy the temple and rebuild it in three days, a clear perversion of the temple as his body (not found in Matthew). They exhort him to save himself, and chide him for claiming to save others (vv. 40, 42). Reflecting the precise words of the devil, they tell him to come down of the cross "if you are the son of God" (27:40). The chief priests, scribes, and elders also mock him, and also exhort him to come down of the cross (vv. 42–43). Even the criminals mock him (v. 44). Following the human judgment of condemnation, God speaks with utter darkness (v. 45) and Jesus is forsaken by his God (v. 46). But here too the bystanders misunderstand (vv. 47–49) before Jesus at last dies (v. 50). He dies the death of a criminal based on accusations that are true, and it is by not succumbing to these last-ditch efforts by the devil—albeit not personally—that Jesus displays the true character of the God whose son He is.

32a Ἐξερχόμενοι δὲ εὗρον ἄνθρωπον Κυρηναῖον ὀνόματι Σίμωνα·
Lit. But going out they found a person Cyrenian to name Simon;
And as they were going out, they found a man, a Cyrenian—by name Simon;

Ἐξερχόμενοι   going out
ptcp: pres mid/pass ptcp nom pl masc ἐξέρχομαι "(those) going/coming out"

δὲ   and
conj: δέ "but/now/and"

εὗρον   they found
verb: aor act ind 3rd pl εὑρίσκω "they found"

ἄνθρωπον   person/ man
noun: acc sg masc ἄνθρωπος "a man/person"

Κυρηναῖον   Cyrenian
noun: acc sg masc Κυρηναῖος "a Cyrenian"

ὀνόματι   to name/ by name
noun: dat sg neut ὄνομα "to a name"

Σίμωνα   Simon
noun: acc sg masc Σίμων "Simon"

Explanation. ἄνθρωπος is typically a general term for "person" or "human." Here the reference is to a particular male, so it is translated "man."

Matthew commonly uses an adverbial participle ahead of the main verb which it modifies, here Ἐξερχόμενοι and εὗρον.

ἄνθρωπον and Κυρηναῖον are in apposition.

The ὀνόματι is a dative of reference.

Σίμωνα is an accusative singular in apposition with ἄνθρωπον.

32b τοῦτον ἠγγάρευσαν ἵνα ἄρῃ τὸν σταυρὸν αὐτοῦ.
Lit. this they forced that he might carry the cross of him.
this (one) they forced in order that he should carry his cross.

τοῦτον   this
dem pron: acc sg masc οὗτος "this"

ἠγγάρευσαν   they forced/ pressed into service
verb: aor act ind 3rd pl ἀγγαρεύω "they forced/compelled"

ἵνα   that/ in order that
conj: ἵνα "in order that"

ἄρῃ   he should carry
verb: aor act subj 3rd sg αἴρω "he/she/it should begin to take away/lift up"

τὸν   the
article: acc sg masc ὁ "the"

σταυρὸν   cross
noun: acc sg masc σταυρός "a cross"

MATHEW 27:32-50

αὐτοῦ   of him/ his
pers pron: gen sg masc αὐτός "of him/it"

Explanation. τοῦτον is a demonstrative pronoun, the antecedent of which is Simon.

The αὐτοῦ refers to Jesus; the cross intended for him.

Matthew's ἵνα plus subjunctive ἄρῃ indicates purpose.

33a Καὶ ἐλθόντες εἰς τόπον λεγόμενον Γολγοθά,
Lit. And having come to the place called Golgotha,
And having come to the place called Golgotha

Καὶ   and
conj: καί "and"

ἐλθόντες   having come/
ptcp: aor act ptcp nom pl masc ἔρχομαι "(the men) having come"

εἰς   into/ to
prep: εἰς "into/for"

τόπον   place/ location
noun: acc sg masc τόπος "a place"

λεγόμενον   being called
ptcp: pres pass ptcp acc sg masc λέγω "(he) being said"

Γολγοθά   Golgotha
prop noun: indecl Γολγοθᾶ "Golgotha"

Explanation. Matthew commonly uses an adverbial participle ahead of the main verb which it modifies, here ἐλθόντες and λεγόμενον.

Γολγοθά is presumably a Hebrew or Aramaic word transliterated here, since its meaning is explained below.

AN EXPOSITOR'S HANDBOOK TO THE GREEK TEXT OF MATTHEW

33b ὅ ἐστιν Κρανίου Τόπος λεγόμενος,
Lit. which is of Skull Place called,
(which is called Skull Place),

ὅ	which
rel pron:	nom sg neut ὅς "which"

ἐστιν	is
verb:	pres act ind 3rd sg εἰμί "(he/she/it) is"

Κρανίου	of skull
noun:	gen sg neut κρανίον "of a skull"

Τόπος	place
noun:	nom sg masc τόπος "a place"

λεγόμενος	being said/ when said
ptcp:	pres pass ptcp nom sg masc λέγω "(one) being said"

Explanation. ὅ ἐστιν ... λεγόμενος is literally, "which is ... when said," meaning translated into Greek from the transliterated word Γολγοθά.

ὅ is a relative pronoun and subject of the verb ἐστιν.

34a ἔδωκαν αὐτῷ πιεῖν οἶνον μετὰ χολῆς μεμιγμένον·
Lit. they gave to him to drink wine with gall mixed;
they gave to him wine mixed with gall to drink;

ἔδωκαν	they gave
verb:	aor act ind 3rd pl δίδωμι "they gave"

αὐτῷ	to him
pers pron: dat sg masc αὐτός "to him"	

πιεῖν	to drink
verb:	aor act inf πίνω "to begin to drink"

οἶνον	wine
noun:	acc sg masc οἶνος "a wine"

μετὰ	with
prep:	μετά "with/after"

χολῆς	gall
noun:	gen sg fem χολή "of gall"

μεμιγμένον	having been mixed
ptcp:	perf pass ptcp acc sg masc μίγνυμι "(one) having been mingled/mixed"

Explanation. ἔδωκαν is the verb with πιεῖν being the complementary infinitive describing the verb.

The word αὐτῷ is in the dative case and is the indirect object, indicating to whom it was given.

The word οἶνον is in the accusative case, indicating it is what is given.

μετά χολῆς μεμιγμένον is a prepositional phrase describing the οἶνον.

34b καὶ γευσάμενος οὐκ ἠθέλησεν πιεῖν.
Lit. and having tasted not willing to drink.
and having tasted (it), he did not want to drink (it).

καὶ	and
conj:	καί "and"

γευσάμενος	having tasted/ when he tasted
ptcp:	aor mid ptcp nom sg masc γεύομαι "(he) having (for himself) tasted"

οὐκ	not
neg particle:	οὐ "no/not"

ἠθέλησεν he willed/ wanted/ desired
verb: aor act ind 3rd sg θέλω "he/she/it willed"

πιεῖν to drink
verb: aor act inf πίνω "to begin to drink"

Explanation. γευσάμενος is likely temporal, indicating when he tasted or upon tasting. The point is that the tasting is what lead to his refusal to drink.

35 Σταυρώσαντες δὲ αὐτὸν διεμερίσαντο τὰ ἱμάτια αὐτοῦ βάλλοντες κλῆρον,
Lit. *Having crucified but him they distributed the garments of him casting a lot,*
And when they had crucified him, they distributed his garments by casting a lot,

Σταυρώσαντες having crucified/ when they crucified
ptcp: aor act ptcp nom pl masc σταυρόω "(they) having crucified"

δὲ and/ but
conj: δέ "but/now/and"

αὐτὸν him
pers pron: acc sg masc αὐτός "him"

διεμερίσαντο the distributed
verb: aor mid ind 3rd pl διαμερίζω "(they themselves) distributed/delivered"

τὰ the
article: acc pl neut ὁ "the (ones)"

ἱμάτια garments
noun: acc pl neut ἱμάτιον "(outer) garments"

278

MATHEW 27:32-50

αὐτοῦ   of him/ his
pers pron: gen sg masc αὐτός "of him/it"

βάλλοντες   by throwing/ by casting
ptcp: pres act ptcp nom pl masc βάλλω "(those) throwing/casting"

κλῆρον   a lot
noun: acc sg masc κλῆρος "a lot/allotted portion"

Explanation. The participle σταυρώσαντες is a temporal participle, subordinate to the main verb διεμερίσαντο.

They were distributing Jesus' garments by means of βάλλοντες κλῆρον, literally "throwing a lot" or "casting lots."

The passage is influenced by LXX Ps 21:19: "they divided my clothes among themselves, and for my clothing they cast lots" (NETS; διεμερίσαντο τὰ ἱμάτιά μου ἑαυτοῖς καὶ ἐπὶ τὸν ἱματισμόν μου ἔβαλον κλῆρον).

36 καὶ καθήμενοι ἐτήρουν αὐτὸν ἐκεῖ.
Lit. and sitting they were observing him there.
and, as they were sitting down, they were keeping watch over him there.

καὶ   and
conj: καί "and"

καθήμενοι   sitting
ptcp: pres mid/pass ptcp nom pl masc κάθημαι "(those) sitting"

ἐτήρουν   they were observing/ keeping watch over
verb: impf act ind 3rd pl τηρέω "(they) continually kept/observed"

αὐτὸν   him
pers pron: acc sg masc αὐτός "him"

ἐκεῖ   there
adv: ἐκεῖ "there"

Explanation. ἐτήρουν is in the imperfect indicating a continuous past action.

37a Καὶ ἐπέθηκαν ἐπάνω τῆς κεφαλῆς αὐτοῦ τὴν αἰτίαν αὐτοῦ γεγραμμένην·
Lit. and they placed above of the head of him the chart of him having been written:
And they placed over his head the written charge against him:

Καὶ   and
conj: καί "and"

ἐπέθηκαν   they placed on/ placed upon/ placed over
verb: aor act ind 3rd pl ἐπιτίθημι "they placed upon"

ἐπάνω   above
adv: ἐπάνω "above"

τῆς   the
article: gen sg fem ὁ "of the"

κεφαλῆς   of head
noun: gen sg fem κεφαλή "of a head"

αὐτοῦ   of him/ his
pers pron: gen sg masc αὐτός "of him/it"

τὴν   the
article: acc sg fem ὁ "the"

αἰτίαν   charge/ accusation
noun: acc sg fem αἰτία "a charge/cause"

αὐτοῦ   of him/ his/ against him
pers pron: gen sg masc αὐτός "of him/it"

γεγραμμένην   having been written
ptcp: perf pass ptcp acc sg fem γράφω "(one) having been written"

Explanation. ἐπιτίθημι is a compound verb from ἐπί, "on, upon" and τίθημι, "I put, I place" to form ἐπιτίθημι, "I place upon."

αἰτία is the legal charge against Jesus.

37b οὗτός ἐστιν Ἰησοῦς ὁ βασιλεὺς τῶν Ἰουδαίων.
Lit. "This is Jesus the king of the Jews."
"This is Jesus, the king of the Jews."

οὗτός   this
dem pron: nom sg masc οὗτος "this"

ἐστιν   is
verb: pres act ind 3rd sg εἰμί "(he/she/it) is"

Ἰησοῦς   Jesus
noun: nom sg masc Ἰησοῦς "Jesus"

ὁ   the
article: nom sg masc ὁ "the"

βασιλεὺς   king
noun: nom sg masc βασιλεύς "a king"

τῶν   the
article: gen pl masc ὁ "of the (ones)"

Ἰουδαίων of Jews
adj: gen pl masc Ἰουδαῖος "of Jewish (ones)"

Explanation. Ironically, the charge against Jesus is true (Matt 2:2; 27:11).

38a Τότε σταυροῦνται σὺν αὐτῷ δύο λῃσταί,
Lit. Then they crucified with him two robbers,
At that time two robbers were crucified with him,

Τότε then/ at that time
adv: τότε "then"

σταυροῦνται they were crucified
verb: pres pass ind 3rd pl σταυρόω "(they) are crucified"

σὺν with/ together with
prep: σύν "with"

αὐτῷ to him/ him
pers pron: dat sg masc αὐτός "to him"

δύο two
adj: num δύο "two"

λῃσταί robbers
noun: nom pl masc λῃστής "robbers"

Explanation. σταυροῦνται is a historical present.

λῃσταί is probably robbers or, more generally, criminals. There is no indication what their crimes were, but brigands were common in and around Judea and Galilee dating back to the time of Herod the Great and since. These were groups who banded together to rob caravans of traders and seeking refuge in small towns and villages, bringing Roman wrath down hard on entire communities. Perhaps these people were from that class of criminal, but the word itself only raises the possibility, and Matthew provides us with no further information.

38b εἷς ἐκ δεξιῶν καὶ εἷς ἐξ εὐωνύμων.
Lit. one of right and one of left.
one at his right and one at his left.

εἷς	one
adj:	nom sg masc εἷς "one"
ἐκ	from/ of
prep:	ἐκ "from/out of"
δεξιῶν	of right
adj:	gen pl masc δεξιός "of right (hands/sides)"
καὶ	and
conj:	καί "and"
εἷς	one
adj:	nom sg masc εἷς "one"
ἐξ	from/ of
prep:	ἐκ "from/out of"
εὐωνύμων	of left
adj:	gen pl masc εὐώνυμος "of left (hands/sides)"

Explanation. εἷς is an adjective meaning "one," not to be confused with the preposition εἰς, "in" or "into."

39-40a Οἱ δὲ παραπορευόμενοι ἐβλασφήμουν αὐτὸν κινοῦντες τὰς κεφαλὰς αὐτῶν καὶ λέγοντες·

Lit. The's but passing by blasphemed him shaking the's heads of them and saying

And the ones passing by were blaspheming him, shaking their heads and saying,

Οἱ   The
article: nom pl masc ὁ "the (ones)"

δὲ   and/ but
conj: δέ "but/now"

παραπορευόμενοι   ones passing by
ptcp: pres mid/pass ptcp nom pl masc παραπορεύομαι "(those) passing by"

ἐβλασφήμουν   were blaspheming
verb: impf act ind 3rd pl βλασφημέω "(they) continually blasphemed"

αὐτὸν   him
pers pron: acc sg masc αὐτός "him"

κινοῦντες   moving/ shaking
ptcp: pres act ptcp nom pl masc κινέω "(those) moving/removing"

τὰς   the
article: acc pl fem ὁ "the (ones)"

κεφαλὰς   heads
noun: acc pl fem κεφαλή "heads"

αὐτῶν   of them/ their
pers pron: gen pl masc αὐτός "of them"

καὶ   and
conj: καί "and"

λέγοντες   saying
ptcp: pres act ptcp nom pl masc λέγω "(those) saying"

Explanation. παραπορεύομαι is a compound verb from παρα, "beside" and πορεύομαι, "I go" to form παραπορεύομαι, "I go by" or "I pass by."

Crucifixion by the Romans was a public event, a crime-deterrent technique by which they warn enemies of the state what can happen to them should they be guilty of a crime like that of these crucified criminals.

κινοῦντες τὰς κεφαλὰς αὐτῶν, literally "moving their heads" means "shaking their heads" in disapproval.

ἐβλασφήμουν is an imperfect verb meaning continuous past action. The root βλασφημέω often means to utter contemptuous words to God. Here, though, the passers-by do not recognize Jesus as God but presume he is a fraud, so the sense is rather to utter reproach and degrading words against Jesus. Ironically, their mere contempt is in reality blasphemy, since Jesus is God.

40b ὁ καταλύων τὸν ναὸν

Lit. The destroying the temple

The one destroying the temple

ὁ   the
article: nom sg masc ὁ "the"

καταλύων   one destroying
ptcp: pres act ptcp nom sg masc καταλύω "(one) destroying/being at naught"

τὸν   the
article: acc sg masc ὁ "the"

ναὸν   temple
noun: acc sg masc ναός "a sanctuary"

Explanation. The definite article ὁ belongs to both participles, καταλύων and οἰκοδομῶν (v. 40c), indicating that the one destroying and the one building are the same individual.

This part of the charge comes from the accusation against Jesus in Matt 26:61.

40c καὶ ἐν τρισὶν ἡμέραις οἰκοδομῶν,
Lit. and in three days building,
and in three days building (it again),

καὶ   and
conj: καί "and"

ἐν   in
prep: ἐν "in/by/with"

τρισὶν   three
adj: dat pl fem τρεῖς "to three"

ἡμέραις   days
noun: dat pl fem ἡμέρα "to days"

οἰκοδομῶν   building
ptcp: pres act ptcp nom sg masc οἰκοδομέω "(one) building"

Explanation. In Matthew's gospel Jesus predicates he will be raised on the third day three times (Matt 16:21; 17:23; 20:19).

40d σῶσον σεαυτόν,
Lit. save yourself,
save yourself!

σῶσον	you (sg) save
verb:	aor act imv 2nd sg σῴζω "begin (you) to save/deliver"

σεαυτόν	yourself (sg)
reflexive pron: 2nd acc sg masc σεαυτοῦ "yourself"	

Explanation. The passers-by exhort Jesus to save himself (σῶσον σεαυτόν). It is by *not* saving himself from the crucifixion Jesus is *saving his people* from their sins (Matt 1:21).

40e εἰ υἱὸς εἶ τοῦ θεοῦ,
Lit. *if son you are of God,*
If you are God's Son,

εἰ	If
conditional: εἰ "if"	

υἱὸς	son
noun:	nom sg masc υἱός "a son"

εἶ	you (sg) are
verb:	pres act ind 2nd sg εἰμί "(you) are"

τοῦ	the
article:	gen sg masc ὁ "of the"

θεοῦ	of God
noun:	gen sg masc θεός "of God/a god"

Explanation. The conditional εἰ υἱὸς εἶ τοῦ θεοῦ is exactly the same charge by the devil in the Temptation (Matt 4:3, 6). No mention is made here of the devil or Satan, but his influence is surely present.

40f καὶ κατάβηθι ἀπὸ τοῦ σταυροῦ.
Lit. *and come down from of the cross."*
and come down from the cross."

καί	and	
conj:	καί "and"	

κατάβηθι	you (sg) get down/ come down/ descend	
verb:	aor act imv 2nd sg καταβαίνω "begin (you) to go down/descend"	

ἀπὸ	from	
prep:	ἀπό "(away) from"	

τοῦ	the	
article:	gen sg masc ὁ "of the"	

σταυροῦ	of cross	
noun:	gen sg masc σταυρός "of a cross"	

Explanation. The means by which Jesus is exhorted to save himself is by descending from the cross (κατάβηθι ἀπὸ τοῦ σταυροῦ).

41 ὁμοίως καὶ οἱ ἀρχιερεῖς ἐμπαίζοντες μετὰ τῶν γραμματέων καὶ πρεσβυτέρων ἔλεγον·

Lit. *Likewise also the chief priests mocking with the scribes and elders were saying,*

Likewise also the chief priests, mocking along with the scribes and elders, were saying,

ὁμοίως	likewise/ in this way/ similarly	
adv:	ὁμοίως "similarly/likewise"	

καί	and/ also	
conj:	καί "and/also"	

οἱ	the	
article:	nom pl masc ὁ "the (ones)"	

ἀρχιερεῖς   chief priests
noun: nom pl masc ἀρχιερεύς "high/chief priests"

ἐμπαίζοντες   were mocking/ were ridiculing
ptcp: pres act ptcp nom pl masc ἐμπαίζω "(those) ridiculing/mocking"

μετὰ   with
prep: μετά "with/after"

τῶν   the
article: gen pl masc ὁ "of the (ones)"

γραμματέων   of scribes
noun: gen pl masc γραμματεύς "of scribes"

καὶ   and
conj: καί "and"

πρεσβυτέρων   of elders
adj: gen pl masc πρεσβύτερος "of eldest (ones)"

ἔλεγον   they were saying
verb: impf act ind 3rd pl λέγω "(they) continually said"

Explanation. ὁμοίως καί indicates the chief priests, scribes and elders participated in similar disparagement of Jesus.

The participle ἐμπαίζοντες is a present participle connoting continuous action, and in a past setting suggests a historical present translated like an imperfect verb, "were mocking." This is confirmed by the imperfect verb ἔλεγον.

The chief priests (ἀρχιερεύς) in Matthew are almost always paired with another group, notably the "scribes" (γραμματεῖς) but also the elders (πρεσβύτεροι) and the Pharisees.

Matthew's γραμματεύς is unclear. In the LXX the term γραμματεύς is used for a figure responsible for written records (e.g., Exod 5:6,

14, 15, 19; 2 Kgs 8:17). In the NT they likely had some sort of record-keeping responsibility. But they are not merely archivists but had an integral role in the composition of documents, including legal documents. But in Matthew the scribes are among the few, perhaps the only, opponents of Jesus who exhibit some hope for discipleship.

42a ἄλλους ἔσωσεν,

Lit. "Others he saved,

"He saved others,

ἄλλους	others
adj:	acc pl masc ἄλλος "other (ones)"

ἔσωσεν	he saved
verb:	aor act ind 3rd sg σῴζω "he/she/it saved/delivered"

Explanation. This begins the content of the mockery. The adjective ἄλλους is substantival, acting like a noun, and is placed at the head of the sentence for emphasis. *Others* he saved, but not himself (v. 42b).

42b ἑαυτὸν οὐ δύναται σῶσαι·

Lit. himself not he is able to save;

himself he is not able to save;

ἑαυτὸν himself
reflexive pron: 3rd acc sg masc ἑαυτοῦ "himself"

οὐ not
neg particle: οὐ "no/not"

δύναται	he is able
verb:	pres mid/pass ind 3rd sg δύναμαι "(he/she/it) is able"

σῶσαι   to save
verb: aor act inf σῴζω "to begin to save/deliver"

Explanation. Subject is an implied "he" (αὐτός), the verb is δύναται which is described by a complementary infinitive σῶσαι. The object is ἑαυτόν. The verb δύναται shows that it is the ability of Jesus that is in question.

The verb σῴζω can mean various things, including the salvation of people from their sins (Matt 1:21) and from final judgment (Matt 10:22; cf. 16:25; 19:25; 24:13, 22) as well as rescuing from a deadly peril (Matt 8:25; 14:30; 27:40, 42, 49) or a miraculous healing from a chronic illness (Matt 9:21, 22). The question here pertains to rescue from a deadly situation.

42c βασιλεὺς Ἰσραήλ ἐστιν,
Lit. king of Israel he is
he is the king of Israel,

βασιλεὺς   king
noun: nom sg masc βασιλεύς "a king"

Ἰσραήλ   Israel
proper noun: indecl Ἰσραήλ "Israel"

ἐστιν   is
verb: pres act ind 3rd sg εἰμί "(he/she/it) is"

Explanation. Ἰσραήλ is a proper noun transliterated from Hebrew, and will not change its form regardless of its case or number.

The chiding remark that Jesus is the king of Israel is true (cf. Matt 2:1, 2).

42d καταβάτω νῦν ἀπὸ τοῦ σταυροῦ
Lit. let him come down now from of the cross
let him come down now from the cross,

καταβάτω let him descend/ come down
verb: aor act imv 3rd sg καταβαίνω "let (him/her/it) begin to go down/descend"

νῦν now
adv: νῦν "now"

ἀπὸ from
prep: ἀπό "(away) from"

τοῦ the
article: gen sg masc ὁ "of the"

σταυροῦ of cross
noun: gen sg masc σταυρός "of a cross"

Explanation. This phrase is an implied conditional sentence, "if he comes down" (v. 42d) . . . "then we will believe" (v. 42e).

καταβάτω is a third person imperative, which is awkward in English and translates "let him come down." But the word "let" is not a permissive word, but a command, "he must come down" for us to believe in him (v. 42e).

The adverb νῦν describes the command to come down.

The prepositional ἀπό τοῦ σταυροῦ also describes the command to come down.

42e καὶ πιστεύσομεν ἐπ' αὐτόν.
Lit. and we will believe upon him.
and we will believe in him.

καὶ and
conj: καί "and"

πιστεύσομεν we will believe
verb: fut act ind 1st pl πιστεύω "(we) will believe"

ἐπ'   upon
prep: ἐπί "upon"

αὐτόν   him
pers pron: acc sg masc αὐτός "him"

Explanation. The future tense verb πιστεύσομεν indicates the timing in which they will believe upon him is future, but conditioned upon his descent from the cross (v. 42d).

ἐπ' αὐτόν is a contraction (elision) from ἐπί αὐτόν to aid in pronunciation.

43a πέποιθεν ἐπὶ τὸν θεόν,
Lit. he has trusted upon God,
he has trusted in God,

πέποιθεν he has trusted
verb: perf act ind 3rd sg πείθω "(he/she/it) has persuaded"

ἐπὶ   upon
prep: ἐπί "upon"

τὸν   the
article: acc sg masc ὁ "the"

θεόν   God
noun: acc sg masc θεός "God/god"

Explanation. πέποιθεν is a perfect active verb from πείθω, indicating a past action with present effects. This indicates that they recognized that Jesus has in the past been persuaded by or trusted in God, with the present effects that they anticipate God will rescue him (43b).

Jesus' opponents are prepared to believe ἐπ' αὐτόν ("in him"), knowing that Jesus has trusted ἐπί τὸν θεόν ("in God")

43b ῥυσάσθω νῦν εἰ θέλει αὐτόν·
Lit. let him deliver now if he desires him;
let him deliver him now if he wants him;

ῥυσάσθω	Let him deliver
verb:	aor mid imv 3rd sg ῥύομαι "let (him/her/it for oneself) begin to deliver"

νῦν	now
adv:	νῦν "now"

εἰ	if
conditional:	εἰ "if"

θέλει	he desires
verb:	pres act ind 3rd sg θέλω "(he/she/it) wills"

αὐτόν	him
pers pron:	acc sg masc αὐτός "him"

Explanation. The verb ῥυσάσθω is an imperative verb in the third person.

νῦν is an adverb demanding the activity of God, conditioned upon God's perspective toward Jesus (εἰ θέλει αὐτόν).

The language here reflects Ps 22:9 (LXX 21:9): ἤλπισεν ἐπὶ κύριον ῥυσάσθω αὐτόν σωσάτω αὐτόν ὅτι θέλει αὐτόν ("He hoped in the Lord; let him rescue him; let him save him, because he wants him," NETS, modified). θέλει, translated "he wants," renders the Hebrew חָפֵץ ("to delight") and so the sense here is best, "to take pleasure in." It may recall the voice from heaven at the baptism: "This is my Son, the Beloved, with whom I am well pleased (ἐν ᾧ εὐδόκησα)" (Matt 3:17 NRSV).

43c εἶπεν γὰρ ὅτι θεοῦ εἰμι υἱός.
Lit. he said for 'God I am son.'"
for he said, 'I am God's Son.'"

εἶπεν	he said
verb:	aor act ind 3rd sg λέγω "he/she/it said"

γάρ	for
conj:	γάρ "for/because"

ὅτι	that
conj:	ὅτι "because/that"

θεοῦ	of God
noun:	gen sg masc θεός "of God/a god"

εἰμί	I am
verb:	pres act ind 1st sg εἰμί "(I) am"

υἱός	son
noun:	nom sg masc υἱός "a son"

Explanation. Here Jesus' opponents reason that the rationale for appealing to God's delivery of him is based upon (γάρ) a claim that Jesus said (εἶπεν).

Matthew does not record Jesus explicitly saying θεοῦ εἰμί υἱός, but attributes the claim to Jesus' opponents. Of course, from Matthew's perspective it is surely true.

44 Τὸ δ' αὐτὸ καὶ οἱ λῃσταὶ οἱ συσταυρωθέντες σὺν αὐτῷ ὠνείδιζον αὐτόν.

Lit. the through it also the thieves the with-crucified with him were reviling him.

In the same way also the thieves who were crucified with him were reviling him.

Τὸ	the
article:	acc sg neut ὁ "the"

δ' but/ and
conj: δέ "but/now"

αὐτὸ it
pers pron: acc sg neut αὐτός "it"

καὶ and/ also
conj: καί "and"

οἱ the
article: nom pl masc ὁ "the (ones)"

λῃσταὶ robbers/ thieves
noun: nom pl masc λῃστής "robbers"

οἱ the
article: nom pl masc ὁ "the (ones)"

συσταυρωθέντες ones being crucified together with
ptcp: aor pass ptcp nom pl masc συσταυρόω "(those) having been crucified together"

σὺν with
prep: σύν "with"

αὐτῷ to him
pers pron: dat sg masc αὐτός "to him"

ὠνείδιζον they were insulting/ disparaging
verb: impf act ind 3rd pl ὀνειδίζω "(they) continually insulted/disparaged"

αὐτόν him
pers pron: acc sg masc αὐτός "him"

Explanation. δ' αὐτό is a contraction ("elision") from δέ αὐτό made to aid pronunciation.

τό ... αὐτό means "in the same way"

Even though the criminals (οἱ λῃσταί) were crucified with him (οἱ συσταυρωθέντες σὺν αὐτῷ) they were insulting and disparaging him (ὠνείδιζον αὐτόν). ὠνείδιζον is an imperfect verb connoting continuous past action.

45a Ἀπὸ δὲ ἕκτης ὥρας σκότος ἐγένετο ἐπὶ πᾶσαν τὴν γῆν
Lit. From but sixth hour darkness came upon all the land
Now from the sixth hour darkness came upon all the land

Ἀπὸ	from/ away from
prep:	ἀπό "(away) from"
δὲ	but/ and/ now
conj:	δέ "but/now"
ἕκτης	of sixth
adj:	gen sg fem ἕκτος "of a sixth"
ὥρας	of hour/ of an hour/ hour
noun:	gen sg fem ὥρα "of an hour"
σκότος	darkness
noun:	nom sg neut σκότος "darkness"
ἐγένετο	he/she/it came/ became/ occurred
verb:	aor mid ind 3rd sg γίνομαι "(one oneself) became/occurred"
ἐπὶ	upon
prep:	ἐπί "upon"
πᾶσαν	all
adj:	acc sg fem πᾶς "all"

τὴν	the
article:	acc sg fem ὁ "the"

γῆν	land
noun:	acc sg fem γῆ "earth/land"

Explanation. Ἀπό and ἕως mark the temporal ends of the timeframe.

Time reckoning in the Roman system designated ἕκτης ὥρας to correspond to noon and ὥρας ἐνάτης to three in the afternoon.

Darkness was sometimes associated with the Day of the Lord (e.g., Joel 2:2, 31; Zeph 1:15). It reminds readers of judgment upon Egypt when Pharaoh refused to release Israel (Exod 10:22).

The darkness ἐπὶ πᾶσαν τὴν γῆν likely refers to the land of Israel.

45b ἕως ὥρας ἐνάτης.
Lit. until hour ninth.
until the ninth hour.

ἕως	until
adv:	ἕως "until/while"

ὥρας	of hour/ of an hour/ hour
noun:	gen sg fem ὥρα "of an hour"

ἐνάτης	of ninth/ ninth
adj:	gen sg fem ἔνατος "of a ninth"

46a περὶ δὲ τὴν ἐνάτην ὥραν ἀνεβόησεν ὁ Ἰησοῦς φωνῇ μεγάλῃ λέγων·
Lit. about but the ninth hour cried out the Jesus to voice loud saying,
And about the ninth hour Jesus cried out with a loud voice, saying,

περὶ	concerning/ around
prep:	περί "concerning/around"

δέ   but/ and/ now
conj: δέ "but/now/and"

τὴν   the
article: acc sg fem ὁ "the"

ἐνάτην   ninth
adj: acc sg fem ἔνατος "ninth"

ὥραν   hour
noun: acc sg fem ὥρα "an hour"

ἀνεβόησεν   he, she, it cried out/ shouted out
verb: aor act ind 3rd sg ἀναβοάω "he/she/it shouted"

ὁ   the
article: nom sg masc ὁ "the"

Ἰησοῦς   Jesus
noun: nom sg masc Ἰησοῦς "Jesus"

φωνῇ   to, with a sound/ noise/ voice
noun: dat sg fem φωνή "to a voice/sound"

μεγάλῃ   to, with a great/ great
adj: dat sg fem μέγας "to a great"

λέγων   saying
ptcp: pres act ptcp nom sg masc λέγω "(one) saying"

Explanation. The verb in this sentence is ἐβόησεν. Since it is a third singular verb, it requires a nominative singular subject, which is ὁ Ἰησοῦς. The φωνῇ indicates the manner in which he cried out, "with a voice." This is described by the adjective μεγάλῃ, "great" or "loud."

46b ηλι ηλι λεμα σαβαχθανι;
Lit. "ēli lema sabachthani?"
"ēli lema sabachthani?"

ηλι   ēli
Aramaic ηλι or ἐλωί "ēli/my God"

λεμά   lema
Aramaic λεμά "lema" or λαμά "lama" "why?/ "for what reason?"

σαβαχθανεί   sabachthanei
Aramaic σαβαχθάνι "sabachthani/you have left me"

Explanation. There are no question marks in Greek. Editors of published editions of the Greek NT today use ";" to denote a question, as is natural to the context as well as the source from which this verse is drawn.

Here Jesus is speaking in Aramaic, quoting Ps 22:2, which in the LXX is Ps 21:2.

Greek manuscripts spell this various ways because it is an attempt by the author to render into Greek letters for his reader, what is written in a Semitic language, here Aramaic.

The Hebrew here is אֵלִי אֵלִי לָמָה עֲזַבְתָּנִי.

46c τοῦτ' ἔστιν· θεέ μου θεέ μου,
Lit. this is, God of me, God of me,
this is, "My God, my God,

τοῦτ'   this
dem pron: nom sg neut οὗτος "this"

ἔστιν   he, she, it is
verb: pres act ind 3rd sing εἰμί "(he/she/it) is"

θεέ   God!
noun: voc sg masc θεός "O God!"

μου   of me/ my
pers pron: 1st gen sg ἐγώ "of me/my"

θεέ   God!
noun: voc sg masc θεός "O God!"

μου   of me/ my
pers pron: 1st gen sg ἐγώ "of me/my"

Explanation. Here the evangelist translates for his readers. It differs from the Septuagint, which reads ὁ θεὸς ὁ θεός μου

τοῦτ' ἔστιν literally means "this is," here understood as an explanation of the meaning of the previous verse for Greek readers. Idiomatically, it could be rendered "which means."

θεέ is in the vocative case from the noun θεός. This means that Jesus, following the Psalmist, is speaking directly to God.

46d ἱνατί με ἐγκατέλιπες;

Lit. In order that what me you did forsake?
For what reason did you forsake me?

ἱνατί   for what reason
adv: ἱνατί "why? for what purpose? "

με   me
pers pron: 1st acc sg ἐγώ "me"

ἐγκατέλιπες   you (sg) forsook/ did forsake/ leave
verb: aor act ind 2nd sg ἐγκαταλείπω "you forsook/left"

Explanation. The LXX reads πρόσχες μοι.

47a τινὲς δὲ τῶν ἐκεῖ ἑστηκότων ἀκούσαντες ἔλεγον ὅτι

Lit. some ones but of there standing having heard began saying that,

And some of those who were standing there having heard, began saying that,

τινὲς	some (ones)

indef pron: nom pl masc τίς "some ones"

δὲ	but/ and/ now
conj:	δέ "but/now/and"

τῶν	of the
article:	gen pl masc ὁ "of the (ones)"

ἐκεῖ	there
adv:	ἐκεῖ "there"

ἑστηκότων	of the ones standing
ptcp:	perf act ptcp gen pl masc ἵστημι "of (those) having stood"

ἀκούσαντες	having heard
ptcp:	aor act ptcp nom pl masc ἀκούω "(they) having heard"

ἔλεγον	they were saying
verb:	impf act ind 3rd pl λέγω "(they) continually said"

ὅτι	that
conj:	ὅτι "because/that"

Explanation. ἔλεγον is an inceptive imperfect, meaning that they began saying something upon the occasion of hearing.

47b Ἡλίαν φωνεῖ οὗτος.

Lit. "Elijah he calls this."

"He is calling Elijah."

Ἠλίαν	Elijah
noun:	acc sg masc Ἠλίας "Elijah"
φωνεῖ	he is calling/ he calls
verb:	pres act ind 3rd sing φωνέω "(he/she/it) invites/calls"
οὗτος	this/ he
dem pron:	nom sg masc οὗτος "this"

Explanation. οὗτος is a demonstrative pronoun ("this"), here functioning like a personal pronoun, like αὐτός ("he/ him")

Some of those standing there hear Jesus' Ἐλωί ("My God") and confuse it with Ἠλίας ("Elijah"), whom Matthew has already identified with John the Baptist (Matt 11:14). Elijah was thought to come first in preparation of the way of the Lord (Matt 17:10–12; Mal 4:5–6).

"Lo, I will send you the prophet Elijah before the great and terrible day of the LORD comes. He will turn the hearts of parents to their children and the hearts of children to their parents, so that I will not come and strike the land with a curse" (Mal 4:5–6 NRSV).

48a καὶ εὐθέως δραμὼν εἷς ἐξ αὐτῶν

Lit. *And immediately running one of them*

And immediately, running, one of them

καί	and
conj:	καί "and"
εὐθέως	immediately
adv:	εὐθέως "immediately/next"
δραμών	running
ptcp:	aor act ptcp nom sg masc τρέχω "(he) having ran/raced"
εἷς	one
adj:	nom sg masc εἷς "one"

ἐξ	from/ out of
prep:	ἐκ "from/out of"

αὐτῶν	of them
pers pron:	personal gen pl masc αὐτός "of them"

Explanation. ἐξ αὐτῶν is partitive, describing the adjective εἷς.

δραμὼν is a participle describing attendant circumstances to the main action ἐπότιζεν (v. 48c).

48b καὶ λαβὼν σπόγγον πλήσας τε ὄξους
Lit. and taking a sponge filling sour wine
and taking a sponge, filling (it) with sour wine,

καὶ	and
conj:	καί "and"

λαβὼν	taking
ptcp:	aor act ptcp nom sg masc λαμβάνω "(he) having taken/received"

σπόγγον	a sponge
noun:	acc sg masc σπόγγος "a sponge"

πλήσας	filling
ptcp:	aor act ptcp nom sg masc πλήθω "(he) having fulfilled/ended"

τε	*no translation*
particle:	τέ "both/even"

ὄξους	sour wine
noun:	gen sg neut ὄξος "of a sour wine"

Explanation. λαβών is a participle describing attendant circumstances to the main action ἐπότιζεν (v. 48c).

πλήσας is a participle describing attendant circumstances to the main action ἐπότιζεν (v. 48c).

τε is an untranslated connective conjunction, indicating a close relationship between a sequence of events.

48c καὶ περιθεὶς καλάμῳ ἐπότιζεν αὐτόν.
Lit. and putting to reed he was giving him.
and putting (it) on a reed, he was giving him a drink.

καὶ	and
καί	conj: "and"

περιθεὶς	putting/ placing
ptcp:	aor act ptcp nom sg masc περιτίθημι "(he) having placed around/bestowed"

καλάμῳ	to a reed/ on a reed
noun:	dat sg masc κάλαμος "to a reed/pen"

ἐπότιζεν	he was giving to drink
verb:	impf act ind 3rd sg ποτίζω "(he/she/it) continually drank"

αὐτόν	him

pers pron: acc sg masc αὐτός "him"

Explanation. περιθεὶς is a participle describing attendant circumstances to the main action ἐπότιζεν (v. 48c).

ἐπότιζεν is an imperfect verb, connoting a continuous past action.

49a οἱ δὲ λοιποὶ ἔλεγον·
Lit. the's but rests were saying,
And the rest were saying,

οἱ	the
article:	nom pl masc ὁ "the (ones)"

δὲ	but/ and
conj:	δέ "but/now"

λοιποὶ	the rest/ remaining
adj:	nom pl masc λοιπός "remaining (ones)"

ἔλεγον	they said
verb:	impf act ind 3rd pl λέγω "they were saying"

Explanation. λοιποί is a noun from λοιπός, here functioning as the subject of the sentence.

οἱ . . . λοιποί, "the rest," refers to those other than the one handling the sponge of wine.

49b ἄφες ἴδωμεν εἰ ἔρχεται Ἠλίας σώσων αὐτόν.
Lit. "Let us see if he comes Elijah saving him."
"Let us see if Elijah comes to save Him."

ἄφες	(you sg) permit/ allow
verb:	aor act imv 2nd person sg ἀφίημι "begin (you) to dismiss/forsake"

ἴδωμεν	we should see
verb:	aor act subj 1st pl ὁράω "we should begin to see"

εἰ	if
conditional:	εἰ "if"

ἔρχεται	he comes
verb:	pres mid /pass ind 3rd sg ἔρχομαι "(he/she/it) comes"

Ἠλίας	Elijah
noun:	nom sg masc Ἠλίας "Elijah"

| σώσων | he (who) will have/ to save |
| ptcp: | fut act ptcp nom sg masc σῴζω "(he) who will save/deliver" |

| αὐτόν | him |
| pers pron: acc sg masc αὐτός "him" |

Explanation. ἄφες ἴδωμεν, literally "leave (you sg) we may see," is probably a hortatory construction not so much addressed to the singular person who offered the sponge (v. 48b) but to all the bystanders to step back and await developments.

Here they still think Jesus is calling for Elijah, and naturally regard Jesus' intent as to be delivered from the cross. Readers already know that the Elijah, who is John the Baptist, is dead (cf. Matt 14:2, 10) and that Jesus has no intent even now to depart from the agonies of his crucifixion, since it is the will of his father (Matt 26:39).

σώσων is a rare future participle, here indicating purpose (σῴζω, "to save").

50 ὁ δὲ Ἰησοῦς πάλιν κράξας φωνῇ μεγάλῃ ἀφῆκεν τὸ πνεῦμα.
Lit. The but Jesus again crying out to voice to great gave up the spirit.
And Jesus again crying out in a loud voice, gave up the spirit.

| ὁ | the |
| article: | nom sg masc ὁ "the" |

| δὲ | but/ and |
| conj: | δέ "but/now/and" |

| Ἰησοῦς | Jesus |
| noun: | nom sg masc Ἰησοῦς "Jesus" |

| πάλιν | again |
| adv: | πάλιν "again" |

κράξας	crying out/ having cried out
ptcp:	aor act ptcp nom sg masc κράζω "(he) having cried out/shouted"

φωνῇ	to a voice/ sound
noun:	dat sg fem φωνή "to a voice/sound"

μεγάλῃ	to great/ to a great/ great
adj:	dat sg fem μέγας "to a great"

ἀφῆκεν	forsook/ gave up/ yielded/ dismissed
verb:	aor act ind 3rd sg ἀφίημι "he/she/it dismissed/forsook"

τὸ	the
article:	acc sg neut ὁ "the"

πνεῦμα	spirit
noun:	acc sg neut πνεῦμα "a spirit"

Explanation. So far readers are not told that Jesus had cried out at all, but Matthew here uses πάλιν to indicate it was so.

Here the content of the cry is not recorded, as before, but simply a description of it as φωνῇ μεγάλῃ.

There are several ways to say someone has died in the Greek language. ἀφῆκεν τό πνεῦμα is perhaps unexpected, especially since it omits any reference to *his* spirit (τό πνεῦμα αὐτοῦ), which is supplied in some translations. Perhaps the notion here is that Jesus yielded up the spirit in the sense that his commissioned messianic task, for which he received the spirit at his baptism ("the Spirit of God descending like a dove and alighting on him," Matt 3:16 NRSV) is now complete.

Preaching the Text

1. **Main idea:** The Mission and Ministry of Christ is seen in the charges against Him

2. **Text to Sermon:**
    a. We often think about how unjust and cruel the abuses against Jesus are, and rightly so! But the focus of this passage is on the *accusations* that lead to the abuses. And, the accusations are either *true*, or distortions of *true statements* that we as readers should consider. Nevertheless, throughout this passage, we see *true* statements made:
    b. Jesus' Roman executioners recognize that he is "King of the Jews" (Matt 27:37) and the "King of Israel" (v. 42), though they obviously ascribe that to him in mockery. Unknown to them, it is true! This was already recognized long ago, even by the Magi as Jesus' birthright (Matt 2:2), much to the consternation of King Herod (Matt 2:3), whose kingship had been appointed to him by the Roman senate. And besides, we as readers know that Jesus is the Son of David and heir to the Davidic throne (2 Sam 7:12-13; Matt 1:1; 9:27; 12:23; 15:22; 20:30, 31; 21:9, 15).
    c. It is also true that Jesus spoke about destroying the temple and raising it in three days, as the accusation states (Matt 27:40; cf. 26:61). The Gospel of John tells us that he was speaking about the temple of his body (John 2:21). We know that the charge that he is the "Son of God" (Matt 27:40, 42) because, well, He is! And remember this phrase is exactly the same as that of the devil or Satan from the temptation narrative:

    Matt 4:3, 6: "if you are the son of God" (εἰ υἱὸς εἶ τοῦ θεοῦ)

    Matt 27:40: "if you are the son of God" (εἰ υἱὸς εἶ τοῦ θεοῦ)

    d. The mockery that Jesus saved others (v. 42) but cannot save himself is false, since He is fully *capable* of saving himself from crucifixion (v. 42). But, in *not* saving Himself from crucifixion, this is *exactly* how Jesus fulfills His mission of His father (Matt 26:42) to save His people from their sins (Matt 1:21).

e. Despite all that Jesus has done, his opponents will only believe in him if he comes down off the cross (v. 42). Jesus does indeed trust in God (v. 43) and though he asks that he be spared from his sufferings (Matt 26:39), he does not ask God to deliver him from the cross. Instead he stays, cries out to God (v. 46) and ultimately dies (v. 50).

3. **Tip for Preaching:** There are plenty of injustices in this scene, of course. But that may distract listeners from the focus, which is on who Jesus really is. All of the accusations conjure up for the readers in rapid-fire fashion and in a very brief section the things that Jesus has done and the mission that He has accomplished. So, focusing on the *true* accusations and the *truth behind* the distorted accusations can help an exposition of this passage draw attention to the glories of Christ's mission coming to a climax in Matthew.

13
Matthew 28:1–10
The Empty Tomb

Matthew does not actually describe the resurrection of Jesus. There is no depiction of a corpse coming back to life. Instead, the evangelist shows the *evidence* for the resurrection—the tomb in which Jesus was buried is now empty. Previously readers of Matthew have seen an angel at the birth of Jesus, appearing to Joseph in a dream to direct his course of action with respect to the infant Jesus (Matt 1:20; 2:13, 19). Now an angel descends from heaven and rolls back the stone which covered the entrance to the tomb. The angel's appearance was dazzlingly bright with heavenly glory (cf. Jesus in Matt 17:2). Ironically, the guards become *like dead men* in their fear of the angel (28:4), whereas the man who *had been dead*—Jesus—is alive again. With the soldiers seemingly out of their wits, the angel addresses the women: he knows they are looking for the crucified Jesus, but he has risen "as he said" (v. 6a). Then he implores them to *see for themselves the place where he lay* (v. 6b). Then the angel tells the women to announce to Jesus' other disciples that he has been raised from the dead and will meet them in Galilee (v. 7). On their way they met Jesus, who tells them in the same way as the angel (vv. 8–10).

1a Ὀψὲ δὲ σαββάτων,
    Lit. *After but sabbath,*
    And after the Sabbath,

       Ὀψὲ   late/ after
       adv: ὀψέ "late/after"

       δὲ   but/ now/ and
       conj: δέ "but/now/and"

       σαββάτων   of Sabbaths
       noun: gen pl neut σάββατον "of Sabbaths"

Explanation. Ὀψέ is typically an adverb, but here serves as a preposition, "after."

σάββατον can occur in either singular or plural and can refer to a particular day, "the Sabbath" or, more generally, a week.

The Sabbath was instituted in Exodus 20, where the Lord commands Moses to instruct the Israelites to do all their work in six days, "but the seventh day is a sabbath to the Lord your God. On it you shall not do any work" (Exod 20:10). This law was patterned after God's activity in creation, where he finished the entirety of his work in six days and rested on the seventh (Exod 20:11; cf. Gen 2:2–3).

In Matthew the disciples pick grain on the Sabbath (Matt 12:1), much to the consternation of the Pharisees (12:2). But Jesus declares that he is Lord of the Sabbath (Matt 12:8), and that it is lawful to do good on the Sabbath (12:12).

1b τῇ ἐπιφωσκούσῃ εἰς μίαν σαββάτων,
     Lit. to the dawning in first of week,
     at dawn on the first day of the week,

       τῇ   the
       article: dat sg fem ὁ "to the"

       ἐπιφωσκούσῃ   to the growing light
       ptcp: pres act ptcp dat sg fem ἐπιφώσκω "to (one) dawning/ growing light"

εἰς   into
prep: εἰς "into/for"

μίαν   one
adj: acc sg fem εἷς "one"

σαββάτων   Sabbath
noun: gen pl neut σάββατον "of Sabbaths"

Explanation. τῇ ἐπιφωσκούσῃ is a present participle from ἐπιφώσκω, literally "to the one growing light" or "at the one growing light," clearly meaning "at the growing of light" which, in English, is commonly, "at dawn."

εἰς μίαν is literally "into one," with ἡμέραν, "day" implied. This is perhaps a Semitic idiom where one would typically expect the ordinal πρῶτος, "first."

1c ἦλθεν Μαριὰμ ἡ Μαγδαληνὴ καὶ ἡ ἄλλη Μαρία θεωρῆσαι τὸν τάφον.
Lit. she came Mary the Magdalene and the other Mary to see the tomb.
Mary Magdalene and the other Mary came to see the tomb.

ἦλθεν   came
verb: aor act ind 3rd sg ἔρχομαι "he/she/it came"

Μαριὰμ   Mary
noun: nom sg fem Μαριάμ "Mary"

ἡ   the
article: nom sg fem ὁ "the"

Μαγδαληνὴ   Magdalene
noun: nom sg fem Μαγδαληνή "Magdalene"

καί			and
conj:		καί "and"

ἡ			the
article:		nom sg fem ὁ "the"

ἄλλη		other
adj:		nom sg fem ἄλλος "another"

Μαρία		Mary
noun:		nom sg fem Μαρία "Mary"

θεωρῆσαι	to behold/ gaze at/ look at
verb:		aor act inf θεωρέω "to begin to behold/gaze at"

τὸν			the
article:		acc sg masc ὁ "the"

τάφον		grave/ tomb
noun:		acc sg masc τάφος "a grave/tomb"

Explanation. θεωρῆσαι is an infinitive of purpose modifying ἦλθεν and indicating the purpose for which they came: to look at the tomb (τὸν τάφον).

Mary Magdalene is thought to come from Magdala, a Jewish town located on the western shore of the Sea of Galilee, north of Tiberias. Its name is from the Hebrew word for "tower" (*migdal*, מגדל); its full name being "tower of fish" (*Migdal Nunayya*) in reference to the major role that fishing industry played there. In antiquity it was also known as *Taricheai* (Ταριχέαι), a Greek term for a particular manner of preserving fish.

2a	καὶ ἰδοὺ σεισμὸς ἐγένετο μέγας·
	Lit. and behold earthquake occurred great;
	And behold a great earthquake occurred,

καὶ   and
conj: καί "and"

ἰδοὺ   behold
verb: aor mid imv 2nd sg ὁράω "begin (you for yourself)
        to see"

σεισμὸς earthquake
noun: nom sg masc σεισμός "an earthquake"

ἐγένετο occurred
verb: aor mid ind 3rd sg γίνομαι "(one oneself)
        became/occurred"

μέγας   great
adj: nom sg masc μέγας "great"

Explanation. Earthquakes are sometimes used as signs of God's judgment (cf. Matt 24:7; Rev 11:13, 19; 16:18). In other contexts, earthquakes may accompany the appearance of God or display his power (e.g., Acts 16:26).

2b ἄγγελος γὰρ κυρίου καταβὰς ἐξ οὐρανοῦ
    Lit. angel for of the Lord descending from of heaven
    for an angel of the Lord, descending from heaven

ἄγγελος angel
noun: nom sg masc ἄγγελος "an angel"

γὰρ   for
conj: γάρ "for/because"

κυρίου of Lord
noun: gen sg masc κύριος "of the Lord/a lord"

καταβὰς having come down/ having descended
ptcp: aor act ptcp nom sg masc καταβαίνω "(he) having come down/ descended"

ἐξ from/ out of
prep: ἐκ "from/out of"

οὐρανοῦ of heaven
noun: gen sg masc οὐρανός "of the heaven"

Explanation. The reason for the great earthquake (v. 2a) is given in v. 2b (γάρ). Here the "angel of the Lord" (ἄγγελος κυρίου) appears. In the Bible this figure appears often, but it is debated whether he is the Lord himself, the Lord's agent, or something else. Sometimes he is an agent of destruction and judgment (2 Sam 24:16; 2 Kgs 19:25; Ps 35:5–6; Acts 12:7) or of protection and deliverance (Exod 14:19; Ps 34:7; Isa 63:9; cf. Dan 3:28; 6:22; Acts 5:19; 12:7, 11). Sometimes biblical authors can transition seamlessly from speaking of the "Lord" and the "angel of the Lord." It is the angel of the Lord (ἄγγελος κυρίου, מַלְאַךְ יְהוָה) who speaks to Hagar regarding her son Ishmael (Gen 16:7–11). The same figure intercedes with Abraham to prevent him from harming Isaac (Gen 22:11, 15), and later appears to Moses in the burning bush (Exod 3:2).

In the NT the ἄγγελος κυρίου is seen only in Luke-Acts, where he appears in the temple to Zechariah (Luke 1:11) and later to the shepherds watching their flocks by night (Luke 2:9). In Acts the angel of the Lord awakens Peter and directs him to escape from prison (Acts 12:7) and strikes Herod dead for receiving the accolades due to a god (Acts 12:23).

Outside of this passage, the ἄγγελος κυρίου appears in Matthew only to Joseph, only in dreams, and intervenes directly in the affairs of Jesus (Matt 1:20, 24; 2:13, 19).

His appearance is described as having descended from heaven (καταβὰς ἐξ οὐρανοῦ).

2c   καὶ προσελθὼν ἀπεκύλισεν τὸν λίθον
Lit. and approaching rolled away the stone
and approaching, rolled away the stone

καὶ	and
conj:	καί "and"

προσελθὼν	coming toward/ approaching
ptcp:	aor act ptcp nom sg masc προσέρχομαι "(he) having come toward"

ἀπεκύλισεν	he rolled away
verb:	aor act ind 3rd sg ἀποκυλίω "he/she/it rolled away"

τὸν	the
article:	acc sg masc ὁ "the"

λίθον	stone
noun:	acc sg masc λίθος "a stone"

Explanation. "Descending" (καταβάς) and "approaching" (προσελθών) are both participles describing the main verb, ἀπεκύλισεν.

Tombs in the first century were often family tombs, with a forechamber where the recently dead were laid, and a back chamber where the remains of others were laid. The tomb was often a cave, with a large circulate stone rolled to cover the entrance.

2d   καὶ ἐκάθητο ἐπάνω αὐτοῦ.
Lit. and was sitting upon of it.
and was sitting above it.

καὶ	and
conj:	καί "and"

ἐκάθητο   he was sitting
verb: impf mid/pass ind 3rd sg κάθημαι "(he/she/it) continually sat"

ἐπάνω   above
adv: ἐπάνω "above"

αὐτοῦ   of it
pers pron: gen sg masc αὐτός "of him/it"

Explanation. Having rolled away the stone (τόν λίθον) which covered the entrance to the tomb, the angel was sitting above it.

ἐκάθητο is an imperfect, indicating a continuous past action.

Matthew's ἐπάνω αὐτοῦ is an adverbial phrase describing where the angel was sitting.

3a ἦν δὲ ἡ εἰδέα αὐτοῦ ὡς ἀστραπὴ
Lit. it was but he appearance of him as lightening
And his appearance was like lightning

ἦν   it was
verb: impf act ind 3rd sg εἰμί "(he/she/it) continually was"

δὲ   and/ but
conj: δέ "but/now"

ἡ   the
article: nom sg fem ὁ "the"

εἰδέα   appearance/ form
noun: nom sg fem ἰδέα "an appearance/form"

αὐτοῦ   of him
pers pron: gen sg masc αὐτός "of him/it"

ὡς   as
adv: ὡς "as"

ἀστραπὴ   lightning
noun: nom sg fem ἀστραπή "lightning"

Explanation. Lightning commonly depicts the presence of God (e.g., Exod 19:16; 20:18; etc.).

3b καὶ τὸ ἔνδυμα αὐτοῦ λευκὸν ὡς χιών.
    Lit. and the clothing of him white as snow.
    and his clothing white as snow.

καὶ   and
conj: καί "and"

τὸ   the
article: nom sg neut ὁ "the"

ἔνδυμα   clothing
noun: nom sg neut ἔνδυμα "clothing"

αὐτοῦ   of him/ his
pers pron: gen sg masc αὐτός "of him/it"

λευκὸν   white
adj: nom sg neut λευκός "white"

ὡς   as
adv: ὡς "as"

χιών   snow
noun: nom sg fem χιών "a snow"

Explanation. A similar description is made of the Ancient of Days, whose clothing was "as white as snow" (Dan 7:9).

4a ἀπὸ δὲ τοῦ φόβου αὐτοῦ ἐσείσθησαν οἱ τηροῦντες
Lit. *from but of fear of him they were shaking the ones keeping watch*
And from fear those keeping watch were shaking

ἀπὸ	from/ away from
prep:	ἀπό "(away) from"
δὲ	and
conj:	δέ "but/now/and"
τοῦ	the
article:	gen sg masc ὁ "of the"
φόβου	of fear
noun:	gen sg masc φόβος "of fear"
αὐτοῦ	his/ of him
pers pron:	gen sg masc αὐτός "of him/it"
ἐσείσθησαν	they were shaken
verb:	aor pass ind 3rd pl σείω "(they) were shaken"
οἱ	the
article:	nom pl masc ὁ "the (ones)"
τηροῦντες	ones keeping watch
ptcp:	pres act ptcp nom pl masc τηρέω "(those) keeping/observing"

Explanation. The prepositional phrase ἀπό . . . τοῦ φόβου is fronted for emphasis.

οἱ τηροῦντες is the subject of the verb, ἐσείσθησαν.

Fear is a common response to the appearance of a supernatural being (cf. Rev 1:17; Gen 28:17; Matt 14:27).

MATTHEW 28:1–10

4b καὶ ἐγενήθησαν ὡς νεκροί.
Lit. and they became like deads.
and they became like dead (people).

καὶ	and
conj:	καί "and"

ἐγενήθησαν	they became
verb:	aor pass ind 3rd pl γίνομαι "(they) have become/occurred"

ὡς	as
adv:	ὡς "as"

νεκροί	dead
adj:	nom pl masc νεκρός "dead (ones)"

5a Ἀποκριθεὶς δὲ ὁ ἄγγελος εἶπεν ταῖς γυναιξίν·
Lit. Answering but the angel said to the women;
But the angel, answering, said to the women,

ἀποκριθεὶς	having answered/ answering
ptcp:	aor pass ptcp nom sg masc ἀποκρίνομαι "(he) having been answered"

δὲ	but/ and
conj:	δέ "but/now"

ὁ	the
article:	nom sg masc ὁ "the"

ἄγγελος	angel
noun:	nom sg masc ἄγγελος "an angel"

εἶπεν	said
verb:	aor act ind 3rd sg λέγω "he/she/it said"

ταῖς   the
article: dat pl fem ὁ "to the (ones)"

γυναιξίν   to women
noun: dat pl fem γυνή "to women/wives"

Explanation. Matthew commonly places a participle ahead of the verb it modifies, here ἀποκριθείς before εἶπεν.

Matthew's ταῖς γυναιξίν is an indirect object, since it is in the dative case. This means that the angel spoke (εἶπεν) *to* the women. What he says is recounted in v. 5b.

5b μὴ φοβεῖσθε ὑμεῖς,
Lit. Do not fear you (pl),
Do not be afraid,

μὴ   not
neg particle: μή "no/not (stop)"

φοβεῖσθε you (pl) be afraid
verb: pres mid/pass imv 2nd pl φοβέω "fear/be afraid (you [pl])"

ὑμεῖς   you
pers pron: 2nd nom pl σύ "you (pl)"

Explanation. ὑμεῖς is unnecessary since it is implied in the verb φοβεῖσθε, suggesting it is emphatic.

The phrase "do not be afraid" occurs dozens of times in the Bible, many of which are exhortations to take courage because of something God is about to do on behalf of his people.

5c οἶδα γὰρ ὅτι Ἰησοῦν τὸν ἐσταυρωμένον ζητεῖτε·

Lit. I know for that Jesus the one having been crucified you (pl) seek; for I know that you are looking for Jesus, the one having been crucified;

οἶδα	I know
verb:	perf act ind 1st sg εἰδώ "(I) have known"

γὰρ	for
conj:	γάρ "for/because"

ὅτι	that
conj:	ὅτι "because/that"

Ἰησοῦν	Jesus
noun:	acc sg masc Ἰησοῦς "Jesus"

τὸν	the
article:	acc sg masc ὁ "the"

ἐσταυρωμένον	one having been crucified
ptcp:	perf pass ptcp acc sg masc σταυρόω "(one) having been crucified"

ζητεῖτε	you (pl) seek
verb:	pres act ind 2nd pl ζητέω "(you [pl]) seek"

Explanation. The γάρ indicates here the angel gives the reason not to fear.

The subject of οἶδα is an implied I (ἐγώ), in reference to the angel. What the angel knows is introduced by Matthew's ὅτι.

ἐσταυρωμένον is a perfect passive participle, here acting substantivally as indicated by the definite article τόν and functioning in apposition to Ἰησοῦν, "Jesus, the one having been crucified."

6a οὐκ ἔστιν ὧδε,
Lit. *not he is here,*
He is not here,

οὐκ	not
neg particle:	οὐ "no/not"

ἔστιν	is
verb:	pres act ind 3rd sg εἰμί "(he/she/it) is"

ὧδε	here
adv:	ὧδε "here"

Explanation. The women seek (ζητεῖτε), but the angel clarifies that he is not here.

The ὧδε indicates the tomb.

6b ἠγέρθη γὰρ καθὼς εἶπεν·
Lit. *he was raised for just as he said;*
for he was raised up, just as he said;

ἠγέρθη	he was raised up
verb:	aor pass ind 3rd sg ἐγείρω "(he/she/it) was raised up"

γὰρ	for
conj:	γάρ "for/because"

καθὼς	as/ just as
adv:	καθώς "just as"

εἶπεν	he said
verb:	aor act ind 3rd sg λέγω "he/she/it said"

Explanation. γάρ introduces the reason why Jesus is not in the tomb.

ἠγέρθη is an aorist passive verb, indicating that the act was done to Jesus and implicitly by God.

MATTHEW 28:1–10

The phrase καθὼς εἶπεν is adverbial, describing ἠγέρθη. καθώς is a comparative word. This means that Jesus' resurrection is in precise accord with what Jesus said. Previously Jesus mentioned his eventual resurrection several times in Matthew (Matt 16:21; 17:9, 23; 20:19; 26:32).

6c δεῦτε ἴδετε τὸν τόπον ὅπου ἔκειτο.
Lit. come see the place where he was lying;
come, see the place where he was lying;

δεῦτε	you (pl) come
verb:	pres act imv 2nd pl δεῦτε "come/come here (you [pl])"
ἴδετε	you (pl) see
verb:	aor act imv 2nd pl ὁράω "begin (you [pl]) to see"
τὸν	the
article:	acc sg masc ὁ "the"
τόπον	place
noun:	acc sg masc τόπος "a place"
ὅπου	where
adv:	ὅπου "where"
ἔκειτο	he was laying/ he was placed
verb:	impf mid/pass ind 3rd sg κεῖμαι "(he/she/it) continually is laid/set/placed"

Explanation. The announcement (v. 6b) is followed by a two-fold imperative, δεῦτε ἴδετε.

The women are beckoned to see τὸν τόπον which is described by the adjectival phrase ὅπου ἔκειτο. ἔκειτο is an imperfect verb from κεῖμαι, indicating a continuous past action ("he was laying").

7a καὶ ταχὺ πορευθεῖσαι εἴπατε τοῖς μαθηταῖς αὐτοῦ ὅτι
Lit. *and quickly going tell to the disciples of him that*
and, quickly, going, tell his disciples, that

καί	and
conj:	καί "and"

ταχύ	quickly
adv:	ταχύ "quickly"

πορευθεῖσαι	going
ptcp:	aor pass ptcp nom pl fem πορεύομαι "(those) having been gone/proceeded"

εἴπατε	you (pl) tell
verb:	aor act imv 2nd pl λέγω "begin (you [pl]) to say"

τοῖς	the
article:	dat pl masc ὁ "to the (ones)"

μαθηταῖς	to disciples
noun:	dat pl masc μαθητής "to disciples"

αὐτοῦ	of him/ his
pers pron:	gen sg masc αὐτός "of him/it"

ὅτι	that
conj:	ὅτι "because/that"

Explanation. The adverb ταχύ is fronted for emphasis.

Again, Matthew uses a participle (πορευθεῖσαι) followed by the verb it modifies, εἴπατε.

The verb εἴπατε is a second plural imperative, indicating that the angel is instructing the women to tell Jesus' disciples.

7b ἠγέρθη ἀπὸ τῶν νεκρῶν,

Lit. He was raised from of the deads,

He was raised from the dead,

ἠγέρθη	he was raised/ raised up
verb:	aor pass ind 3rd sg ἐγείρω "(he/she/it) was raised up"
ἀπὸ	from
prep:	ἀπό "(away) from"
τῶν	the
article:	gen pl masc ὁ "of the (ones)"
νεκρῶν	of dead (ones)
adj:	gen pl masc νεκρός "of dead (ones)"

Explanation. v. 7b is the content of what they are to say to the disciples.

The prepositional phrase ἀπὸ τῶν νεκρῶν is adverbial and describes from where he was raised (ἠγέρθη).

7c καὶ ἰδοὺ προάγει ὑμᾶς εἰς τὴν Γαλιλαίαν,

Lit. and behold he goes before you (pl) into the Galilee,

and, behold, he is going before you into Galilee,

καὶ	and
conj:	καί "and"
ἰδοὺ	behold
verb:	aor mid imv 2nd sg ὁράω "begin (you for yourself) to see"
προάγει	he goes ahead/ is going ahead
verb:	pres act ind 3rd sg προάγω "(he/she/it) leads before/precedes"

ὑμᾶς   you (pl)
pers pron: 2nd acc pl σύ "you (pl)"

εἰς   into
prep: εἰς "into/for"

τὴν   the
article: acc sg fem ὁ "the"

Γαλιλαίαν Galilee
noun: acc sg fem Γαλιλαία "Galilee"

Explanation. προάγω is a compound verb from προ, "before" and ἄγω, "I proceed" or "I go" to προάγω, "I go before."

That Jesus is going ahead of them into Galilee indicates that they are to go to Galilee as well.

This was already promised in Matt 26:32, prior to Jesus' crucifixion and at the Mount of Olives, when he said, " . . . after I am raised, I will go before you to Galilee." The angel is perhaps reminding them of what he had said beforehand.

Prior to the first revolt (AD 67–73) Galilee was a predominantly, but not exclusively, Jewish region. At the time of the revolt against Rome the general Vespasian quickly conquered it (AD 67) on his way to Jerusalem. Its principal cities were Sepphoris and Tiberius, each with several thousand residents. These were major cities in the first century, but modest by Roman standards.

7d ἐκεῖ αὐτὸν ὄψεσθε·

Lit. there him you (pl) will see;

there you (pl) will see him;

ἐκεῖ   there
adv: ἐκεῖ "there"

αὐτὸν   him
pers pron: acc sg masc αὐτός "him"

ὄψεσθε	you (pl) will see
verb:	fut mid ind 2nd pl ὁράω "(you [pl]) will (for yourselves) see"

Explanation. The women expected to see Jesus at the tomb, but the angel indicates that there, ἐκεῖ, in Galilee, they will see him.

The αὐτόν is the direct object of ὄψεσθε, a future tense verb second plural from ὁράω.

7e ἰδοὺ εἶπον ὑμῖν.
Lit. Behold, I said to you."
Behold, I told you."

ἰδοὺ	behold
verb:	aor mid imv 2nd sg ὁράω "begin (you for yourself) to see"

εἶπον	I said/ told
verb:	aor act ind 1st sg λέγω "I said"

ὑμῖν	to you (pl)
pers pron:	2nd dat pl σύ "to you (pl)"

8a Καὶ ἀπελθοῦσαι ταχὺ ἀπὸ τοῦ μνημείου
Lit. *and going away quickly from of the tomb*
And going away quickly from the tomb

καὶ	and
conj:	καί "and"

ἀπελθοῦσαι	going away
ptcp:	aor act ptcp nom pl fem ἀπέρχομαι "(the women) having come/gone away"

ταχὺ quickly
adv: ταχύ "quickly"

ἀπὸ from/ away from
prep: ἀπό "(away) from"

τοῦ the
article: gen sg neut ὁ "of the"

μνημείου of tomb/ of grave
noun: gen sg neut μνημεῖον "of a tomb/grave"

Explanation. The inclusion of ταχὺ probably suggests immediate obedience to the instruction in v. 7a.

The prepositional phrase ἀπὸ τοῦ μνημείου is directional, modifying ἀπελθοῦσαι.

8b μετὰ φόβου καὶ χαρᾶς μεγάλης ἔδραμον
Lit. with fear and joy great they ran
with fear and great joy, they ran

μετὰ with / after
prep: μετά "with/after"

φόβου of fear
noun: gen sg masc φόβος "of fear"

καὶ and
conj: καί "and"

χαρᾶς joy
noun: gen sg fem χαρά "of joy"

μεγάλης great
adj: gen sg fem μέγας "of a great"

ἔδραμον   they ran
verb: aor act ind 3rd pl τρέχω "they ran/raced"

Explanation. The noun χαρά, "joy," in Matthew occurs in a few strategic locations: first when the magi see the star (Matt 2:10), also at the initial reception of the seed in the parable of the sower (Matt 13:20), the joy in finding the kingdom of heaven (Matt 13:44), and the joy of the master's reception in the parable of the talents (Matt 25:21, 23).

8c   ἀπαγγεῖλαι τοῖς μαθηταῖς αὐτοῦ.
Lit. to report to the disciples of him.
to announce (it) to his disciples.

ἀπαγγεῖλαι   to announce/ proclaim/ report
verb: aor act inf ἀπαγγέλλω "to begin to report/announce"

τοῖς   the
article: dat pl masc ὁ "to the (ones)"

μαθηταῖς to disciples
noun: dat pl masc μαθητής "to disciples"

αὐτοῦ   his/ of him
pers pron: gen sg masc αὐτός "of him/it"

Explanation. ἀπαγγεῖλαι is an infinitive of purpose.

9a   καὶ ἰδοὺ Ἰησοῦς ὑπήντησεν αὐταῖς λέγων· χαίρετε·
Lit. And behold Jesus met to them saying, "Greetings";
And, behold, Jesus met them, saying, "Greetings!"

καὶ   and
conj: καί "and"

ἰδοὺ	behold
verb:	aor mid imv 2nd sg ὁράω "begin (you for yourself) to see"

Ἰησοῦς	Jesus
noun:	nom sg masc Ἰησοῦς "Jesus"

ὑπήντησεν	met
verb:	aor act ind 3rd sg ὑπαντάω "he/she/it met"

αὐταῖς	to them
pers pron:	dat pl fem αὐτός "to them"

λέγων	saying
ptcp:	pres act ptcp nom sg masc λέγω "(one) saying"

χαίρετε	you (pl) rejoice/greetings
verb:	pres act imv 2nd pl χαίρω "rejoice (you [pl])/greetings"

Explanation. χαίρω means "I rejoice," but is commonly used in Greek as a greeting without any connotation of rejoicing. In these settings, like here, it simply means "Greetings."

9b αἱ δὲ προσελθοῦσαι ἐκράτησαν αὐτοῦ τοὺς πόδας
Lit. The's but approaching clasped of him the feet
And the ones approaching clasped his feet

αἱ	the
article:	nom pl fem ὁ "the (ones)"

δὲ	and/ but
conj:	δέ "but/now/and"

προσελθοῦσαι	approaching/ coming toward
ptcp:	aor act ptcp nom pl fem προσέρχομαι "(the women) having come toward"

ἐκράτησαν   they grasped/ held fast
verb: aor act ind 3rd pl κρατέω "they held fast/grasped"

αὐτοῦ   of him/ his
pers pron: gen sg masc αὐτός "of him/it"

τοὺς   the
article: acc pl masc ὁ "the (ones)"

πόδας   feet
noun: acc pl masc πούς "feet"

Explanation. Matthew's participle προσελθοῦσαι is substantival because of the presence of the definite article αἱ.

9c καὶ προσεκύνησαν αὐτῷ.
Lit. and they worshiped to him.
and they worshiped him.

καὶ   and
conj: καί "and"

προσεκύνησαν   they worshipped
verb: aor act ind 3rd pl προσκυνέω "they worshiped/ prostrated"

αὐτῷ   to him
pers pron: dat sg masc αὐτός "to him"

10a τότε λέγει αὐταῖς ὁ Ἰησοῦς·
Lit. Then he said to them the Jesus
Then Jesus said to them,

τότε   then
adv: τότε "then"

λέγει	he said
verb:	pres act ind 3rd sg λέγω "(he/she/it) says"

αὐταῖς	to them
pers pron: dat pl fem αὐτός "to them"	

ὁ	the
article:	nom sg masc ὁ "the"

Ἰησοῦς	Jesus
noun:	nom sg masc Ἰησοῦς "Jesus"

Explanation. λέγει is a historical present.

The αὐταῖς, in reference to the women, is the indirect object of the verb λέγει indicating to whom Jesus spoke.

10b μὴ φοβεῖσθε·
Lit. Do not fear;
Do not be afraid;

μὴ	not
neg particle: μή "no/not (stop)"	

φοβεῖσθε	you (pl) fear/ be afraid
verb:	pres mid/pass imv 2nd pl φοβέω "fear/be afraid (you [pl])"

Explanation. the same exhortation, μὴ φοβεῖσθε, is given by the angel (v. 5b).

10c ὑπάγετε ἀπαγγείλατε τοῖς ἀδελφοῖς μου
Lit. go announce to the brothers of me
go, announce to my brothers

ὑπάγετε you (pl) go
verb: pres act imv 2nd pl ὑπάγω "depart/go forth (you [pl])"

ἀπαγγείλατε you (pl) announce/ report
verb: aor act imv 2nd pl ἀπαγγέλλω "begin (you [pl]) to report/announce"

τοῖς   to
article: dat pl masc ὁ "to the (ones)"

ἀδελφοῖς to brothers/ to brethren
noun: dat pl masc ἀδελφός "to brothers"

μου   of me/ my
pers pron: 1st gen sg ἐγώ "of me/my"

Explanation. The command by Jesus is twofold, ὑπάγετε and ἀπαγγείλατε.

The noun ἀδελφός tends to be gender-specific, "brother."

10d ἵνα ἀπέλθωσιν εἰς τὴν Γαλιλαίαν,
Lit. *that they may go into the Galilee,*
that they may go into Galilee,

ἵνα   that
conj: ἵνα "in order that"

ἀπέλθωσιν they may go
verb: aor act subj 3rd pl ἀπέρχομαι "they should begin to come/go away"

εἰς   into
prep: εἰς "into/for"

τὴν   the
article: acc sg fem ὁ "the"

Γαλιλαίαν   Galilee
noun: acc sg fem Γαλιλαία "Galilee"

Explanation. The purpose of their going and announcing (v. 10d) is given with ἵνα plus the subjunctive verb ἀπέλθωσιν, "that they may come."

The prepositional phrase εἰς τὴν Γαλιλαίαν describes where they are to go.

10e κἀκεῖ με ὄψονται.
Lit. *and there me they will see.*
and there they will see me."

κἀκεῖ   and there
adv: κἀκεῖ "and there"

με   me
pers pron: 1st acc sg ἐγώ "me"

ὄψονται   they will see
verb: fut mid ind 3rd pl ὁράω "(they) will (for themselves) see"

Explanation. κἀκεῖ is a contraction of καί and ἐκεῖ.

The position of με is emphatic.

The verb ὄψονται is a future tense verb, indicating they will see Jesus in Galilee when they go to meet him there.

Preaching the Text

1. **Main idea:** Raised Up, Just as He Said

2. **Text to Sermon:**
   a. Jesus has already told His disciples that he will raise from the dead three times. These are sometimes called His "passion" (meaning "suffering") predictions. But this is not a *prediction*, this is entirely planned. In fact, it was ordained in the Scriptures. When Jesus was about to be arrested in the Garden of Gethsemane, he knows ahead of time that He is about to be betrayed (Matt 26:45–46). As they come to arrest Jesus, he rebukes those who defend Him and aim to shield him from arrest. This arrest could easily be avoided, Jesus explains. His Father at once could send more than twelve legions of angels, Jesus explains (Matt 27:53). But Jesus does not ask Him for even one. Why? Because the Scriptures must be fulfilled (Matt 26:54). So, Jesus is not *predicting* His crucifixion, death, and resurrection, He is telling His disciples some of what God's plan is.
   b. Jesus explains God's plan three times:
      1. Matt 16:21: From that time Jesus began to show his disciples that he must go to Jerusalem and suffer many things from the elders and chief priests and scribes, and be killed, and on the third day be raised." (RSV)
      2. Matt 17:9: "And as they were coming down the mountain, Jesus commanded them, 'Tell no one the vision, until the Son of man is raised from the dead.'" (RSV)
      3. Matt 20:18–19: "Behold, we are going up to Jerusalem; and the Son of man will be delivered to the chief priests and scribes, and they will condemn him to death, and deliver him to the Gentiles to be mocked and scourged and crucified, and he will be raised on the third day." (RSV)
   c. Notice the responses:
      1. Response to announcement of suffering, being killed and rising on first day (16:21). Peter rebukes Jesus: "God forbid, Lord!" he says. "This shall never happen to you." (Matt 16:22).

2. Response to Jesus' instruction not to tell anyone about the transfiguration until He is raised from the dead (Matt 17:9). They ask about Elijah coming first (Matt 17:10), because they completely missed the fact that John the Baptist was preparing the way (Matt 17:11-13).

3. Response to announcement of brutal crucifixion (20:18–19): the mother of the sons of Zebedee ask that her sons sit at his right and left hand in his kingdom (20:20–21).

d. This passage is commonly preached on Eastern Sunday, for obvious reasons. The best way to preach it may simply be to follow the sequence of the passage. Notice that there is a great deal of supernatural, extraordinary descriptions happening here. There is an earthquake, which usually signals the appearance of God. Here, though, it is the angel of the Lord, who came down from heaven. Whether the rolling of the stone was thought to cause the earthquake, or the mere appearance of the angelic figure did so is probably irrelevant for Matthew. God caused it, and it displays that He has done something monumental. The angel sits on the rolled-back stone, and his appearance was "like lightening" and clothing "white as snow" (28:3). Though there is no dead man in the tomb any longer, the guards became *like* dead men from fear when they saw the angel (v. 4). Then the angel addresses the women, not the guards, telling them not to fear, and explains that he knows they are looking for the crucified Jesus. The angel explains (1) Jesus is not in the tomb, (2) he has been raised, (3) that this is just as Jesus said previously, and (4) he invites the women to see for themselves the place where he lay. The angel then dispatches the women in haste to tell the disciples, and to meet him in Galilee (v. 7). Presumably convinced by the evidence and the testimony of the angel—how could they not be?—they go to tell the disciples (v. 8) when they come upon Jesus (v. 9a). They fall to his feet and worship him; and rightly so (v. 9b). Then Jesus too tells them not to be afraid, and instructs the women—like the angel did—to tell the disciples to meet him in Galilee (v. 10). The rapid-pace narrative and emotional enthusiasm one can imagine from this scene is of course deliberate—it is the culmination of what Jesus had promised, even though they misunderstood it.

3. **Tip for Preaching:** In addition to explaining this passage verse by verse, it is sometimes helpful to explaining the theological significance of the resurrection of Jesus for Christians by using other texts of Scripture. Here Paul's letters are especially helpful, notably 1 Cor 15:1-26. In that letter, written before Matthew wrote his gospel, Paul explains the importance of the bodily resurrection of Jesus in conquering death itself, and what is accomplished for Christians by the resurrection. Importantly, Paul is telling them nothing new. In fact, he is merely reminding them (1 Cor 15:1) of what he already told them "as of first importance" (1 Cor 15:3). And this urgent message even was passed down to Paul (1 Cor 15:3). You are an expositor of a very ancient and sacred message.

14
Matthew 28:16–20

From Jesus' Mission to Our Great Commission

The "Great Commission" is familiar to many readers; the disciples meet Jesus in Galilee, at a mountain (28:16) just as Jesus and the angel directed the women at the empty tomb (Matt 28:1–10). There are only eleven, since Judas is now gone (Matt 27:3–5). They worship him, but some doubted (28:17). But Matthew says nothing further about the doubt, only proceeding to give the famous "Great Commission." Surprisingly, Jesus says that all authority "in heaven and on earth" has been given to him (v. 18), but says nothing about what that means, who gave it to him, or what it has to do with the ensuing commands. Yet he makes a clear connection by saying "therefore" and giving two commands. In other words, Jesus sees His own comprehensive authority as the grounds for two-fold command to (1) go and (2) make disciples of all nations (v. 19a). This entails primarily two things: first, baptizing them (v. 19b) and, second, teaching them to obey (v. 20a). And finally, he reminds his disciples of his enduring presence with them (v. 20b), though in what way also is not said. There is a great deal of familiar teaching in this passage, but also some things that are unexplained and ambiguous.

> **16a** Οἱ δὲ ἕνδεκα μαθηταὶ ἐπορεύθησαν εἰς τὴν Γαλιλαίαν εἰς τὸ ὄρος
> *Lit. The's but eleven disciples went out into the Galilee into the mountain*
>
> Now the eleven disciples went out into Galilee, into the mountain

MATTHEW 28:16-20

Οἱ	the
article:	nom pl masc ὁ "the (ones)"

δὲ	but / now
conj:	δέ "but/now"

ἕνδεκα	eleven
adj:	num ἕνδεκα "eleven"

μαθηταὶ	disciples
noun:	nom pl masc μαθητής "disciples"

ἐπορεύθησαν	went out
verb:	aor pass ind 3rd pl πορεύομαι "(they) went/proceeded"

εἰς	into
prep:	εἰς "into/for"

τὴν	the
article:	acc sg fem ὁ "the"

Γαλιλαίαν	Galilee
noun:	acc sg fem Γαλιλαία "Galilee"

εἰς	into
prep:	εἰς "into/for"

τὸ	the
article:	acc sg neut ὁ "the"

ὄρος	mountain
noun:	acc sg neut ὄρος "a mountain"

Explanation. Οἱ μαθηταί is the subject, while the ἕνδεκα is an adjective modifying μαθηταί. δέ is always the second element in a sentence.

The disciples were first called together as twelve in number (Matt 10:1, 2, 5; 11:1) and are sometimes referred to simply as "the Twelve" (Matt 20:17; 26:14, 20, 47). Only once (here, 28:16) are they referred to as "the eleven," since Judas, who had betrayed Jesus (Matt 26:25, 47, 49; 27:3), had by now hanged himself (Matt 27:5).

16b οὗ ἐτάξατο αὐτοῖς ὁ Ἰησοῦς,
Lit. where he designated to them the Jesus,
where Jesus designated to them

οὗ   where
adv: οὗ "where"

ἐτάξατο   he directed/ designated
verb: aor mid ind 3rd sg τάσσω "(one oneself) designated/set"

αὐτοῖς   to them
pers pron: dat pl masc αὐτός "to them"

ὁ   the
article: nom sg masc ὁ "the"

Ἰησοῦς   Jesus
noun: nom sg masc Ἰησοῦς "Jesus"

Explanation. οὗ is a relative pronoun, and this entire sentence is a relative clause describing the mountain.

17a καὶ ἰδόντες αὐτὸν προσεκύνησαν,
Lit. and beholding him they worshipped,
and, when they saw him, they worshiped,

καὶ   and
conj: καί "and"

ἰδόντες   having seen/ when they saw
ptcp: aor act ptcp nom pl masc ὁράω "(the men) having seen"

αὐτὸν   him
pers pron: acc sg masc αὐτός "him"

προσεκύνησαν   they worshipped
verb: aor act ind 3rd pl προσκυνέω "they worshiped/ prostrated"

Explanation. The main verb here is προσεκύνησαν, which is modified by ἰδόντες αὐτόν. The verb προσκυνέω can sometimes mean simply to pay reverence to someone, or homage as a newly arisen king (e.g. Matt 2:2, 8, 11). At other times it can be used for bowing in entreaty (Matt 8:2; 9:18; 15:25; 18:26; 20:20). At other times it is used for "worship" as a religious devotion expressed to a deity, which God alone should receive (e.g., Matt 4:9, 10; 14:33; 28:9, 17).

17b οἱ δὲ ἐδίστασαν.
Lit. the's but doubted.
but some doubted.

οἱ   the
article: nom pl masc ὁ "the (ones)"

δὲ   but
conj: δέ "but/now"

ἐδίστασαν   they doubted
verb: aor act ind 3rd pl διστάζω "they doubted"

Explanation. They οἱ δὲ ἐδίστασαν is literally "but they doubted." However, the participle is likely partitive, meaning only *some* doubted. This is sensible since the general response is that of worship (v. 17a).

18a καὶ προσελθὼν ὁ Ἰησοῦς ἐλάλησεν αὐτοῖς λέγων·
Lit. *And coming toward the Jesus he spoke to them saying;*
And coming toward, Jesus spoke to them, saying;

καί	and
conj:	καί "and"

προσελθών	coming toward/ approaching
ptcp:	aor act ptcp nom sg masc προσέρχομαι "(he) having come toward"

ὁ	the
article:	nom sg masc ὁ "the"

Ἰησοῦς	Jesus
noun:	nom sg masc Ἰησοῦς "Jesus"

ἐλάλησεν	he spoke
verb:	aor act ind 3rd sg λαλέω "he/she/it spoke"

αὐτοῖς	to them
pers pron:	dat pl masc αὐτός "to them"

λέγων	saying
ptcp:	pres act ptcp nom sg masc λέγω "(one) saying"

18b ἐδόθη μοι πᾶσα ἐξουσία ἐν οὐρανῷ καὶ ἐπὶ τῆς γῆς.
Lit. *It has been given to me all authority in heaven and upon of the earth;*
All authority in heaven and on earth was given to me;

ἐδόθη	it was given
verb:	aor pass ind 3rd sg δίδωμι "(he/she/it) was given"

μοι	to me
pers pron:	1st dat sg ἐγώ "to me"

πᾶσα	all
adj:	nom sg fem πᾶς "all"
ἐξουσία	authority
noun:	nom sg fem ἐξουσία "an authority"
ἐν	in
prep:	ἐν "in/by/with"
οὐρανῷ	to heaven
noun:	dat sg masc οὐρανός "to the heaven"
καί	and
conj:	καί "and"
ἐπί	on/ upon
prep:	ἐπί "upon"
τῆς	the
article:	gen sg fem ὁ "of the"
γῆς	of earth
noun:	gen sg fem γῆ "of earth/land"

Explanation. The passive voice ἐδόθη implies that it is given by God. The μοι is a dative and so serves as the indirect object, indicating to whom it is given.

What is given is a comprehensive authority (πᾶσα ἐξουσία ἐν οὐρανῷ καὶ ἐπὶ τῆς γῆς).

19a πορευθέντες οὖν μαθητεύσατε πάντα τὰ ἔθνη,
Lit. going then make disciples all the Gentiles,
Going, therefore, make disciples of all the nations,

πορευθέντες   going/ having been gone
ptcp: aor pass ptcp nom pl masc πορεύομαι "(those) having been gone/proceeded"

οὖν   therefore
conj: οὖν "therefore"

μαθητεύσατε   you (pl) make disciples of
verb: aor act imv 2nd pl μαθητεύω "begin (you [pl]) to make disciples of"

πάντα   all
adj: acc pl neut πᾶς "all (ones)"

τὰ   the
article: acc pl neut ὁ "the (ones)"

ἔθνη   nations/ gentiles
noun: acc pl neut ἔθνος "gentiles/nations"

Explanation. οὖν indicates that what follows is an inference of all authority being given to Jesus. The authority in view here draws from Jesus being the "Son of Man," who in Daniel's vision approaches the Ancient of Days and "was given authority, glory and sovereign power; all nations and peoples of every language worshiped him. His dominion is an everlasting dominion that will not pass away, and his kingdom is one that will never be destroyed" (Dan. 7:14 NIV). The authority is given to Jesus *after* his resurrection, and the Great Commission (28:18–20) pertains to the claim Jesus now has upon "all nations (LXX πάντα τὰ ἔθνη) and peoples of every language" (Dan 7:14).

The command is to μαθητεύσατε πάντα τὰ ἔθνη. Previously the disciples and Jesus went only to the lost sheep of the house of Israel (Matt 10:6; 15:24). Now, presumably because of the resurrection and the comprehensive authority Jesus has, the mission is expanded.

πορευθέντες is an adverbial participle describing the main verb. It describes the context for the main verb.

MATTHEW 28:16-20

19b βαπτίζοντες αὐτοὺς εἰς τὸ ὄνομα τοῦ πατρὸς καὶ τοῦ υἱοῦ καὶ τοῦ ἁγίου πνεύματος,

Lit. baptizing them in the name of the father and of the son and of the holy spirit,

baptizing them in the name of the Father and of the Son and of the Holy Spirit,

βαπτίζοντες	baptizing
ptcp:	pres act ptcp nom pl masc βαπτίζω "(those) baptizing"

αὐτοὺς	them
pers pron: acc pl masc αὐτός "them"	

εἰς	in/ into
prep:	εἰς "into/for"

τὸ	the
article:	acc sg neut ὁ "the"

ὄνομα	name
noun:	acc sg neut ὄνομα "a name"

τοῦ	the
article:	gen sg masc ὁ "of the"

πατρὸς	of father
noun:	gen sg masc πατήρ "of a father"

καὶ	and
conj:	καί "and"

τοῦ	the
article:	gen sg masc ὁ "of the"

υἱοῦ	of son
noun:	gen sg masc υἱός "of a son"

καί   and
conj: καί "and"

τοῦ   the
article: gen sg neut ὁ "of the"

ἁγίου   of holy
adj: gen sg neut ἅγιος "of a holy"

πνεύματος   of spirit
noun: gen sg neut πνεῦμα "of a spirit"

Explanation. Matthew likely views making disciples as two-fold in this verse, first βαπτίζοντες.

The antecedent of αὐτοὺς is πάντα τὰ ἔθνη (v. 19a).

20a δıδάσκοντες αὐτοὺς τηρεῖν πάντα ὅσα ἐνετειλάμην ὑμῖν·
Lit. teaching them to observe all that which I commanded you (pl);
teaching them to obey everything that I commanded you (pl);

δıδάσκοντες teaching
ptcp: pres act ptcp nom pl masc δıδάσκω "(those) teaching"

αὐτοὺς   them
pers pron: acc pl masc αὐτός "them"

τηρεῖν   to keep/ observe/ obey
verb: pres act inf τηρέω "to keep/observe"

πάντα   all
adj: acc pl neut πᾶς "all (ones)"

ὅσα   as much as/ that which/ that
correlative pron: acc pl neut ὅσος "as many as"

| ἐνετειλάμην | I commanded |
| verb: | aor mid ind 1st sg ἐντέλλω "(I myself) commanded" |

| ὑμῖν | you (pl) |
| pers pron: 2nd dat pl σύ "to you (pl)" | |

Explanation. The second aspect Matthew regards as making disciples is διδάσκοντες.

The αὐτούς is the object of "teaching." Matthew's infinitive τηρεῖν describes the teaching, "teaching them to keep." What they are to keep is πάντα, "everything," which is described by the phrase ὅσα ἐνετειλάμην ὑμῖν. A defining element of the Great Commission is teaching disciples to obey what Jesus commanded them.

20b καὶ ἰδοὺ ἐγὼ μεθ' ὑμῶν εἰμι πάσας τὰς ἡμέρας
Lit. and behold I with you (pl) I am all the days,
and, behold, I am with you all the days,

| καὶ | and |
| conj: | καί "and" |

| ἰδοὺ | behold |
| verb: | aor mid imv 2nd sg ὁράω "begin (you for yourself) to see" |

| ἐγὼ | I |
| pers pron: 1st nom sg ἐγώ "I" | |

| μεθ' | with |
| prep: | μετά "with/after" |

| ὑμῶν | of you (pl) |
| pers pron: 2nd gen pl σύ "of you (pl)" | |

| εἰμὶ | I am |
| verb: | pres act ind 1st sg εἰμί "(I) am" |

πάσας   all
adj: acc pl fem πᾶς "all (ones)"

τὰς   the
article: acc pl fem ὁ "the (ones)"

ἡμέρας   days
noun: acc pl fem ἡμέρα "days"

Explanation. Previously readers saw that Jesus was Immanuel, "God with us." Now he promises to be "with you" (ἐγὼ μεθ' ὑμῶν εἰμι)

μεθ' ὑμῶν is a contraction ("elision") from μετά ὑμῶν, used to aid in pronunciation.

πάσας τὰς ἡμέρας indicates the extent or measure of Jesus being with them.

20c ἕως τῆς συντελείας τοῦ αἰῶνος.
Lit. until of the completion of the age.
until the completion of the age.

ἕως   until
adv: ἕως "until/while"

τῆς   the
article: gen sg fem ὁ "of the"

συντελείας   of completion/ termination
noun: gen sg fem συντέλεια "of completion/termination"

τοῦ   the
article: gen sg masc ὁ "of the"

αἰῶνος   of age
noun: gen sg masc αἰών "of an age/eternity/forever"

Preaching the Text

1. **Main idea:** How Jesus got authority; Why Jesus commands to go.

2. **Text to Sermon:**

   a. We know this verse and many of us love it. But do we know what it means? What does Jesus mean by the authority given to Him? By whom, and why? And what is that "therefore" there for? That is, what does the fact that Jesus is *given authority* have to do with His command to *send people out* to do what He tells them to do? The "therefore" indicates that the authority given to him has an *implication* or is the *basis upon which* He is giving this command. How does that work? That *must* be clear and explained to get this passage right.

   b. This familiar text is perhaps best preached verse-by-verse, in its order. The eleven disciples (without Judas, see Matt 27:3–5) come to Galilee, where they were to meet the resurrected Jesus (Matt 26:32; 28:7, 10). Which "mountain" in Galilee is not said (28:16), though it is traditionally thought to be Mount Tabor.

   c. The appropriate response to seeing the resurrected Jesus is worship (v. **17**), yet some doubted. Διστάζειν is not unbelief (ἀπιστία, Matt 13:58; 17:17), but a hesitancy. The same term is used when Peter walks on water (Matt 14:31). He certainly has faith to step out, yet the wind causes fear and he is addressed by Jesus as ὀλιγόπιστε, "O little faith," and asks εἰς τί ἐδίστασας.

   d. Then Jesus comes to them (v. **18**) with an announcement that, as familiar as it is to us, perhaps was understood as obscure to the disciples. Jesus declares, "All authority in heaven and on earth has been given to me. The passive voice ἐδόθη and emphatic position of μοι underscore that God is the giver, and Jesus himself the recipient. Previously readers knew that Jesus as Son of Man was given "authority" (ἐξουσία) on earth to forgive sins (Matt 9:6, 8). And later Jesus will assert, "All things have been handed over to me by my Father" (Matt 11:27 Πάντα μοι παρεδόθη ὑπὸ τοῦ πατρός μου). But now that the ministry and words of Jesus have been vindicated by God through his resurrection from the dead, Jesus receives a comprehensive authority, in which Daniel sees one like a Son of Man presented before the Ancient One (Dan 7:13). "And royal authority was given to him, and all the nations of the earth according to posterity, and all honor was serving him. And his authority is an everlasting authority, which shall never be removed— and his kingship, which will never perish" (Dan 7:14 NETS καὶ ἐδόθη αὐτῷ ἐξουσία καὶ πάντα τὰ ἔθνη τῆς γῆς κατὰ γένη καὶ πᾶσα δόξα αὐτῷ λατρεύουσα καὶ ἡ ἐξουσία αὐτοῦ ἐξουσία αἰώνιος ἥτις οὐ μὴ ἀρθῇ καὶ ἡ βασιλεία αὐτοῦ ἥτις οὐ μὴ φθαρῇ). Jesus is this Son of Man; his resurrection has occasioned the receipt of this honor and the basis for the claim upon which Jesus makes upon making disciples of all nations.

e. Verse **19** is the inference ("therefore") for Jesus' claim of comprehensive, God-given authority in terms of a two-fold command to (1) go and (2) make disciples of all nations. The concern is not restricted to the lost sheep of the house of Israel (Matt 10:6; 15:24), but rather πάντα τὰ ἔθνη, Jews and gentiles. The universal authority is the basis for universal mission. How they are to do making disciples is described in terms of baptism (v. 19) and teaching to obey (v. **20**). But how does one deal with "obedience," especially in the West? In Matthew there is no ambiguity, and is all tied to the universal and unrivalled authority of King Jesus. In Matthew Jesus is always obedient to the will of the Father, and discipleship is obedience following in Jesus' example (e.g., Matt 4:23; 5:2; 7:29; 9:35; 11:1; 13:34; 21:23; 26:55). Obedience is a defining element of following after Jesus in discipleship (cf. Matt 5:17–20; 7:21–27). Obedience in order to be saved is legalism. Obedience *because* one is saved is discipleship. Jesus is constantly *telling people to do things* in the Gospel of Matthew. Here one must come to terms with Jesus' demands of his disciples, then and now. The promise of Jesus (ἐγὼ μεθ' ὑμῶν εἰμι) recalls that Jesus is Immanuel, God with us (Matt 1:23), and reflect the character of God's presence among his covenant people (Gen 28:15; Exod 3:12; Josh 1:5, 9; Isa 41:10).

3. **Tip for Preaching:** As indicated at the beginning, familiarity with this passage can sometimes be our biggest obstacle. What is the *logic* of this passage. What is Matthew *saying*? Where did Jesus get authority on heaven and on earth? Did He not have it before? Why was it given

to Him? Who gave it to Him? And why is it the *basis* ("therefore") for His command to make disciples? What exactly are the commands that disciples are to obey? These and other questions that are raised by the text and can be answered by the text itself. In your efforts to pursue these answers in the text, pursue Christ in your own faith. Find more of Christ and pray for Christ-likeness in your own sanctification, and let the wealth of our exposition of these sacred words flow from careful study as well as the crucible of a refined heart, for the glory and praise of God.

Biblical and Ancient Text Index

Old Testament / Hebrew Bible

Genesis

2:2–3	312
16:7–11	316
22:11	316
22:15	316
28:15	352
28:17	320

Exodus

3:2	316
3:12	352
5:6	289
5:14	290
5:15	290
5:19	290
6:6–7	262
10:21	88
10:22	88, 298
12	258
12:11	258
12:12–13	258
14:19	316
14:20	88
19:3	55
19:16	319
20	312
20:1–17	32
20:3–7	185
20:10	312
20:11	312
20:12–16	204
20:12	195
20:13–17	185
20:13	193
20:14	194
20:15	193
20:16	194
20:18	319
24	271
24:7	264
24:8	264, 270
24:18	55
29:12	265
33:20	66
34:4	55
34:28	28
34:14	99

Leviticus

4:5	160
4:7	265
4:16	160
4:18	265
4:25	265
4:30	265
6:15	160
19:18 LXX	196
19:18	205
21:10	160
21:12	160

BIBLICAL AND ANCIENT TEXT INDEX

Numbers

12:3	61

Deuteronomy

5:1	32
5:16	195
5:17	193
5:18	193
5:19	194
5:20	194
6:13	52
6:13a	47
6:13b	48
6:16	41, 51
8:2–3	51
8:3	32, 51
10:20	52
10:20a	47
10:20b	48
20:8 LXX	107
22:20–24	22
28:29	88

Joshua

1:5	352
1:9	352

Judges

7:3	107

1 Samuel

2:10	160
2:35	160
12:3	160
12:5	160
16:6	160
24:7	160
24:11	160
26:9	160
26:11	160
26:16	160
26:23	160

2 Samuel

1:14	160
1:16	160
2:5 LXX	160
7	9, 229
7:12–17	229
7:12–13	309
19:22	160
20:20	160
22:29	88
23:1	160
23:17	160
24:16	316

2 Kings

8:17	290
19:25	316

1 Chronicles

11:19	178

2 Chronicles

6:42	160
13:7	107

Nehemiah

11:1	34

Job

11:18–19	105

Psalms

2:2	160
2:7	24
3:5–6	105
19:7 LXX	160
20:6	160
21:2 LXX	300
21:9 LXX	294
21:19 LXX	279

22:2	300	118:14	230
22:9	294	118:15–18	230
24:3	66	118:19–21	230
24:4	66	118:26	230
23:4 LXX	66	118:29 LXX	236
24:5	66	119	236
27:8 LXX	160	119:1	236
28:8	160	119:5–28	236
33:3 LXX	61	119:29	236
34:3	61	132:10	160
34:7	316	134:3	204
35:5–6	326	147:6	61
36:11 LXX	61, 62	146:6 LXX	61
37:11	61	149:4	61
65:5	112		
65:7	112		
75:10 LXX	61	## Proverbs	
76:10	61	3:24–26	105
83:10 LXX	160	20:20	88
84:9	160		
88:39 LXX	160	## Isaiah	
88:52 LXX	160		
89:8–9	112	6:9–10	149
89:38	160	7	16
89:51	160	7:1–2	16
90:11	38	7:3–9	16
90:11 LXX	37, 39	7:14	16
91	51	7:16	16
91:3–16	53	8:22	88
91:11–12	51	29:18	88
91:11	37, 38, 39	40:3	26
106 LXX	64	41:10	352
107	64	42:16	88
106:5 LXX	64	50:10	88
106:6a LXX	64	52:1	34
106:9 LXX	64	53:1–12	265
107:29	112	53:4	265
117:25 LXX	229	53:5	265
118	230	53:10	265
118 LXX	236	53:11	265
118:1	230	53:12	265
118:1 LXX	236	61:1	59
118:25	229	62:1–10	236
118:2–4	230	62:11–12	218
118:5–28 LXX	236	62:11	218, 236
118:6–7	230	62:12	236
118:8–13	230	63:9	316

Jeremiah

31	271
31:31	264, 270

Lamentations

3:2	88
3:25	204
4:20	160

Ezekiel

12:2	144

Daniel

3:28	316
6:22	316
7:9	319
7:13	352
7:13–14	154
7:14	346, 352
9:26	160

Hosea

2:17 LXX	203

Joel

1:11	203
2:2	298
2:31	298

Amos

4:14 LXX	160

Micah

7:8	88

Habakkuk

3:13	160

Zephaniah

1:15	298

Zechariah

9	218
9:1–3	218
9:4	218
9:5–7	218
9:8	218
9:9	207, 218, 219, 220, 236
9:9–13	236
9:9–10	236
9:9 LXX	218, 220
9:10–16	218
9:11	218
9:14–17	236
9:16	218
14:3–4	209

Malachi

4:5	156
4:5–6	303

New Testament

Matthew

1–3	235
1:1–17	1, 2
1:1	2, 229, 309
1:6	229
1:17	229
1:18–25	1
1:18	22
1:18a	1
1:18b	2
1:18c	3
1:18d	4
1:19a	5
1:19b	5
1:19c	6

1:20	22, 107, 229, 311, 316	4:3b	29
		4:3c	30
1:20a	7	4:4	51
1:20b	7	4:4a	31
1:20c	7	4:4b	31
1:20d	9	4:4c	33
1:20e	10	4:5–6	51
1:21	106, 236, 266, 287, 291, 309, 312	4:5a	33
		4:5b	34
1:21a	11	4:6	49, 287, 309
1:21b	12	4:6a	35, 38
1:22	13	4:6b	36
1:23	185, 352	4:6c	37
1:23a	15	4:6d	38
1:23b	15	4:6e	39
1:23c	17	4:7	51
1:24	316	4:7a	40
1:24a	18	4:7b	40
1:24b	19	4:7c	41
1:25a	20	4:8	52
1:25b	21	4:8a	41
		4:8b	43
2:1	291	4:9	52, 343
2:2	291, 309, 343	4:9a	44
2:3	232, 309	4:9b	44
2:4	240	4:10	343
2:8	343	4:10a	46
2:10	331	4:10b	46
2:11	343	4:10c	48
2:13	311, 316	4:11a	48
2:19	311, 316	4:11b	49
2:22	107	4:11c	49, 50
		4:12–25	57
3:1	24	4:12–17	54
3:15	63	4:13	101
3:16	308	4:16	88
3:17	24, 294	4:17	44, 54
		4:18–25	54
4–20	235	4:19	180
4:1–11	24, 25, 54, 55, 181	4:20	76, 103, 201
4:1a	24	4:22	76, 103, 201
4:1b	26	4:23	352
4:2	31	4:25	103, 201
4:2a	27		
4:2b	28	5–7	54, 147
4:3	287, 309	5:1–12	54
4:3a	28	5:1–2	76

Matthew (continued)

5:1	54
5:1a	54
5:1b	56
5:2–12	54
5:2	57, 75, 352
5:3	161
5:3a	58
5:3b	59
5:4a	60
5:4b	60
5:5	62, 236
5:5a	61
5:5b	61
5:6	63
5:6a	62, 63
5:6b	63
5:7a	64, 65
5:7b	64, 65
5:8a	65
5:8b	66
5:9a	66
5:9b	67
5:10	63, 71
5:10a	68
5:10b	69
5:11	72, 75
5:12	75
5:12a	72
5:12b	72
5:12c	73
5:17–20	352
5:20	63
5:29	138
5:30	138
5:46	73
6	77, 81
6:1	63, 73
6:2–4	77
6:2	73
6:4	77
6:5–15	77
6:5	73
6:6	77
6:16–18	27, 77
6:16	73
6:18	77
6:19–25	77
6:19–24	94
6:19–21	84, 85, 86, 99, 200
6:19–20	77
6:19a	77
6:19b	78, 80
6:19c	79, 80
6:20a	80
6:20b	81
6:20c	82
6:21	77, 83
6:22–24	94
6:22–23	77, 99
6:22a	84, 85
6:22b	85
6:22c	86
6:23	86
6:23a	87
6:23b	87
6:23c	88
6:23d	89
6:24–25	77
6:24	99, 142
6:24a	90
6:24b	91
6:24c	91, 92
6:24d	93
6:25	94, 99, 100
6:25a	94
6:25b	95
6:25c	96
6:25d	97
6:26–32	94
6:26–27	77
6:28–30	77
6:31–34	77
6:33	v, 63, 94, 100, 142, 200
7:21–27	352
7:21	181
7:28–29	75
7:29	352
8:1	103, 201

8:2	343	10:27	88
8:5–6	101	10:37	92
8:5	101	10:38	103, 180, 201
8:7–9	101	10:41	73
8:10–13	101	10:42	73
8:10	103, 201		
8:12	88	11:1	342, 352
8:14–17	101	11:2	155
8:18	101	11:6	138
8:19–20	101	11:7–13	247
8:19	103, 186, 201	11:13	156
8:21–22	101	11:14	303
8:22–23	103, 201	11:27	351
8:23–27	101	11:29	61
8:23	101, 113		
8:24–25	113	12	150
8:24a	103, 105	12:1	209
8:24b	104, 105	12:2	312
8:24c	105	12:8	312
8:25	291	12:12	312
8:25a	105	12:15	103, 201
8:25b	106	12:16	109
8:26a	107	12:23	229, 309
8:26b	108	12:38–40	150
8:26c	109	12:38	186
8:27	113, 236	12:50	181
8:27a	109		
8:27b	110	13	117
8:28–34	114	13:1–9	116, 130
		13:1–8	148
9:1–8	114	13:1–2	116
9:6	351	13:3–9	116
9:8	107, 351	13:3	116
9:9	103, 114, 201, 204, 207	13:3a	117
		13:3b	118
9:18	343	13:4	147
9:19	103	13:4a	118
9:21	291	13:4b	120
9:22	291	13:5–6	147
9:27	103, 229, 309	13:5a	121
9:35	352	13:5b	122
		13:6a	123
10:1	342	13:6b	124
10:2	342	13:7	148
10:5	342	13:7a	124
10:6	346, 352	13:7b	125
10:22	291	13:8–22	116

Matthew *(continued)*

13:8	148
13:8a	126
13:8b	127, 146
13:9–17	148
13:9	128
13:10	148
13:11	148
13:12	116
13:15	149
13:17–23	148
13:18–23	116, 147
13:18	129
13:19	147
13:19a	130
13:19b	131
13:19c	132
13:20–21	147
13:20	331
13:20a	133
13:20b	134, 135, 140, 144
13:20c	135
13:21a	136
13:21b	137
13:22	148
13:22a	139
13:22b	139, 144
13:22c	140, 142
13:22d	142
13:23	147, 148
13:23a	143
13:23b	143
13:23c	145
13:34	352
13:41	181
13:44	331
13:57	138
13:58	351
14:1–2	155
14:2	307
14:3–12	155
14:10	307
14:13	103, 201
14:27	320
14:30	291
14:31	351
14:33	343
15:2	241
15:12	138
15:22	229, 309
15:24	346, 352
15:25	343
15:29–38	150
15:31	110
16	113, 150, 266
16:1–4	150
16:5–12	150
16:13–23	150
16:13–15	183
16:13	150
16:13a	151
16:13b	153, 155
16:14	150
16:14a	154
16:14b	154
16:14c	155
16:14d	156
16:15	150, 157
16:16	150, 183, 236, 272
16:16a	158
16:16b	159
16:17–19	150
16:17a	160
16:17b	161
16:17c	162
16:17d	162, 163
16:18–19	183
16:18a	164
16:18b	164
16:18c	165
16:18d	166
16:19a	167
16:19b	168
16:19c	170
16:20	183
16:20a	171
16:20b	171, 172
16:21–23	183
16:21	151, 184, 240, 241, 272, 286, 325, 337

16:21a	173	19:18–19	185, 205
16:21b	174, 176	19:18a	191
16:21c	174	19:18b	192
16:21d	174, 176	19:18c	192
16:22	151, 183, 337	19:18d	193
16:22a	176	19:18e	193
16:22b	177, 178	19:18f	194
16:22c	177, 178	19:19a	194
16:23	49, 52, 109, 151	19:19b	195
16:23a	179	19:20a	185, 196
16:23b	180	19:20b	185, 196, 197
16:23c	180	19:21	81, 103, 185, 202, 205
16:23d	181		
16:24	103, 180, 201	19:21a	197
16:25	291	19:21b	198, 203
		19:21c	198, 199
17:2	311	19:21d	198, 199
17:9	325, 337, 338	19:21e	198, 200
17:10–12	303	19:21f	198, 200
17:10	338	19:22	81, 185, 205
17:11–13	338	19:22a	201
17:12–13	247	19:22b	202
17:17	351	19:23–26	205
17:18	109	19:23	205
17:23	286, 325	19:24	205
17:27	138	19:25	106, 205
		19:26	205
18:6	138	19:26a	107
18:7	181	19:27–28	103, 201
18:8	138	19:30	236
18:9	99, 138		
18:11	106	20:8	73
18:26	343	20:15	240
		20:17	342
19	185	20:18–19	337, 338
19:2	103, 201	20:18	240
19:13	109	20:19	286, 325
19:16–22	185	20:20–21	338
19:16	185, 204	20:20	343
19:16a	186	20:23	240
19:16b	186, 187	20:27	236
19:17	185, 204	20:28	184, 237, 266
19:17a	188	20:29	103, 201
19:17b	188	20:30–31	109, 229
19:17c	189	20:30	309
19:17d	190	20:31	309
19:17e	191	20:34	103, 201

Matthew (continued)

21–28	235
21:1–11	207
21:1–7	235
21:1	207, 209, 235
21:1a	207
21:1b	208
21:1c–2a	210
21:2	207
21:2b	210
21:2c	211
21:2d	212
21:2e	213
21:3–7	207
21:3a	213, 215
21:3b	214
21:3c	215
21:4	216
21:5	61, 236
21:5a	217
21:5b	217, 218
21:5c	219
21:6	220
21:7a	220
21:7b	222
21:7c	223
21:8	207, 235
21:8a	224, 226
21:8b	225
21:8c	226
21:9	103, 201, 207, 235, 236, 309
21:9a	227, 228
21:9b	227
21:9c	228
21:9d	229, 230
21:9e	230
21:10–11	207
21:10	236
21:10a	231
21:10b	232, 233
21:11	233, 236
21:11a	233
21:11b	233
21:15	309
21:17	209
21:20	110
21:23–27	238
21:23	238, 256, 352
21:23a	238
21:23b	239, 241
21:23c	241
21:23d	241
21:24	238, 256
21:24a	242
21:24b	243
21:24c	244
21:25–26	238
21:25	238
21:25a	245, 256
21:25b–26	256
21:25b	246
21:25c	247
21:26	238
21:26a	248, 256
21:26b	248, 256
21:26c	249
21:26d	250
21:26e	251
21:27	238
21:27a	252, 256
21:27b	252
21:27c	253
21:27d	254
21:32	63
22:13	88, 184
23:15	184
23:16	184, 186
23:17	184
22:22	110
23:23	184
22:24	186
23:25	184
23:27	184
23:29	184
22:36	186
22:42–45	229
24:7	103
24:9	138
24:10	138
24:13	291

BIBLICAL AND ANCIENT TEXT INDEX

24:22	291	27:1	240, 241
24:29	88	27:3-5	340, 351
		27:3	241, 342
25:21	331	27:5	342
25:23	331	27:11	282
25:30	88	27:12	241, 240
		27:14	110
26:3-4	240	27:20	240, 241
26:3	241	27:28	272
26:6	209	27:29	236
26:14	342	27:32-50	272
26:17	258	27:32-33	272
26:20	342	27:32a	273
26:25	342	27:32b	274
26:26-29	258	27:33a	275
26:26	258	27:33b	276
26:26a	258	27:34-36	272
26:26b	259	27:34a	276
26:26c	260	27:34b	277
26:26d	260	27:35	278
26:26e	261	27:36	279
26:27-28	258	27:37	272, 309
26:27a	261	27:37a	280
26:27b	262	27:37b	281
26:27c	263	27:38a	282
26:28	258, 270	27:38b	283
26:28a	263	27:39-40a	284
26:28b	265	27:40	49, 52, 273, 291, 309
26:28c	265		
26:29	258, 270	27:40b	285
26:29a	266	27:40c	286
26:29b	266	27:40d	286
26:29c	268	27:40e	287
26:31	138	27:40f	287
26:32	325, 328, 351	27:41	240, 241, 288
26:33	138	27:42-43	273
26:39	307, 310	27:42	273, 291, 309, 310
26:42	309	27:42a	290
26:45-46	337	27:42b	290
26:47	235, 240, 241, 342, 342	27:42c	291
		27:42d	291, 292, 293
26:49	342	27:42e	292
26:53	52	27:43	52, 310
26:54	337	27:43a	293
26:55	352	27:43b	293, 294
26:57	241	27:43c	295
26:58	103, 201	27:44	273, 295
26:61	286, 309	27:45	88, 273

365

Matthew (continued)

27:45a	297
27:45b	298
27:46	273, 310
27:46a	298
27:46b	300
27:46c	300
27:46d	301
27:47–49	273
27:47a	302
27:47b	302
27:48a	303
27:48b	304
27:48c	304, 305
27:49	291
27:49a	305
27:49b	306, 307
27:50	273, 307, 310
27:53	34, 337
27:54	103, 337
27:55	103
28:1–10	311, 340
28:1a	311
28:1b	312
28:1c	313
28:2	103
28:2a	314, 316
28:2b	315, 316
28:2c	317
28:2d	317
28:3	338
28:3a	318
28:3b	319
28:4	311, 338
28:4a	320
28:4b	321
28:5a	321
28:5b	322, 334
28:5c	323
28:6a	311, 324
28:6b	311, 324, 325
28:6c	325
28:7	311, 338, 351
28:7a	326, 330
28:7b	327
28:7c	327
28:7d	328
28:7e	329
28:8–10	311
28:8	338
28:8a	329
28:8b	330
28:8c	331
28:9	343
28:9a	331, 338
28:9b	332, 338
28:9c	333
28:10	338, 351
28:10a	333
28:10b	334
28:10c	334
28:10d	335, 336
28:10e	336
28:12	241
28:16–20	340
28:16	340, 342, 351
28:16a	340
28:16b	342
28:17	340, 343, 351
28:17a	342, 343
28:17b	343
28:18–20	346
28:18	52, 154, 245, 340, 351
28:18a	344
28:18b	344
28:19	352
28:19a	340, 345, 348
28:19b	340, 347
28:20	235, 352
28:20a	340, 348
28:20b	340, 349
28:20c	350

Mark

1:4	266, 270
1:12–13	25
1:14	24
1:27	111
4:17	137
4:39	109

5:20	110	12:11	316
11:1	209	12:23	316
11:11–12	209	16:26	315
14:3	209	13	166
15:5	110	22:3	242
		26:18	88

Luke

1:11	316
2:9	316
3:3	266, 270
4:1–13	24, 25
4:2	27
4:4	51
8:25	110
8:29	109
9:43	110
11:14	110
14:26	92
19:29	209
20:26	110
22:20	264
24:12	110
24:41	110
24:46–47	270
24:50	209
24:50–51	209

John

1:28	209
2:21	309
6:44	183
6:65	183
11:1	209
11:18	209
12:1	209

Acts

1:11–12	209
1:15	166
1:16–22	166
2:14–36	166
2:38	266, 270
5:19	316
12:7	316

1 Corinthians

7:32	141
7:33	141
7:34	141
10:13	51
10:16	262
11:25	264, 270, 271
15:1–26	339
15:1	339
15:3	339
15:55–57	167

2 Corinthians

3:6	264
4:18	137
11:28	141

Galatians

5:22–24	142

Ephesians

6:5	85

Hebrews

4:15	51
6:7	142
8:6	264
8:8	264
9:15	264
11:24–25	51
12:2	183
12:24	264

James

1:4	198

1 Peter

1:3–4	99
2:9	88
2:20	69
3:4	61

Revelation

1:17	320
1:18	168
11:2	34
11:13	315
11:19	315
16:18	315
21:2	34
21:8	107
21:10	34
22:4	66
22:19	34

Apocrypha & Pseudepigrapha

Sirach

46:19	160

1 Maccabees

2:21	178

Psalms of Solomon

17	9, 229

Other Ancient Jewish Texts

Josephus, *Jewish War*

2.5.3 §322	240
2.16.3 §342	240
5.1.5 §36	240
6.9.3 §42	240

Mishnah Menaḥot

11:2	209

www.ingramcontent.com/pod-product-compliance
Lightning Source LLC
Chambersburg PA
CBHW022227010526
44113CB00033B/526